The I-Series

Microsoft® Office Word 2003

Brief

The I-Series

Microsoft® Office Word 2003

Brief

Stephen Haag
University of Denver

James Perry
University of San Diego

Paige Baltzan
University of Denver

Boston   Burr Ridge, IL   Dubuque, IA   Madison, WI   New York   San Francisco   St. Louis
Bangkok   Bogotá   Caracas   Kuala Lumpur   Lisbon   London   Madrid   Mexico City
Milan   Montreal   New Delhi   Santiago   Seoul   Singapore   Sydney   Taipei   Toronto

Technology Education

THE I-SERIES: MICROSOFT® OFFICE WORD 2003, BRIEF

Published by McGraw-Hill/Technology Education, a business unit of The McGraw-Hill Companies, Inc., 1221 Avenue of the Americas, New York, NY, 10020. Copyright © 2004 by The McGraw-Hill Companies, Inc. All rights reserved. No part of this publication may be reproduced or distributed in any form or by any means, or stored in a database or retrieval system, without the prior written consent of The McGraw-Hill Companies, Inc., including, but not limited to, in any network or other electronic storage or transmission, or broadcast for distance learning.
Some ancillaries, including electronic and print components, may not be available to customers outside the United States.

This book is printed on acid-free paper.

1 2 3 4 5 6 7 8 9 0 WEB/WEB 0 9 8 7 6 5 4 3

ISBN 0-07-282999-0

Editor-in-chief: *Bob Woodbury*
Publisher: *Brandon Nordin*
Senior sponsoring editor: *Donald J. Hull*
Associate sponsoring editor: *Craig S. Leonard*
Editorial assistant: *Veronica Vergoth*
Marketing manager: *Andy Bernier*
Senior producer, Media technology: *David Barrick*
Lead project manager: *Mary Conzachi*
Senior production supervisor: *Rose Hepburn*
Lead designer: *Pam Verros*
Senior supplement producer: *Rose M. Range*
Senior digital content specialist: *Brian Nacik*
Cover design: *Asylum Studios*
Interior design: *Mary Christianson*
Typeface: *10.5/12 Minion*
Compositor: *GAC Indianapolis*
Printer: *Webcrafters, Inc.*

Library of Congress Cataloging-in-Publication Data
Haag, Stephen.
    Microsoft Office Word 2003, brief / Stephen Haag, James Perry, Paige Baltzan.
      p. cm.—(The I-series)
    Includes Index
    ISBN 0-07-282999-0 (acid-free paper)
    1. Microsoft Word. 2. Word processing. I. Perry, James T. II. Baltzan, Paige. III. Title
IV. Series.
Z52.5.M52H325 2004
005.52—dc22   2003062556

www.mhhe.com

MCGRAW-HILL TECHNOLOGY EDUCATION

At McGraw-Hill Technology Education, we publish instructional materials for the technology education market, in particular computer instruction in post-secondary education—from introductory courses in traditional 4-year universities to continuing education and proprietary schools. McGraw-Hill Technology Education presents a broad range of innovative products—texts, lab manuals, study guides, testing materials, and technology-based training and assessment tools.

We realize that technology has created and will continue to create new mediums for professors and students to use in managing resources and communicating information to one another. McGraw-Hill Technology Education provides the most flexible and complete teaching and learning tools available, and offers solutions to the changing world of teaching and learning. McGraw-Hill Technology Education is dedicated to providing the tools for today's instructors and students that will enable them to successfully navigate the world of Information Technology.

- McGraw-Hill/Osborne—This division of The McGraw-Hill Companies is known for its best-selling Internet titles, Harley Hahn's *Internet & Web Yellow Pages*, and the *Internet Complete Reference*. For more information, visit Osborne at www.osborne.com.

- Digital Solutions—Whether you want to teach a class online or just post your "bricks-n-mortar" class syllabus, McGraw-Hill Technology Education is committed to publishing digital solutions. Taking your course online doesn't have to be a solitary adventure, nor does it have to be a difficult one. We offer several solutions that will allow you to enjoy all the benefits of having your course material online.

- Packaging Options—For more information about our discount options, contact your McGraw-Hill sales representative at 1-800-338-3987 or visit our Web site at www.mhhe.com/it.

McGraw-Hill Technology Education is dedicated to providing the tools for today's instructors and students

THE I-SERIES PAGE

By using the I-Series, students will be able to learn and master applications skills by being actively engaged—by *doing*. The "I" in I-Series demonstrates Insightful tasks that will not only Inform students, but also Involve them while learning the applications.

How Will the I-Series Accomplish This for You?

Through relevant, real-world chapter opening cases.

Tasks throughout each chapter incorporating steps and tips for easy reference.

Alternative methods and styles of learning to keep the student involved.

Rich, end-of-chapter materials that support what the student has learned.

I-Series Titles Include:

Computer Concepts

Computing Concepts, 2e, Introductory

Computing Concepts, 2e, Complete

Microsoft Office Applications

Microsoft Office 2003, Volume I

Microsoft Office 2003, Volume II

Microsoft Office Word 2003 (Brief, Introductory, Complete Versions) 11 Total Chapters

Microsoft Office Excel 2003 (Brief, Introductory, Complete Versions) 12 Total Chapters

Microsoft Office Access 2003 (Brief, Introductory, Complete Versions) 12 Total Chapters

Microsoft Office PowerPoint 2003 (Brief, Introductory Versions) 8 Total Chapters

Microsoft Office Outlook 2003 (Brief, Introductory Versions) 8 Total Chapters

Microsoft Office FrontPage 2003 (Brief Version) 4 Total Chapters

Microsoft Office XP, Volume I

Microsoft Office XP, Volume I Expanded (with Internet Essentials bonus chapters)

Microsoft Office XP, Volume II

Microsoft Office Word 2002 (Brief, Introductory, Complete Versions) 12 Total Chapters

Microsoft Office Excel 2002 (Brief, Introductory, Complete Versions) 12 Total Chapters

Microsoft Office Access 2002 (Brief, Introductory, Complete Versions) 12 Total Chapters

Microsoft Office PowerPoint 2002 (Brief, Introductory Versions) 8 Total Chapters

Microsoft Office Internet Explorer 6.0 (Brief Version) 5 Total Chapters

Microsoft Windows

Microsoft Windows 2000 (Brief, Introductory, Complete Versions) 12 Total Chapters

Microsoft Windows XP (Brief, Introductory, Complete Versions) 12 Total Chapters

For additional resources, visit The I-Series Online Learning Center at www.mhhe.com/i-series

GOALS/PHILOSOPHY

The I-Series applications textbooks strongly emphasize that students learn and master applications skills by being actively engaged—by *doing*. We made the decision that teaching how to accomplish tasks is not enough for complete understanding and mastery. Students must understand the importance of each of the tasks that lead to a finished product at the end of each chapter.

Approach

The I-Series chapters are subdivided into sessions that contain related groups of tasks with active, hands-on components. The session tasks containing numbered steps collectively result in a completed project at the end of each session. Prior to introducing numbered steps that show how to accomplish a particular task, we discuss why the steps are important. We discuss the role that the collective steps play in the overall plan for creating or modifying a document or object, answering students' often-heard questions, "Why are we doing these steps? Why are these steps important?" Without an explanation of why an activity is important and what it accomplishes, students can easily find themselves following the steps but not registering the big picture of what the steps accomplish and why they are executing them.

I-Series Applications for 2003

The I-Series offers three levels of instruction. Each level builds upon knowledge from the previous level. With the exception of the running project that is the last exercise of every chapter, chapter cases and end-of-chapter exercises are independent from one chapter to the next, with the exception of Access. The three levels available are

Brief   Covers the basics of the Microsoft application and contains Chapters 1 through 4. The Brief textbooks are typically 200 pages long.

Introductory   Includes chapters in the Brief textbook plus Chapters 5 through 8. Introductory textbooks typically are 400 pages long and prepare students for the <u>Microsoft Office Specialist (MOS) Core Exam</u>.

Complete   Includes the Introductory textbook plus Chapters 9 through 12. The four additional chapters cover advanced-level content and the textbooks are typically 600 pages long. Complete textbooks prepare students for the <u>Microsoft Office Specialist (MOS) Expert Exam</u>. The Microsoft Office User Specialist program is recognized around the world as the standard for demonstrating proficiency using Microsoft Office applications.

In addition, there are two compilation volumes available.

Office I   Includes introductory chapters on Windows and Computing Concepts followed by Chapters 1 through 4 (Brief textbook) of Word, Excel, Access, and PowerPoint. In addition, material from the companion Computing Concepts book is integrated into the first few chapters to provide students with an understanding of the relationship between Microsoft Office applications and computer information systems.

Office II   Includes introductory chapters on Windows and Computing Concepts followed by Chapters 5 through 8 from each of the Introductory-level textbooks including Word, Excel, Access, and PowerPoint. In addition, material from the companion Computing Concepts book is integrated into the introductory chapters to provide students with a deeper understanding of the relationship between Microsoft Office applications and computer information systems. An introduction to Visual Basic for Applications (VBA) completes the Office II textbook.

STEPHEN HAAG

Stephen Haag is a professor and Chair of Information Technology and Electronic Commerce and the Director of Technology in the University of Denver's Daniels College of Business. Stephen holds a B.B.A. and M.B.A. from West Texas State University and a Ph.D. from the University of Texas at Arlington. He has published numerous articles appearing in such journals as *Communications of the ACM, The International Journal of Systems Science, Applied Economics, Managerial and Decision Economics, Socio-Economic Planning Sciences,* and the *Australian Journal of Management.*

Stephen is also the author of 20 other books including *Interactions: Teaching English as a Second Language* (with his mother and father), *Case Studies in Information Technology, Information Technology: Tomorrow's Advantage Today* (with Peter Keen), and *Excelling in Finance.* He is also the lead author of the accompanying I-Series *Computing Concepts* text, released in both an Introductory and a Complete version. Stephen lives with his wife, Pam, and their four sons—Indiana, Darian, Trevor, and Elvis— in Highlands Ranch, Colorado.

JAMES PERRY

James Perry is a professor of Management Information Systems in the University of San Diego's School of Business. He holds a B.S. in mathematics from Purdue University and a Ph.D. in computer science from The Pennsylvania State University. Jim has published several journal and conference papers. He is the co-author of 60 other textbooks and trade books including *Using Access with Accounting Systems, Building Accounting Systems, Understanding Oracle, The Internet,* and *Electronic Commerce.* His books have been translated into Chinese, Dutch, French, and Korean. Jim teaches both undergraduate and graduate courses at the University of San Diego and has worked as a computer security consultant to various private and governmental organizations including the Jet Propulsion Laboratory. He was a consultant on the Strategic Defense Initiative ("Star Wars") project and served as a member of the computer security oversight committee. Jim lives with his wife, Nancy, in San Diego, California. He has three grown children: Jessica, Stirling, and Kelly.

PAIGE BALTZAN

Paige Baltzan is a professor of Information Technology and Electronic Commerce in the University of Denver's Daniels College of Business. Paige holds a B.S.B.A. from Bowling Green State University and an M.B.A. from the University of Denver. Paige's primary concentration focuses on object-oriented technologies and systems development methodologies. She has been teaching Systems Analysis and Design, Telecommunications and Networking, Software Engineering, and The Global Information Economy at the University of Denver for the past three years. Paige has contributed materials for several McGraw-Hill publications including *Using Information Technology* and *Management Information Systems for the Information Age.*

Prior to joining the University of Denver Paige spent three years working at Level(3) Communications as a Technical Architect and four years working at Andersen Consulting as a Technology Consultant in the telecommunications industry. Paige lives in Lakewood, Colorado, with her husband, Tony, and her daughter, Hannah.

AMY PHILLIPS

Amy Phillips is a professor of Information Technology and Electronic Commerce in the University of Denver's Daniels College of Business. She holds a B.S. degree in environmental biology and an M.S. degree in education from Plymouth State College. Amy has been teaching for more than 18 years: 5 years in public secondary education and 13 years in higher education. She has also been an integral part of both the academic and administrative functions within the higher educational system.

Amy's main concentration revolves around database driven Web sites focusing on dynamic Web content, specifically ASP and XML technologies. Some of the main core course selections that Amy teaches at the University of Denver include Analysis and Design, Database Management Systems, Using Technology to Communicate, and Using Technology to Manage Information. Her first book, *Internet Explorer 6.0,* written with Stephen Haag and James Perry, was published in September 2002.

MERRILL WELLS

Merrill Wells is a professor of Information Technology and Electronic Commerce in the University of Denver's Daniels College of Business. Merrill holds a B.A. and M.B.A. from Indiana University. Although her goal was to teach and write, she followed the advice of her professors and set out to gain business experience before becoming a professor herself.

Merrill began her nonacademic career as a business systems programmer developing manufacturing, accounting, and payroll software using relational databases. Throughout her first career Merrill worked in the aerospace, manufacturing, construction, and oil and gas industries. After years of writing technical manuals and training end users, Merrill honored her original goal and returned to academia to become an active instructor of both graduate and undergraduate technology courses.

Merrill is the author of several online books including *An Introduction to Computers, Introduction to Visual Basic,* and *Programming Logic and Design.* Merrill lives with her husband, Rick, in Denver, Colorado. They have four children—Daniel, Dusty, Victoria (Tori), and Evan—and foster twins Connor and Gage.

Each textbook features the following:

Did You Know   Each chapter has six or seven interesting facts—about both high-tech and other topics.

Sessions   Each chapter is divided into two or three sessions.

Chapter Outline   Provides students with a quick map of the major headings in the chapter.

Chapter and Microsoft Office Specialist Objectives   At the beginning of each chapter is a list of 5 to 10 action-oriented objectives. Any chapter objectives that are also Microsoft Office Specialist objectives indicate the Microsoft Office Specialist objective number.

Chapter Opening Case   Each chapter begins with a case. Cases describe a mixture of fictitious and real people and companies and the needs of the people and companies. Throughout the chapter, the student gains the skills and knowledge to solve the problem stated in the case.

Introduction   The chapter introduction establishes the overview of the chapter's activities in the context of the case problem.

Another Way and Another Word   Another Way is a highlighted feature providing a bulleted list of steps to accomplish a task, or best practices—that is, a better or faster way to accomplish a task such as pasting a format onto an Excel cell. Another Word, another highlighted box, briefly explains more about a topic or highlights a potential pitfall.

Step-by-Step Instructions   Numbered step-by-step instructions for all hands-on activities appear in a distinctive color. Keyboard characters and menu selections appear in a **special format** to emphasize what the user should press or type. Steps make clear to the student the exact sequence of keystrokes and mouse clicks needed to complete a task such as formatting a Word paragraph.

Tips   Tips appear within a numbered sequence of steps and warn the student of possible missteps or provide alternatives to the step that precedes the tip.

Task Reference and Task Reference Summary   Task References appear throughout the textbook. Set in a distinctive design, each Task Reference contains a bulleted list of steps showing a generic way to accomplish activities that are especially important or significant. A Task Reference Summary at the end of each chapter summarizes a chapter's Task References.

Microsoft Office Specialist Objectives Summary   A list of Microsoft Office Specialist objectives covered in a chapter appears in the chapter objectives and the chapter summary.

Making the Grade   Short answer questions appear at the end of each chapter's sessions. They test a student's grasp of each session's contents, and Making the Grade answers appear at the end of each chapter so students can check their answers.

Rich End-of-Chapter Materials   End-of-chapter materials incorporating a three-level approach reinforce learning and help students take ownership of the chapter. Level One, Review of Terminology, contains fill in the blank, true/false, and multiple choice questions that enforce review of a chapter's key terms. Level Two, Review of Concepts, contains review questions and a Jeopardy-style create-a-question exercise. Level Three contains Hands-On Projects (see the paragraph following this one). Level Four, Analysis, contains short questions that require students to step back from the details of what they learned and think about higher level concepts covered in the chapter.

Hands-On Projects   Extensive hands-on projects engage the student in a problem-solving exercise from start to finish. There are seven clearly labeled categories that each contain one or two questions. Categories are Practice, Challenge!, E-Business, On the Web, Around the World, and a Running Project that carries throughout all the chapters.

We understand that, in today's teaching environment, offering a textbook alone is not sufficient to meet the needs of the many instructors who use our books. To teach effectively, instructors must have a full complement of supplemental resources to assist them in every facet of teaching, from preparing for class to conducting a lecture to assessing students' comprehension. The **I-Series** offers a complete supplements package and Web site that is briefly described below.

INSTRUCTOR'S RESOURCE KIT

The Instructor's Resource Kit is a CD-ROM containing the Instructor's Manual in both MS Word and .pdf formats, PowerPoint Slides with Presentation Software, Brownstone test-generating software, and accompanying test item files in both MS Word and .pdf formats for each chapter. The CD also contains figure files from the text, student data files, and solutions files. The features of each of the three main components of the Instructor's Resource Kit are highlighted below.

Instructor's Manual Featuring:

- Chapter learning objectives
- Chapter key terms
- Chapter outline and lecture notes
  - Teaching suggestions
  - Classroom tips, tricks, and traps
  - Page number references
- Additional end-of-chapter practice projects
- Answers to all Making the Grade and end-of-chapter questions
- Text figures

PowerPoint Presentation

The PowerPoint presentation is designed to provide instructors with comprehensive lecture and teaching resources that will include

- Chapter learning objectives followed by source content that illustrates key terms and key facts per chapter
- FAQ (frequently asked questions) to show key concepts throughout the chapter; also lecture notes, to illustrate these key concepts and ideas

- End-of-chapter exercises and activities per chapter, as taken from the end-of-chapter materials in the text
- Speaker's Notes, to be incorporated throughout the slides per chapter
- Figures/screen shots, to be incorporated throughout the slides per chapter

Test Bank

The I-Series Test Bank, using Diploma Network Testing Software by Brownstone, contains over 3,000 questions (both objective and interactive) categorized by topic, page reference to the text, and difficulty level of learning. Each question is assigned a learning category:

- Level 1: Key Terms and Facts
- Level 2: Key Concepts
- Level 3: Application and Problem-Solving

The types of questions consist of 20 percent Multiple Choice, 50 percent True/False, and 30 percent Fill-in-the-Blank Questions.

ONLINE LEARNING CENTER/ WEB SITE

To locate the I-Series OLC/Web site directly, go to www.mhhe.com/i-series. The site is divided into three key areas:

- **Information Center**   Contains core information about the text, the authors, and a guide to our additional features and benefits of the series, including the supplements.
- **Instructor Center**   Offers instructional materials, downloads, additional activities and answers to additional projects, answers to chapter troubleshooting exercises, answers to chapter preparation/post exercises posed to students, relevant links for professors, and more.
- **Student Center**   Contains chapter objectives and outlines, self-quizzes, chapter troubleshooting exercises, chapter preparation/post exercises, additional projects, simulations, student data files and solutions files, Web links, and more.

RESOURCES FOR STUDENTS

SimNet

SimNet is a simulated assessment and learning tool for either Microsoft® Office XP or Microsoft® Office 2003. SimNet allows students to study MS Office skills and computer concepts, and professors to test and evaluate students' proficiency, within MS Office applications and concepts. Students can practice and study their skills at home or in the school lab using SimNet, which does not require the purchase or installation of Office software. SimNet includes:

Structured Computer-Based Learning SimNet offers a complete computer-based learning side that presents each skill or topic in several different modes. *Teach Me* presents the skill or topic using text, graphics, and interactivity. *Show Me* presents the skill using an animation with audio narration to show how the skill is used or implemented. *Let Me Try* allows you to practice the skill in SimNet's robust simulated interface.

Computer Concepts Coverage! SimNet includes coverage of 60 computer concepts in both the Learning and the Assessment side.

The Basics and More! SimNet includes modules of content on:

Word	Windows 2000
Excel	Computer Concepts
Access	Windows XP Professional
PowerPoint	Internet Explorer 6
Office XP Integration	FrontPage
Outlook	

More Assessment Questions! SimNet includes over *1,400* assessment questions.

Practice or Pre-Tests Questions! SimNet has a separate pool of over *600* questions for Practice Tests or Pre-Tests.

Comprehensive Exercises! SimNet offers comprehensive exercises for each application. These exercises require the student to use multiple skills to solve one exercise in the simulated environment.

Simulated Interface! The simulated environment in **SimNet** has been substantially deepened to more realistically simulate the real applications. Now students are not graded incorrect just because they chose the wrong submenu or dialog box. The student is not graded until he or she does something that immediately invokes an action—just like the real applications!

DIGITAL SOLUTIONS FOR INSTRUCTORS AND STUDENTS

PageOut PageOut is our Course Web Site Development Center that offers a syllabus page, URL, McGraw-Hill Online Learning Center content, online exercises and quizzes, gradebook, discussion board, and an area for student Web pages. For more information, visit the PageOut Web site at www.pageout.net.

Online Courses Available OLCs are your perfect solutions for Internet-based content. Simply put, these Centers are "digital cartridges" that contain a book's pedagogy and supplements. As students read the book, they can go online and take self-grading quizzes or work through interactive exercises.

Online Learning Centers can be delivered through any of these platforms:

McGraw-Hill Learning Architecture (TopClass)

Blackboard.com

College.com (formerly Real Education)

WebCT (a product of Universal Learning Technology)

CHAPTER

one

1

Creating Worksheets for Decision Makers

Did You Know?

A unique presentation of text and graphics introduces interesting and little-known facts.

did you
know?

one-third *of online shoppers abandon their electronic shopping carts before completing the checkout process.*

goldfish *lose their color if they are kept in a dim light or if they are placed in a body of running water such as a stream.*

electric *eels are not really eels but a type of fish.*

in *1963, baseball pitcher Gaylord Perry said, "They'll put a man on the moon before I hit a home run." Only a few hours after Neil Armstrong set foot on the moon on July 20, 1969, Perry hit the first and only home run of his career.*

Chapter Objectives

- Start Excel and open a workbook
- Move around a worksheet using the mouse and arrow keys
- Locate supporting information (help)—MOS XL03S-1-3
- Select a block of cells
- Type into worksheet cells text, values, formulas, and functions—MOS XL03S-2-3
- Edit and clear cell entries—MOS XL03S-1-1
- Save a workbook
- Add a header and a footer—MOS XL03S-5-7
- Preview output—MOS XL03S-5-5
- Print a worksheet and print a worksheet's formulas—MOS XL03S-5-8
- Exit Excel

Chapter Objectives

Each chapter begins with a list of competencies covered in the chapter.

Task Reference

Provides steps to accomplish an especially important task.

task reference   Opening an Excel Workbook

- Click **File** and then click **Open**
- Ensure that the Look in list box displays the name of the folder containing your workbook
- Click the workbook's name
- Click the **Open** button

SESSION 1.1

Making the Grade

Short-answer questions appear at the end of each session, and answers appear at the end of each chapter.

making *the grade*

1. A popular program used to analyze numeric information and help make meaningful business decisions is called a _____ program.

2. _____ analysis is observing changes to spreadsheets and reviewing their effect on other values in the spreadsheet.

3. An Excel spreadsheet is called a(n) _____ and consists of individual pages called _____.

4. Beneath Excel's menu bar is the _____ toolbar, which contains button shortcuts for commands such as Print, and the _____ toolbar containing button shortcuts to alter the appearance of worksheets and their cells.

5. The _____ cell is the cell in which you are currently entering data.

Modifying the left and right margins:

1. With the Print Preview window still open, click the **Setup** button. The Page Setup dialog box opens

2. Click the **Margins** tab and double-click the **Left spin control box** to highlight the current left margin number

3. Type **0.5** to set the left margin to one-half inch

4. Double-click the **Right spin control box** to highlight the current right margin number

5. Type **0.5** to set the right margin to one-half inch

6. Click **OK** to close the Page Setup dialog box

tip: If you still cannot see the entire worksheet on one page, you can force the worksheet to fit by clicking the **Page** tab in the Page Setup dialog box and then click the **Fit to** option button in the Scaling section of [   ]
it fits on a single page

7. Click the **Close** butt[on]
[ ] and return to the wo[rksheet]

Step-by-Step Instruction

Numbered steps guide you through the exact sequence of keystrokes to accomplish the task.

Tips

Tips appear within steps and either indicate possible missteps or provide alternatives to a step.

---

hands-on projects

practice

LEVEL **THREE**

CHAPTER ONE

1. Creating an Income Statement

Carroll's Fabricating, a machine shop providing custom metal fabricating, is preparing an income statement for its shareholders. Betty Carroll, the company's president, wants to know exactly how much net income the company has earned this year. Although Betty has prepared a preliminary worksheet with labels in place, she wants you to enter the values and a few formulas to compute cost of goods sold, gross profit, selling and advertising expenses, and net income. Figure 1.26 shows an example of a completed worksheet.

1. Open the workbook **ex01Income.xls** in your student disk in the folder Ch01

2. Click **File** and then click **Save As** to save the workbook as **Income2.xls** in the folder Ch01

3. Scan the Income Statement worksheet and type the following values in the listed cells: Cell C5, **987453**; cell B8, **64677**; cell B9, **564778**; cell B10, **-43500**; cell B15, **53223**; cell B16, **23500**; cell B17, **12560**; cell B18, **123466**; cell B19, **87672**

4. In cell C10, write the formula =**SUM(B8:B10)** to sum cost of goods sold

5. In cell C12, type the formula for Gross Profit: =**C5-C10**

6. In cell C19, type the formula to sum selling and advertising expenses: =**SUM(B15:B19)**

7. In cell C21, type the formula =**C12-C19** to compute net income (gross profit minus total selling and advertising expenses)

8. In cell A4, type **Prepared by** <your name>

9. Click the Save button on the Standard toolbar to save your modified worksheet

10. Print the worksheet and print the worksheet formulas

FIGURE 1.26
income statement

www.mhhe.com/i-series

EX 1.41

EXCEL

Screen Shots

Screen shots show you what to expect at critical points.

End-of-Chapter Hands-On Projects

A rich variety of projects introduced by a case lets you put into practice what you have learned. Categories include Practice, Challenge, On the Web, E-Business, Around the World, and a running case project.

---

anotherword   . . . on Cell Ranges

A SUM function can contain more than one cell range. For example, the function =SUM(A1:A5,B42:B51) totals two cell ranges. Place commas between distinct cell ranges within the SUM function. The collection of cells, cell ranges, and values in the comma-separated list between a function's parentheses is its *argument list*

Another Way/ Another Word

Another Way highlights an alternative way to accomplish a task; Another Word explains more about a topic.

---

task reference summary

Task	Location	Preferred Method
Opening an Excel workbook	EX 1.00	• Click **File**, click **Open**, click workbook's name, click the **Open** button
Writing a formula	EX 1.00	• Select cell, type =, type formula, press **Enter**
Entering the SUM function	EX 1.00	• Select cell, type =**SUM(**, type cell range, type), and press **Enter**
Editing a cell	EX 1.00	• Select cell, click formula bar, make changes, press **Enter**
Saving a workbook with a new name	EX 1.00	• Click **File**, click **Save As**, type filename, click **Save** button
Obtaining help	EX 1.00	Obtaining help

Task Reference Summary

Provides a quick reference and summary of a chapter's task references.

The authors want to acknowledge the work and support of the seasoned professionals at McGraw-Hill. Thank you to Bob Woodbury, editor in chief, for his leadership and a management style that fosters creativity and innovation. Thank you to Craig Leonard, associate sponsoring editor. Craig took on the very difficult task of both developmental editor and then sponsoring editor with eagerness and did a splendid job of bringing all the pieces together.

Thanks to Carol Lloyd, who performed an outstanding job editing Word. Carol's feedback and suggestions were invaluable. Thanks also to Deanna Tague for her technical editing efforts on the Word book.

If you would like to contact us about any of the books in the I-Series, we would enjoy hearing from you. We welcome comments and suggestions. You can e-mail book-related messages to us at i-series@McGraw-Hill.com. For the latest information about the I-Series textbooks and related resources, please visit our Web site at www.mhhe.com/i-series.

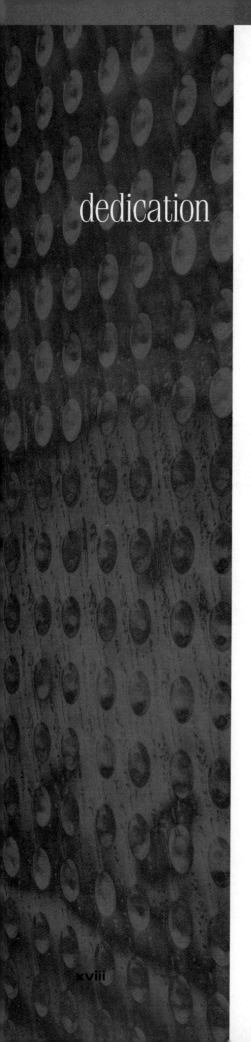

dedication

To Gus and Marme—the cornerstones of our lives

P.B.

brief *brief* contents

table of contents

END-OF-BOOK

The I-Series

Microsoft® Office Word 2003

Brief

1

Working with a Document

know? did you

the *first 1-gigabyte hard drive introduced by IBM in 1980 was the size of three industrial air conditioners and cost $40,000.*

on *October 21, 1938, Chester Floyd Carlson made his first successful copy using the process he called "xerography," meaning "dry writing."*

a *man-made fountain opposite the Gateway Arch in St. Louis is now the world's highest geyser, at 600 feet.*

earthling *is first found in print in 1593. Another surprisingly old word is spaceship (1894).*

one-third *of 95 developing countries have a waiting period of six years or more for a telephone connection, compared with less than a month in developed countries.*

a *sonic boom occurs when molecules come crashing together.*

Chapter Objectives

- Insert and edit text, symbols, and special characters—MOS WW03S-1-1
- Organize documents using file folders—MOS WW03S-5-3
- Save documents in appropriate formats for different uses—MOS WW03S-5-4
- Print documents, envelopes, and labels—MOS WW03S-5-5
- Preview documents and Web pages—MOS WW03S-5-6
- Change and organize document views and windows—MOS WW03S-5-7

Writing a Mission Statement for The Great Outdoor Gear Company

A mission statement describes the primary goals for a business. The mission statement helps to explain the company's purpose, business, customers, and products. You should be able to look at a mission statement and instantly understand the primary purpose and goals of the business. From a mission statement a customer can instantly tell what type of business it is, an employee can instantly tell what values or goals the company thinks are most important, and a competitor can instantly tell where the business is in the marketplace. Microsoft's mission statement is as follows: "To enable people and businesses throughout the world to realize their full potential."

Microsoft's mission statement is clear, concise, and easy to understand. Everyone who reads this mission statement, from customers to competitors, can easily understand Microsoft's primary goal of enabling people and businesses throughout the world to realize their full potential.

Alex Coombe works for The Great Outdoor Gear Company, a brand-new company that produces, markets, and sells high-quality outdoor activity gear over the Internet. The company has five basic product lines including mountaineering, mountain biking, camping, skiing, and rock climbing. Alex joined the company early in July and is the 104th employee. Her first assignment is to brainstorm some ideas for the company mission statement. Once Alex has generated some solid ideas, she will create two different versions of the mission statement. After the statements are completed, the other employees will be asked for their feedback and revisions will be made if necessary.

This is Alex's first assignment with the company and she has never used word-processing software before. Not wanting to jeopardize her new job, she agrees to tackle the project, realizing that she is going to be learning word-processing software as she works on the mission statements. **Word-processing software** helps you create papers, letters, memos, and other basic documents. Paula Logston, the vice president of The Great Outdoor Gear Company, will work with Alex on the content of the mission statements based on her in-depth knowledge of the company. Figure 1.1 displays the draft of the mission statements that Alex will show to Paula before she distributes the mission statements to the rest of the employees.

The Great Outdoor Gear Company Mission Statements

Draft A

Continually offer the highest levels of customer service, strive to exceed our global customer's expectations, and ensure that every item purchased meets our customer's high standards.

Draft B

To exceed our global customer's expectations by delivering the highest quality outdoor activity gear in the world.

Alex Coombe

FIGURE 1.1

Alex's draft of the two mission statements

INTRODUCTION

Word processing is an important skill to build. Once you know how to create papers, letters, memos, and other types of documents, there is no limit to what you will be able to accomplish. This session teaches you the basics of Office Word 2003. In this session, you will:

- Explore the elements in the Word window
- Learn about the menu bar and toolbars
- Learn how to enter and edit text in a document
- Learn how to open, save, and close documents

SESSION 1.1 ALL ABOUT OFFICE WORD 2003

Introduction to Word-Processing Software

Not long ago, typists and secretaries used typewriters to create almost all clerical documents—letters, memos, purchase orders, and so on. By the end of 1974, typewriters had been in successful use for over 100 years. Electric typewriters had largely replaced manual or mechanical typewriters, but it was still a typing job to produce the majority of a company's documents. By 1974 a tidal wave of change was about to sweep the world. Only a few people had the vision to see the coming change.

In 1964, IBM brought out the MT/ST (Magnetic Tape/Selectric Typewriter), which combined the features of the Selectric with a magnetic tape drive. Magnetic tape was the first reusable storage medium for typed information. With this, for the first time, typed material could be edited without having to retype the whole text. On the tape, information could be stored, replayed, corrected, and reprinted as many times as needed, and then erased and reused for other projects. This development marked the beginning of word processing, as it is known today. It also introduced word processing as a definite idea and concept. The term was first used in IBM's marketing of the MT/ST as a "word processing" machine.

In 1969, IBM introduced MagCards, magnetic cards that slipped into a box attached to the typewriter and recorded text as it was typed. About one page of text could be stored on each card. If the user needed to reprint the text, they simply used the card to recall the text. The MagCards were extremely useful for companies that sent out large numbers of form letters.

In 1972, Lexitron and Linolex developed a similar word-processing system that included video display screens and tape cassettes for storage. Text is easy to enter and correct when using a screen. The user could now wait to print the document until they were completely satisfied with the material.

The floppy disk marked a new stage in the evolution of storage media, and the word-processing industry was quick to adopt it. With a floppy disk, the user could now create and edit multiple paged documents and could even save the documents on the disk for retrieval at a later point in time.

Word-processing software became common throughout every industry in the early 1980s. The software featured many editing functions that allowed the user to manipulate text in new and exciting ways. Users could now insert and delete text, search and replace text, and change the size and color of text anywhere in the document. All of these new features allowed users to make multiple changes in a document without extensive retyping. This saved the users an incredible amount of time and businesses a large amount of money. Soon, some word-processing software incorporated a "type-composition" function and a page-layout function, allowing the user to electronically design and lay out a printed page. These are the key features of desktop publishing.

Word-processing software has become the workhorse application for business and personal computing. Document production used to be limited to businesses that employed secretaries and graphic artists and that performed printing/typesetting. Now all of these functions are easily available to all individuals.

Starting Word

Alex is familiar with the functionality of word-processing software, but she has never actually used it before. She must learn how to start Office Word 2003 so she can begin working on the two draft versions of the mission statements. Alex realizes that there will probably be many changes to her initial mission statements. Using word-processing software will help Alex to make the changes quickly and easily. Once she learns how to use the program, she can complete her first task and will be ready to take on additional tasks for the company. Alex is ready to get to work, and she is going to start by taking a quick look at the primary functions used in Word.

Starting Word:

1. Click the **Start** button on the Taskbar to display the Start menu

2. Point to **All Programs** to display the Programs menu

3. Point and click on **Microsoft Word**

tip: *If the Office Assistant appears when you start Word, click Help on the menu bar and then click Hide the Office Assistant. Later, you will learn how the Office Assistant can help you when you have questions*

4. Word should fill the entire screen. If it does not fill the entire screen, then click the **Maximize** ⬜ button found in the upper-right corner of the Word window

5. Your screen should look similar to Figure 1.2

Exploring the Word Window

The Word window contains several important items including:

- Title bar
- Document window
- Horizontal ruler
- Task pane
- Menu bar
- Standard toolbar
- Formatting toolbar
- Status bar
- Scroll bars

Figure 1.2 displays where several of the above items are located on the Word window. The *Title bar* is the area that displays the current document name and the program. The *document window* is where you will enter text, tables, charts, and graphics. The flashing cursor at the insertion point is a vertical blinking bar that indicates where text, tables, charts, or graphics are placed when you begin your work.

Just above the document window is the horizontal ruler. The *horizontal ruler* is a bar marked off in units of measure (inches in this example; other units can be selected) that is displayed across the top of the document window. You can use the horizontal ruler to view and set paragraph indents, tab stops, page margins, and column widths.

Task Pane

A *task pane* is a dockable dialog window that provides a convenient way to use a command, gather information, and modify a document. The task pane automatically

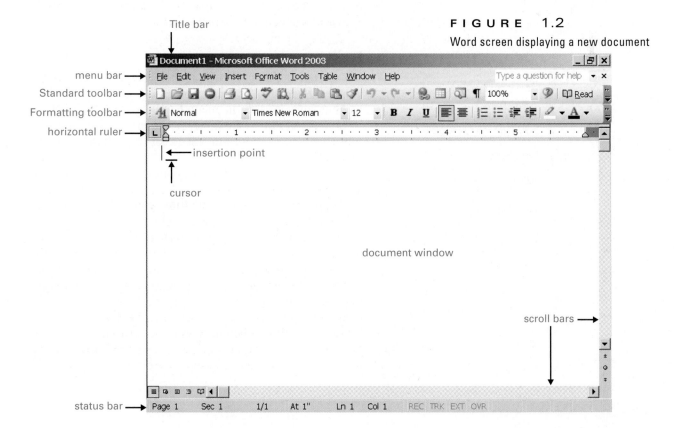

FIGURE 1.2

Word screen displaying a new document

FIGURE   1.3

Task pane

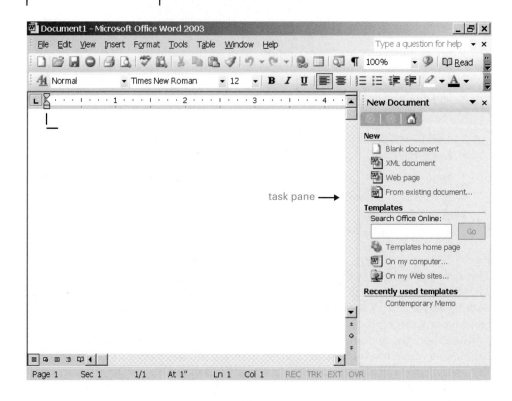

task pane ⟶

FIGURE   1.4

Menu bar revealing File commands

File menu ⟶

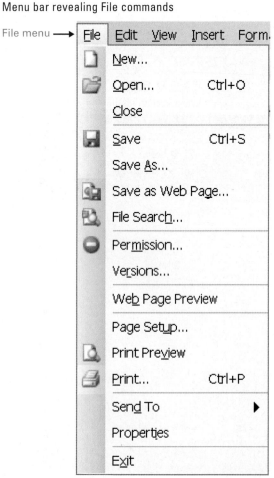

appears when a user performs an action that uses the task pane (see Figure 1.3). The task pane gives users easy access to important tasks. From the task pane, which appears on the right side of the screen in Figure 1.3, users can perform searches, open or start a new document, format documents, or even access document templates on the Web.

Menu Bar

The *menu bar* is a horizontal menu that appears on top of the window. Normally, the menu bar appears just below the Title bar, but you can click the menu handle at the left end of the menu bar and *drag* (hold down on the left mouse button and move the mouse pointer) the menu bar to any location on the screen.

The menu bar contains nine options including File, Edit, View, Insert, Format, Tools, Table, Window, and Help. Each option in the menu bar is associated with a drop-down list. Clicking one of the menu items will reveal a drop-down list displaying all the functions associated with that particular menu item. For example, clicking the File menu reveals the New, Open, Close, Save, Save As, and other functions (see Figure 1.4). If you click on any of these items, you can perform that particular task. For example, if you want to save a document, you can click on File, and then the Save menu item. Word offers many different ways to perform the same function. Oftentimes the same function can be performed by using the menu bar, toolbars, or keyboard shortcuts.

Toolbars

The Standard toolbar performs many of the same functions as the menu bar, but allows you to execute the commands with a single click on an icon. An *icon* is a small button on the toolbar that executes a command when the button is clicked. The ***Standard toolbar***, which normally appears below the menu bar, contains buttons representing the most popular commands such as Open, Save, Print, Cut, and Paste.

The ***Formatting toolbar*** contains buttons that change the appearance of text in a document. For example, you can bold, italicize, underline, number, or bullet text by simply pressing the appropriate button on the Formatting toolbar. Figure 1.5 presents an overview of each icon on the Standard and Formatting toolbars.

If Standard and Formatting toolbars are on one line and you want them on two lines, click Tools, Customize, Options, and remove the checkmarks from the top two boxes. This also turns off the Adaptive menus.

Status Bar

The ***status bar*** is located at the bottom of the window and displays information about a command or toolbar button, an operation in progress, or the location of the insertion point. For example, the status bar displays, from left to right, the page number, the section number, the page currently visible in the document window, and the number of pages in the document. It also displays your position on the page and tells you about the current state of any selected keys on the keyboard (see Figure 1.2).

Scroll Bars

The ***scroll bars*** allow you to view or display different parts of your document in the document window by scrolling up and down, or left to right. The scroll bars are the shaded bars along the right side and bottom of a document window that allow scrolling to another part of a document by dragging the scroll box or clicking the scroll arrows. On the right side of the screen is the vertical scroll bar. At the bottom of the screen is the horizontal scroll bar (see Figure 1.2).

FIGURE 1.5

Standard and Formatting toolbars

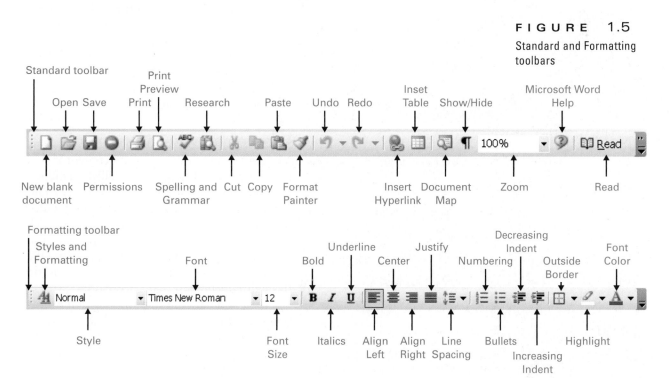

> ***anotherword***   . . . on the Mouse Pointer
>
> You can display a toolbar icon's function, or Screen Tip, by placing the pointer over the icon

Mouse Pointer

The ***mouse pointer*** indicates the current position of the mouse as you move it around the screen. It changes shape to indicate which duties you can perform at that particular mouse pointer location. For example, when the mouse is over a menu item, it changes to an arrow, indicating that you can select that item by clicking the mouse.

The Insertion Point

When you move the mouse over an area that has text, it changes into an I-beam shape. When you click, you position the ***insertion point***, which indicates the place where you will be entering text. When you first open a document, the insertion point is always at the top left corner.

Moving around a Document

You can use either the keyboard or the mouse to move around a document. As you begin using Word, you will decide which way works the best for you.

FIGURE 1.6

Keyboard keys for moving around a document

Press	To move
Left Arrow	One character to the left
Right Arrow	One character to the right
Ctrl+Left Arrow	One word to the left
Ctrl+Right Arrow	One word to the right
Ctrl+Up Arrow	One paragraph up
Ctrl+Down Arrow	One paragraph down
Up Arrow	Up one line
Down Arrow	Down one line
End	To the end of a line
Home	To the beginning of a line
Alt+Ctrl+Page Up	To the top of the window
Alt+Ctrl+Page Down	To the end of the window
Page Up	Up one screen (scrolling)
Page Down	Down one screen (scrolling)
Ctrl+Page Down	To the top of the next page
Ctrl+Page Up	To the top of the previous page
Ctrl+End	To the end of a document
Ctrl+Home	To the beginning of a document
Shift+F5	To a previous revision
Shift+F5	To the location of the insertion point when the document was last closed

Using the Keyboard

The arrow keys move you one space up, down, right, or left. The Control key (Ctrl) + the arrow keys moves you one word to the left or right, or one paragraph up or down. Figure 1.6 displays a number of different ways you can move around your document using the keyboard.

Using the Mouse

You can use your mouse as a quick and easy way to move around your document. Simply move the insertion point around your document by using your mouse. Once you are in the place where you want to enter or edit text, simply left-click on the mouse to insert the insertion point. Figure 1.7 displays a number of different ways you can enter or select text using your mouse.

Scrolling around a Document

Moving through a document to content that is not currently displayed is called scrolling. ***Scrolling*** means you are moving left and right, and up and down, through a document. A quick way to scroll through your document is to click on the arrows in the vertical and horizontal scroll bars. Figure 1.8 summarizes how you can use the vertical and horizontal scroll bars to move through a document.

After you have finished scrolling to the location you want, you can simply click the mouse to position the insertion point and start typing. You can also scroll up or down by pages by simply clicking on the Select Browse Object on the lower right of the vertical scroll bar (see Figure 1.9).

FIGURE   1.7

Mouse moves for entering and selecting text

To select	Do this
Any amount of text	Drag over the text.
A word	Double-click the word.
A line of text	Move the pointer to the left of the line until it changes to a right-pointing arrow, and then click.
Multiple lines of text	Move the pointer to the left of the lines until it changes to a right-pointing arrow, and then drag up or down.
A sentence	Hold down Ctrl key, and then click anywhere in the sentence.
A paragraph	Move the pointer to the left of the paragraph until it changes to a right-pointing arrow, and then double-click. Or triple-click anywhere in the paragraph.
Multiple paragraphs	Move the pointer to the left of the paragraphs until it changes to a right-pointing arrow, and then double-click and drag up or down.
A large block of text	Click at the start of the selection, scroll to the end of the selection, and then hold down **Shift** key and click.
An entire document	Move the pointer to the left of any document text until it changes to a right-pointing arrow, and then triple-click.
A vertical block of text (except within a table cell)	Hold down **Alt** key, and then drag over the text.

To	Do this
Scroll up one line	Click the up scroll arrow
Scroll down one line	Click the down scroll arrow
Scroll up one screen	Click above the scroll box
Scroll down one screen	Click below the scroll box
Scroll to a specific page	Drag the scroll box
Scroll left	Click the left scroll arrow
Scroll right	Click the right scroll arrow
Scroll left, beyond the margin, in Normal view	Hold down **Shift** key and click the left scroll arrow

FIGURE   1.8

Summary of scrolling through a document

FIGURE   1.9

Select Browse Object button on the vertical scroll bar

help yourself *Click the **Ask a Question** combo box lo-cated in the upper-right corner of the screen, type **Scroll Bars**, and press **Enter**. Click the hyperlink **Display or Hide Scroll bars** to display information on how you can hide the scroll bars from your document window. Click the Help screen **Close** button when you are finished*

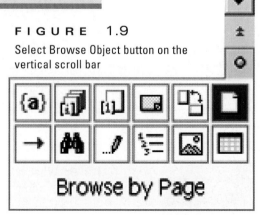

Browse by Page

*another*way
... to Get Help

Using the "Ask a Question box" is a great way to find help quickly and easily (see Figure 1.10). Type a question directly into the "Ask a Question" box in the upper-right corner of the application and the answer appears in the Answer Wizard

Finding Help

If you have any questions about how to use Word, you can find the answers in the on-line Help function. If you are unfamiliar with a function, or have a question about how to complete a task, you can ask the Office Assistant. The ***Office Assistant*** provides a wide variety of help and tips on Word features and functions. The Office Assistant pops up when you click the Help button on the Standard toolbar. You can type your question directly in the space provided and the Office Assistant will return several answers to your screen. Be sure to take advantage of the extensive Help features offered in Word.

Obtaining help from the Office Assistant:

1. Click **Help** on the menu bar
2. Click **Show the Office Assistant** to open the Office Assistant
3. Click on the Office Assistant
4. Type **how do I open a document** in the question box
5. Click on **Search** to start searching
6. Click **Open a file** in the list of alternative Help responses
7. Read the information
8. Click the **Close** button on the Title bar of the Help window to close
9. To hide the Office Assistant, click **Help** on the menu bar and click **Hide the Office Assistant**

F I G U R E   1.10

Ask a Question box

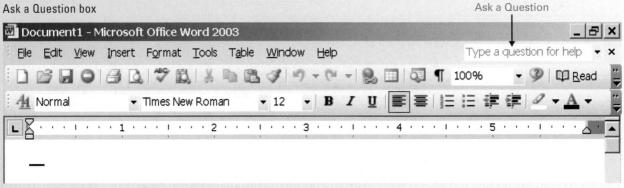

S E S S I O N   1 . 1

making the grade

1. _____ helps you create papers, letters, memos, and other basic documents.
2. What keys are used to move up and down, and right and left, one space at a time?
3. Where do you enter text, tables, charts, and graphics?
4. The _____ bar contains the commands File, Edit, View, Insert, Format, Tools, Table, Window, and Help.
5. What are the shaded bars along the right side and bottom of a document window that allow you to scroll to another part of a document?

SESSION 1.2 CREATING AND WORKING WITH DOCUMENTS

One of the most useful word-processing features is the ability to make changes and corrections. In the past, if you wanted to change one word on a typed page, you had to retype the entire page. Now, with the use of word-processing software, you can make corrections without retyping the entire document. You can quickly edit your document on the screen and print it when all the corrections are completed. If you spot mistakes in your printed copy, the document is still on the screen and can be easily corrected. You can even store your document for editing and revising at a later point in time. In this session you are going to help Alex create her mission statements in Word.

Opening a Document

When you start Word, it opens to a new blank document. By default, this new document is named "Document1" until you save it with a new name. In fact, you can open several new documents and they will be named "Document1," "Document2," "Document3," and so on, until you save and rename them or close them without saving. In addition, when you create or open a document in Word, the document opens in a separate window.

> **anotherword... on Creating a Blank Document**
>
> You can create a blank document by clicking **New** on the File menu and then click on the **Blank Document** icon in the task pane. You can also click on the **Blank Document** icon in the Standard toolbar

---

task reference   Opening a Word Document

- Click on the **File** menu

- Click **Open**

- Ensure that the Look in list box displays the name of the folder containing your document

- Click on the document's name

- Click the **Open** button located on the Open dialog box

Open Dialog Box

The Open dialog box allows you to choose which file you want to open. Let's get started so Alex can begin typing her mission statements for The Great Outdoor Gear Company. Alex created a document called "wd01Mission.doc" containing her first two drafts of the mission statements. Let's open the document as displayed in Figure 1.11.

FIGURE 1.11

Open dialog box displaying wd01Mission.doc

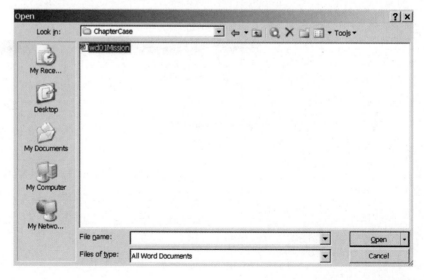

WORD

*another**way***
. . . **to Open a Document**

At the bottom of the File menu Word maintains a list of recently used documents (see Figure 1.12). You can quickly open a recently used document by clicking on it in the File menu. To specify the number of recently used files that appear on the File menu, click on **Tools**, **Options**, and the **General** tab. Increase or decrease the number of documents you wish to display on the File menu using the **Recently used file list** list box

F I G U R E   1.12
Recently used files listed at the bottom of the File menu

Opening an existing document:

1. Identify the drive and folder where you are storing your Word documents

2. Click **File** on the menu bar

3. Click **Open**

4. Click on the arrow next to the **Look in** list to display a list of available disk drives

5. Locate and click on the drive containing your data

6. The window displays a list of folders and Word document filenames

7. Locate and double-click the correct folder

8. Click the Word file **wd01Mission.doc**

9. Click the **Open** button located on the Open dialog box

or

1. Click the **Open** ⬜ button on the Standard toolbar

2. Locate and select the Word file **wd01Mission.doc**

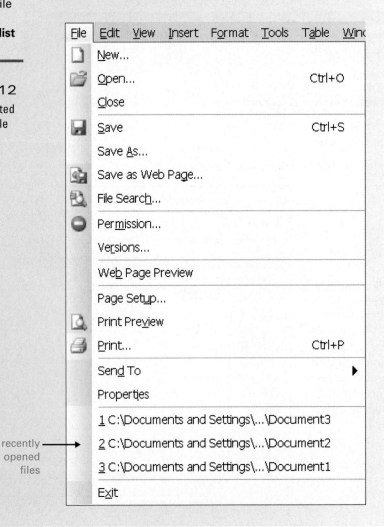

recently opened files →

FIGURE 1.13

Zoom

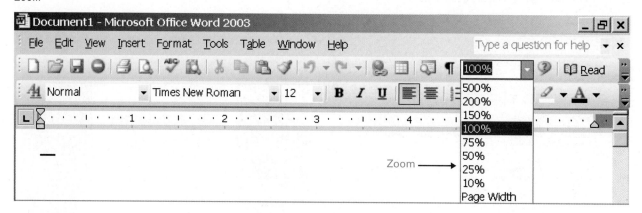

FIGURE 1.14

Document view icons

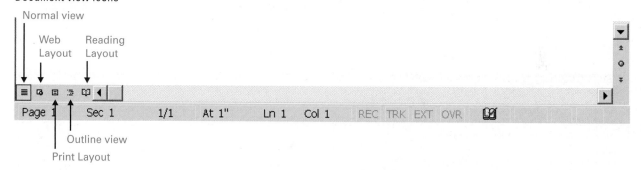

Zooming In on or Out of a Document

If you zoom in on a document, you will get a closer look at the document. If you zoom out of a document, you will see more of the document at a smaller size. To zoom in and out of your document simply click the arrow next to the Zoom drop-down on the Standard toolbar (see Figure 1.13).

Changing Document Views

Word offers five different ways that you can view your documents. The icons (buttons) for these different views are in the lower-left corner on the horizontal scroll bar (see Figure 1.14). The five views include, from left to right:

1. Normal
2. Web Layout
3. Print Layout
4. Outline
5. Reading Layout

Normal View

You should work in Normal view for typing, editing, and formatting text. Normal view shows text formatting but simplifies the layout of the page so that you can type and edit quickly (see Figure 1.15).

FIGURE   1.15

Four different views of the same document

Normal view

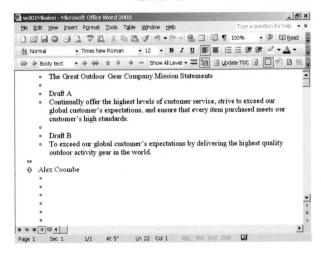

Print Layout view

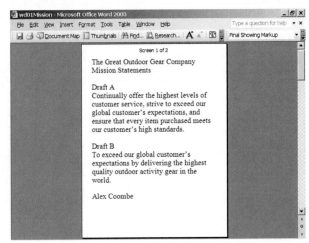

Reading Layout view

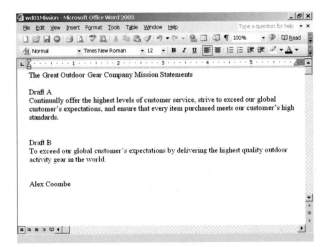

Outline view

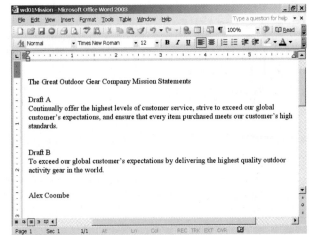

Web Layout View

You should work in Web Layout view when you are creating a Web page or a document that is viewed on the screen. In Web Layout view, you can see backgrounds, text is wrapped to fit the window, and graphics are positioned just as they are in a Web browser such as Microsoft Explorer or Netscape.

Print Layout View

When you want to see how text, graphics, and other elements are positioned on the printed page, you should work in the Print Layout view. This view is useful for showing formatting symbols, editing headers and footers, adjusting margins, and working with columns and drawing objects (see Figure 1.15).

Reading Layout View

Figure 1.15 shows a document in Reading Layout. The Reading Layout view is new to Word 2003. Reading Layout view hides all toolbars except for the Reading Layout and Reading Layout Markup toolbars. The goal of Reading Layout view is to increase legibility. You can easily increase or decrease the size of the text without affecting the size of the font in the document.

Outline View

Figure 1.15 shows a document in Outline view. You should work in Outline view to look at the structure of a document and to move, copy, and reorganize text by dragging headings. In Outline view, you can collapse a document to see only the main headings, or you can expand it to see all headings and even body text. You will learn more about Outline view in future chapters.

Inserting Text in a Document

All you do to enter text in a document is type it on the keyboard. The insertion point indicates where the text will be entered in your document. The flashing cursor will move across the screen in front of your text. Simply press the Enter key if you want to add blank lines in between your text.

Word Wrap

Word automatically wraps your text to the next line when you are typing a paragraph. *Word wrap* is the flow of text between the right and left margins without pressing Enter. You do not have to press the Enter key when you are at the end of the right margin if you wish to continue within a paragraph. If you want to begin a new paragraph, you must press the Enter key to take the cursor to a new line. The only time you need to press Enter is to create blank lines, to split a paragraph, or to end a paragraph.

Insert and Overtype Modes

You can insert text in a document using either the insert mode or overtype mode. The insert mode enters text as you type and moves any existing text to the right. If you are using the insert mode, you will not be typing over any existing text; you will be inserting text directly into your document, which is the most common way to type documents. If you are inserting text using the overtype mode, then you will be typing over any text that already exists in your document.

You can switch between the insert and overtype modes by pressing the Insert key on your keyboard. To find out which mode you are in, look at the OVR button on the status bar (see Figure 1.16). If the OVR button is bold, then you are in overtype mode.

Editing Text in a Document

To change or correct text you can use the four arrow keys, or your mouse, to move the cursor to the place where you want to edit the text.

help yourself *Click the Ask a Question combo box, type* **Selecting Text**, *and press* **Enter**. *Click the hyperlink* **Select Text** *and graphics to display information on how to select items that are not next to each other. Click the Help screen* **Close** *button when you are finished*

FIGURE 1.16

OVR button

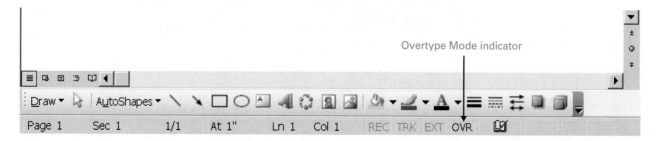

Overtype Mode indicator

Selecting Text

You can select any amount of text to edit. When selected, the text appears on the screen highlighted as white characters on a black background. **_Highlighted text_** is text selected by the user that is marked with a colored background and white lettering. Probably the most common method of selecting text is to use the mouse. To do this, you position the mouse pointer at the start of the text you want selected and hold down on the left mouse button as you drag the mouse across the text you want to select. When you stop moving the mouse pointer and release the left mouse button, your selected text will be highlighted (see Figure 1.17).

When you select text and start typing, Word will replace the entire selection with the first character you type. This saves editing time because you can delete and replace text in one step. If you make a mistake and want to unselect (deselect) the text, click the mouse pointer anywhere outside of the selected text and start over.

After reviewing Alex's first version of the mission statement, Paula makes a few changes in wording as displayed in Figure 1.18. Try to make Paula's suggested changes by using the select and insert functions.

FIGURE 1.17

Selected text in wd01Mission.doc

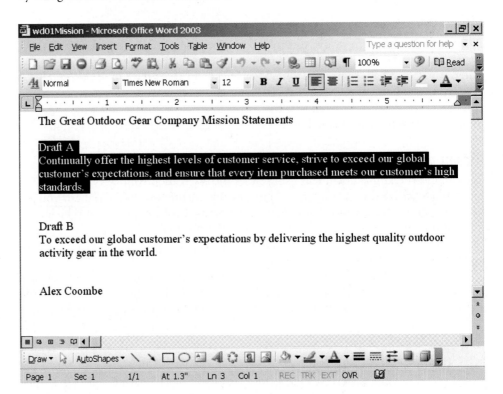

FIGURE 1.18

Mission statement drafts with Paula's changes

The Great Outdoor Gear Company Mission Statements

Draft A
Continually offer the highest levels of customer service and satisfaction, strive to exceed our global customer's expectations, and ensure that every item purchased meets the industries' high standards.

Draft B
To exceed our global customer's expectations by quickly delivering the highest quality outdoor activity gear in the world.

Alex Coombe

Making changes to a mission statement:

1. Make sure that the document wd01Mission.doc is the active document on the screen and you are using the Normal view

2. Insert the cursor behind the word **service** in the first sentence in Draft A

3. Press the **Spacebar** and type **and satisfaction**

4. Insert the cursor before the words **our customer's high standards** in Draft A

5. Select and highlight the words **our customer's**

6. Type **the industries'**

7. Insert the cursor before the word **delivering** in the first sentence of Draft B

8. Type **quickly**

9. Press the **Spacebar**

10. Figure 1.19 displays the revised wd01Mission.doc document

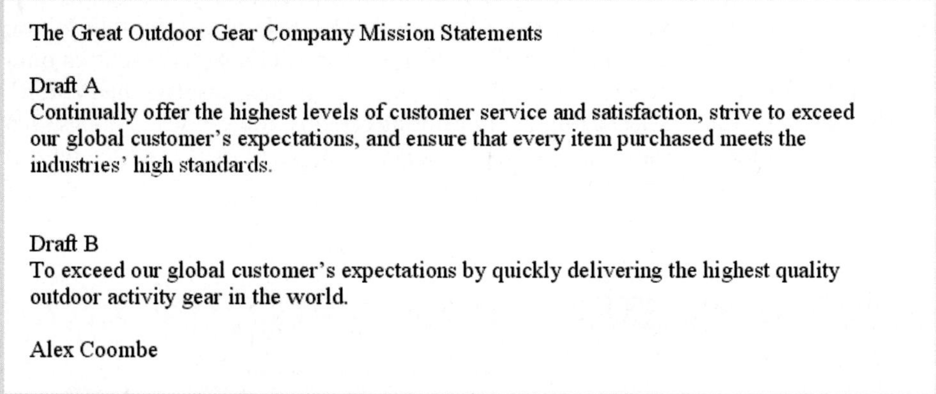

FIGURE 1.19

Mission statement with final changes completed

The Great Outdoor Gear Company Mission Statements

Draft A
Continually offer the highest levels of customer service and satisfaction, strive to exceed our global customer's expectations, and ensure that every item purchased meets the industries' high standards.

Draft B
To exceed our global customer's expectations by quickly delivering the highest quality outdoor activity gear in the world.

Alex Coombe

Delete and Backspace Keys

The *Backspace key* moves the cursor to the left while deleting a single character one space at a time. The *Delete key* moves the cursor to the right while deleting a single character one space at a time.

---

task reference   Deleting Text

- Select the text you would like to delete

- Press the **Delete** key on your keyboard

or

- Insert the cursor behind the text you want to delete

- Press the **Backspace** key on your keyboard

WORD

SESSION 1.2

making the grade

1. What is one of the most useful word-processing features?
2. What is the default name for a new document?
3. If you zoom out of a document, you will see more of the document at a __________ size.
4. There are __________ different views you can use depending on your project.
5. Word wrap is the flow of text between the right and left margins without pressing __________.

SESSION 1.3 PRINTING AND SAVING DOCUMENTS AND EXITING WORD

Printing Files

Printing provides you with a hard copy of your document. You can print a Word document using the Print command in the File menu, or by clicking the Print button on the Standard toolbar. The Standard toolbar Print button is handy because it's a one-click way to print your document. The File menu Print command displays the ***Print dialog*** box allowing you to select a number of printing options. You can select things such as the number of copies you want printed, the specific pages to print, and the type of paper to print on (see Figure 1.20).

FIGURE 1.20
Print dialog box

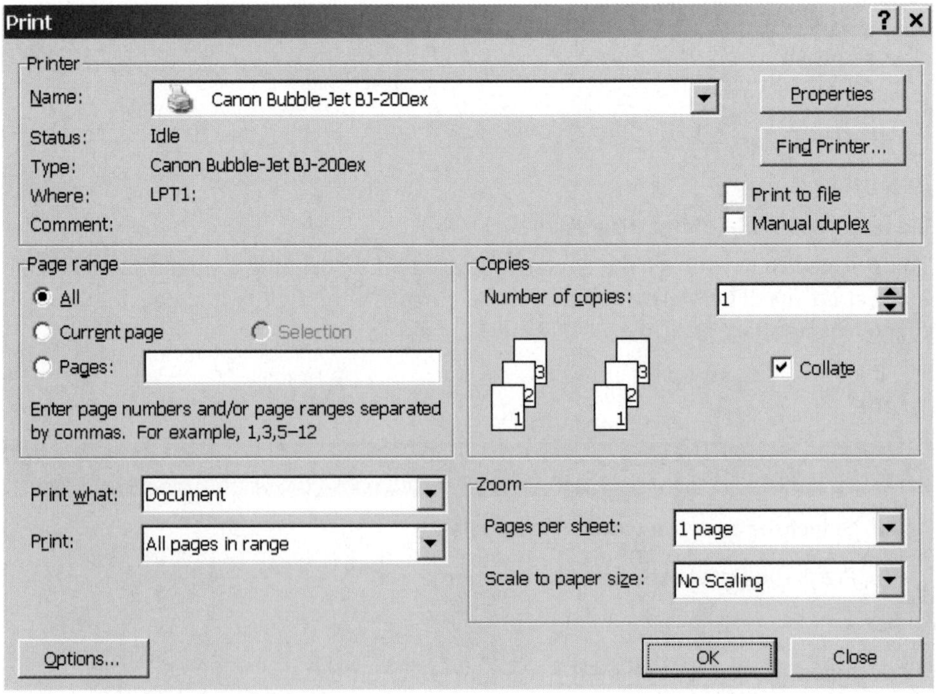

> ### *task reference*   Printing the Active Word Document
>
> - Click **Print** on the Standard toolbar
>
> or
>
> - Click **Print** on the File menu
> - Make any needed changes in the Print dialog box
> - Click the **OK** button in the Print dialog box (see Figure 1.20)

Print Preview

You can click on the File menu and select Print Preview to preview how your document is going to look when it is printed. *Print Preview* displays text and graphics as they will appear when printed on paper. This allows you to make editing and formatting changes before you print the document. This is a great way to save paper because you can correct many of your mistakes before printing (see Figure 1.21).

FIGURE 1.21

Print Preview of Alex's mission statements

Previewing a document:

1. Click on the **File** menu
2. Click **Print Preview** and the first page of output appears on the screen (see Figure 1.21)
3. Click **Close** to exit Print Preview and return to the previous view of the document

tip: *You can also edit text in Print Preview. Display the page you want to edit. Click the text in the area you want to edit. Word zooms in on the area. Click Magnifier. When the pointer changes from a magnifying glass to an I-beam and flashing cursor, make your changes to the document. Then return to the original magnification, click Magnifier, and click on the document*

anotherway

... to Save a Document

You can use the **Save As** item in the **File** menu to save an unnamed document. You can also use the keyboard short cut of **Ctrl+S** to save an unnamed document

WORD

Saving Files

You'll notice in the File menu that you have two primary options for saving documents using Word, Save and Save As. Save is used as a quick way to save changes and updates to a document that has already been saved. Save As is used the first time you save a new unnamed document. There are multiple ways that you can save documents using Word including:

- You can save a new unnamed document
- You can save changes and updates to an active document
- You can save all open documents at the same time
- You can save a copy of the active document with a different name or in a different location

It is important to save your work in the correct folder and to save it often. There is nothing worse than working on a document for several hours and having your computer crash. If your computer crashes and you forgot to save your documents, you will lose all of your work.

It's also important to save different versions of your documents. For example, you might save the initial draft of a mission statement as Mission1.doc. As you continue working on your document, you might save the file with the same name and a new version number, for example, Mission2.doc. Saving a file with a new version number will allow you to go back to your original document, if you ever need to.

For the exercises in this text you will be asked to save the original document with the same name and a new version number. This will allow you to always have the opportunity to go back to your original unedited document.

---

task reference　　　　Saving a New Unnamed Word Document

- Click the **Save As** item in the File menu
- Change the folder if you want to save the document in a different location than the default folder
- Type the document's name in the File name box
- Click **Save**

task reference　　Saving an Active Word Document

- Click the **Save** item in the File menu

Save As Dialog Box

The Save As dialog box offers you several different options for saving files. You can create a new folder by clicking on the new folder button in the Save As dialog box. This will allow you to organize your documents by folders.

One of the most important features of the Save As dialog box is the Save As Type drop-down list. Word allows you to share documents with people who use different types of word-processing software or different versions of Word. Other types of word-processing software include Word Perfect, Works, and Macintosh. If you want to send a document to a friend who is using different word-processing software you can save the document in a different file format. For example, you can open a document created in Word Perfect, make changes to it in Word, and then save it in either Word or Word Perfect format (see Figure 1.22).

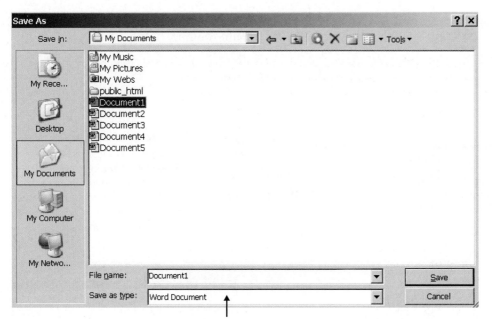

Save As dialog box

choose file type to Save As

Saving a document:

1. Determine which drive and folder will be used to save your documents

2. Click on the **File** menu

3. Click **Save As** to open the Save As dialog box

4. If you want to save the document in a different folder, locate and open the folder

5. In the File name box type the new name for the document **Mission1** (see Figure 1.23). Adding the new version number will allow you to return to the original document at a future point in time

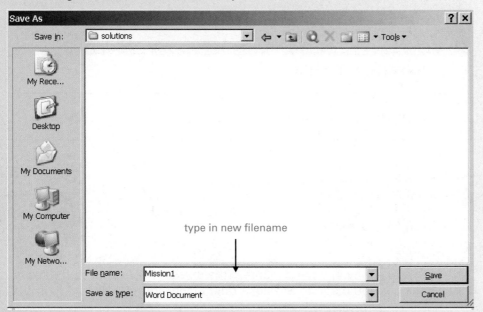

type in new filename

Saving the document as Mission1.doc

WORD

6. Click **Save** to save your document with the new name

tip: *Word adds the default extension of ".doc" to your filename. Using descriptive file-names will help you easily recognize your files in a drop-down list*

---

anotherword ... on Closing Documents

Hold down the **Shift** key and click **Close All** on the File menu to close all open documents without exiting Word

---

help yourself *Click the Ask a Question combo box, type* **Saving a File***, and press* **Enter***. Click the hyperlink* **Save a document** *to display information on how to save a document. Be sure to read the Note on the bottom explaining how to save all open documents at the same time. Click the Help screen Close button when you are finished*

---

task reference   Closing a Document

- Click **Close** on the File menu
- Click **Yes** to save changes

Closing and Exiting Word

Once you are finished working on your document, you can close it. If you made changes to the document that you have not saved, Word will automatically display a dialog box asking if you want to save the document before closing it. Normally, you should affirm saving a changed document even if you cannot remember making any changes to it. That way you are sure to save the most current version.

At this point Word remains available, allowing you to create new documents or to open existing ones. Alternatively, you can close Word if you have finished working on all of your documents. Closing Word unloads it from memory and closes any open documents. When you are finished using Word, it is a good practice to close the application so that the internal memory it occupies becomes available to other programs. Follow these steps to close Word.

---

task reference   Exiting Word

- Click **Exit** on the File menu

or

- Click the **Close** button at the top right of the screen

Closing a Word document:

1. Click on the **File** menu

2. Click **Close**

3. A dialog box may open and displays the message "Do you want to save the changes you made to Mission1.doc?" (see Figure 1.24)

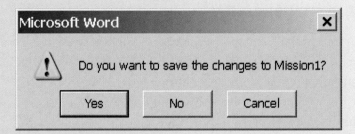

FIGURE 1.24
Save Changes dialog box

4. Click **Yes** to save the changes you made since you last saved the document before closing it. (If you click No, then Word does not save the changes before closing the document. If you click Cancel, then Word cancels the close operation and redisplays the active document.)

To exit Word:

1. Click on the **File** menu

2. Click **Exit**

tip: *You can close Word by clicking the Close button on Word's Title bar. If any documents have unsaved changes, you will be asked if you want to save those changes before the documents are closed and Word is exited*

tip: *If you do not see the Exit command, simply click on the double arrows at the bottom of the list to display additional commands*

---

making the grade

SESSION 1.3

1. What allows you to select a number of printing options?

2. What displays text and graphics as they will appear when printed on paper?

3. Does Word allow you to save files for other types of word-processing software?

4. Word will _____ display a dialog box asking if you want to save changes before closing an edited document.

5. _____ provides you with a hard copy of your document.

SESSION 1.4 SUMMARY

Word processing has come a long way since the days of the electric typewriter. Each new version of word-processing software turns the personal computer into a more powerful tool for creating, saving, and editing documents.

One of the most important things someone new to Word can do is to learn all of the features and functions on the menu and toolbars. A new user should also become familiar with the Help features in Word. After reading this chapter, you should be able to open, change, save, and print documents. These tasks represent the initial steps toward becoming a Word expert.

WORD

MICROSOFT OFFICE SPECIALIST OBJECTIVES SUMMARY

- Insert and edit text, symbols, and special characters—MOS WW03S-1-1
- Organize documents using file folders—MOS WW03S-5-3
- Save documents in appropriate formats for different uses—MOS WW03S-5-4
- Print documents, envelopes, and labels—MOS WW03S-5-5
- Preview documents and Web pages—MOS WW03S-5-6
- Change and organize document views and windows—MOS WW03S-5-7

making the grade *answers*

SESSION 1.1

1. Word-processing software

2. Arrow keys

3. Document window

4. Menu

5. Scroll bars

SESSION 1.2

1. Ability to quickly and easily make changes and corrections

2. Document1

3. Smaller

4. Five

5. Enter

SESSION 1.3

1. Print dialog

2. Print Preview

3. Yes

4. Automatically

5. Printing

task reference *summary*

Task	Page #	Preferred Method
Opening a Word document	WD 1.11	• Click on the **File** menu, click **Open**, click on the document's name, click the **Open** button located on the Open dialog box, or double-click on the document's name
Deleting text	WD 1.17	• Select the text you would like to delete, press the **Delete** key on your keyboard, or insert the cursor behind the text you want to delete, press the **Backspace** key on your keyboard
Printing the active Word document	WD 1.19	• Click **Print** on the Standard toolbar, or click **Print** on the File menu, make any needed changes in the Print dialog box, click the **OK** button in the Print dialog box (see Figure 1.20)
Saving a new unnamed Word document	WD 1.20	• Click the **Save As** item in the File menu, change the folder if you want to save the document in a different location than the default folder, type the document's name in the File name box, click **Save**
Saving an active Word document	WD 1.20	• Click the **Save** item in the File menu
Closing a document	WD 1.22	• Click **Close** on the File menu, click **Yes** to save changes
Exiting Word	WD 1.22	• Click **Exit** on the File menu, or Click the **Close** button at the top right of the screen

TRUE/FALSE

1. Word-processing software helps you create papers, letters, memos, and other basic documents.

2. The Title bar is a bar marked off in units of measure (such as inches) that is displayed across the top of the document window.

3. The mouse pointer indicates the current position of the mouse as you move around the screen.

4. An icon is a drop-down menu list that executes a command when the menu item is selected.

5. A scroll bar allows the user to move diagonally around the document.

6. The Enter key must be used every time you advance to a new line.

FILL-IN

1. _____ and _____ are toolbars found on the Word screen.

2. The Edit command is found in the _____ bar.

3. _____ text is text selected by the user that is marked with a colored background and white lettering.

4. To open a specific previously saved file, you must know the _____ name.

5. The Print _____ box allows you to change some of the printing options.

MULTIPLE CHOICE

1. Which of the following can be created using word-processing software?
   a. Papers
   b. Letters
   c. Memos
   d. All of the above

2. Which of the following displays the current document name?
   a. Title bar
   b. Status bar
   c. Menu bar
   d. Formatting bar

3. Which of the following contains buttons that can change the appearance of text?
   a. Title bar
   b. Status bar
   c. Menu bar
   d. Formatting bar

4. What allows you to select a number of different printing options?
   a. Save As dialog box
   b. Print dialog box
   c. Print Preview
   d. All of the above

5. Which of the following describes the function of the Backspace key?
   a. Deletes single characters to the left
   b. Deletes single characters to the right
   c. Deletes multiple characters to the right
   d. All of the above

REVIEW QUESTIONS

1. Name two toolbars on the Word screen.

2. List four commands on the menu bar.

3. Which view will you use most frequently?

4. How many scroll bars are normally on the Word screen? Name them.

5. Identify two ways of opening a document.

CREATE THE QUESTION

For each of the following answers, create an appropriate, short question.

ANSWER	QUESTION
1. Office Assistant	_____
2. Document window	_____
3. Status bar	_____
4. Formatting marks	_____
5. Normal view	_____
6. Highlighted text	_____
7. View modes	_____

FACT OR FICTION

1. The Formatting toolbar normally appears below the Standard toolbar and contains buttons that change the appearance of text in a document, for example, bold, italicize, underline, justify, number, or bullet text.

2. The status bar normally appears below the menu bar and contains buttons representing the most popular commands such as Open, Save, Print, Cut, and Paste.

3. After you highlight text using the mouse pointer, the text is highlighted with white characters displayed on a black background.

4. Depending on the project you are working on you can view your documents four different ways including Normal, Web Layout, Print Layout, and Standard.

5. The scroll bars are shaded bars that appear on the right side and bottom of a document window and allow you to scroll to another part of a document by dragging the box or clicking the arrows in the scroll bar.

1. Creating Your Personal Mission Statement

Now that you are familiar with Word, let's practice creating, saving, editing, and printing a document. Recall that a mission statement describes the primary goals for a business. A personal mission statement will describe the primary goals you have set for yourself. Your personal mission statement explains who you want to be, what you want to accomplish, and what's most important to you. Once you have completed your personal mission statement, you can use it as the opening line on your resume. This statement helps your future employer instantly understand your values, principles, and goals.

The first step to writing your personal mission statement is to brainstorm. On a piece of paper create a list of everything that is important to you including family, friends, careers, sports, dreams, and goals. Take a good look at your list and decide which items you want to include in your personal goals and ambitions. Finally, write a few short sentences that describe your personal goals and communicate what you really want to do with your life. Try to keep the statement reasonably short with only a few sentences. Once you have your personal mission statement complete, you can begin typing it in Word.

1. Open a blank document in Word

2. Click on the **File** menu

3. Click **Save As** and save the new document as **MyMission1.doc**

4. On the first line type your name

5. Press the **Enter key** once to advance to the next line

6. On the second line type **Personal Mission Statements**

7. Press the **Enter key** once to advance to the next line

8. You suddenly realize that you made a mistake on the second line. *Statements* should not be plural. Insert the cursor at the end of the text on the second line

9. Hit the **Backspace key** once to delete the extra **s**

10. Press the **Enter key** once to advance to the next line

11. On the third line type the date

12. Press the **Enter key** twice to advance two lines

13. Type in your personal mission statement. See Figure 1.25 for an example of Alex's personal mission statement.

14. Click the **Save** button on the Standard toolbar to save your modified document

15. Click the **File** menu

16. Click **Print** to display the Print dialog box

17. Print your personal mission statement

FIGURE 1.25

Alex's Personal Mission Statement

Alex Coombe
Personal Mission Statement
01/01/04

I want to challenge myself by continually learning new and exciting things. I want to become a computer software engineer in the telecommunications industry and work in different countries all over the world.

2. Writing a Business Memo

Let's practice opening, saving, editing, and printing a business memo. A business memo helps employees communicate in an effective and efficient manner. A business memo is similar to a business letter, except a memo is written in a very specific format and you do not sign your name on the bottom of the memo. Instead, you simply place your initials next to your name at the top of the memo.

Alex decided to create a business memo to distribute to her fellow employees along with her two draft versions of the mission statements for The Great Outdoor Gear Company (see Figure 1.26). Alex would like your professional opinion regarding her memo before she distributes it to the rest of the employees. After reviewing the memo, you notice several errors that must be corrected. Let's open Alex's memo so you can help her make the necessary changes. See Figure 1.26 to review how the final memo is going to look.

1. Open the document **wd01Memo.doc**

2. Click on the **File menu**

3. Click **Save As** to save the new document as **Memo1.doc**

4. Insert the cursor at the end of the first line

5. Press the **backspace** key twice to remove **02**

6. Type in the current year

7. Using the mouse pointer, highlight the word **Everyone** on the third line after To:

8. Press the **backspace key** to delete the word **Everyone**

9. Type in **All Employees**

10. Using the mouse pointer, highlight the word **Personal** on the seventh line after RE:

11. Press the **delete key** to delete the word **Personal**

12. Using the mouse pointer, highlight the words **Paula Logston** in the final sentence of the first paragraph

13. Type in the name **Alex Coombe**

14. Type in <**your name**> at the bottom left corner of the memo

tip: Be sure to include your name on the bottom of every document you create. Including your name on the bottom of every document you create will allow your instructor to easily recognize your work

15. Click the **Save** button on the Standard toolbar to save your modified document

16. Click on the **File menu**

17. Click **Print** to display the Print dialog box

18. Print the memo

19. Compare your printed memo to Figure 1.26

FIGURE 1.26

The Great Outdoor Gear Company Mission Statement memo

01/01/04

To: All Employees

From: Alex Coombe

Re: The Great Outdoor Gear Company Mission Statements

As many of you know, we are attempting to develop the mission statement for our company. We are currently seeking any feedback you have on the two potential mission statements below. If you have any question please contact Alex Coombe directly.

Draft A
Continually offer the highest levels of customer service and satisfaction, strive to exceed our global customer's expectations, and ensure that every item purchased meets the industries high standards.

Draft B
To exceed our global customer's expectations by quickly delivering the highest quality outdoor activity gear in the world.

1. Creating a Meeting Agenda for the Madison County Fair and Rodeo

The annual Madison County Fair and Rodeo is held in Twin Bridges, Montana. The fair is one of the largest events held in Montana attracting people from all over the country. A few of the fair's activities include a petting zoo, two-day rodeo, youth rodeo, stock horse show, carnival, and even a parade. People travel from all over to see the animals, ride the rides, and eat the delicious food.

You are excited to find out that you recently received the job of executive assistant for the entire Madison County Fair Board. The position has many challenges as well as great opportunities. The majority of your job consists of using word-processing software to create all kinds of business documents.

The president of the board, Max Fischer, has put together the agenda for the upcoming monthly meeting. Max is unfamiliar with word-processing software and uncomfortable handing out a handwritten agenda to the rest of the board members. Max has asked you to help him transfer his handwritten agenda into Word. You can find Max's handwritten version of the agenda in Figure 1.27. The handwritten copy reflects the format he would like on the typed version.

Open a new Word document and save the file as **Agenda1.doc**. Type in Max's agenda exactly as it is displayed in Figure 1.27. Be sure to add your name in the bottom left corner of the document. When you are finished, save and print out a copy of the agenda.

Below you will find a detailed listing of all the different activities offered at the fair. Max would also like to include this detailed listing along with the agenda so the board members can review the different activities to decide if they want to make any changes. Please open and save a new file with the name **Activities1.doc**. Type in the list below, add your name to the bottom, and save and print a copy of the document.

Activities
Carnival
Fair
Photography
Horse Show
Livestock Show
Parade
Rodeo
Auction
Barbeque
Exhibits
Arts & Crafts
Dancing
Stage Show

FIGURE 1.27

Max Fischer's handwritten agenda for the Madison County Fair Board meeting

Agenda

Monthly Meeting of Madison County Fair Board

Report on assignments made last meeting

Renovation of produce display building

New ticket booth

Contracts for food vendors

Prize money

Review of admission price

Assignments for next meeting

2. Creating and Editing a Letter for the Best Ever Gaming Company

Your good friend Jack Geller is crazy about computer games. He has been playing computer games for the majority of his life and his all-time favorite games are produced by The Best Ever Gaming Company. Jack wants to send the company a letter to find out if the company has a Web site or a catalog. The only problem is that Jack doesn't know how to use word-processing software to create his letter.

Jack convinced his sister, Monica, to type the letter for him. Monica did a great job creating Jack's letter. After Jack had a chance to review the letter, he wanted to make several changes to it. Monica was going to make the changes for him when she realized that she never saved the original letter. Monica did not have the time to retype the entire letter over again.

Jack is now begging you to take the time to retype the letter for him. You decide that you can't let your good friend Jack down, and you agree to take on the task. Figure 1.28 displays the letter with Jack's hand-written changes. Open a new Word document and save the file as **Gameletter1.doc**. Type in Jack's letter and be sure to include all of the handwritten changes. Add your name to the bottom of the letter and save and print a copy of the letter for Jack when you are finished.

FIGURE 1.28

Jack's edited letter to the Best Ever Gaming Company

1. What's This Thing Called the Internet?

According to Webopedia, the Internet is a global network connecting millions of computers in more than 100 countries. Most businesses today have an Internet presence. They have Web sites where you can browse their products, read service reports, and review company information. Businesses that are not on the Internet probably have a hard time competing in today's electronic business world.

You are the public relations specialist at the Old Record Superstore Company. The company has been in business for 40 years and its primary business is to buy and sell albums. The company currently has three superstores in Chicago, New York, and San Francisco. The owner of the company, Gus Marmer, has come to you as the local computer expert. Gus has been working in the album business for the last 40 years and he is unfamiliar with the Internet. He realizes that he needs to develop an Internet presence so that customers can be-

gin purchasing albums online. Gus knows that there are many other advantages to using the Internet, but he is not sure what they are. Gus has asked you to put together a memo describing how the company can use the Internet to generate more business. The memo should address the following three questions:

1. What is the Internet?

2. Internet features

3. How the Internet will help the business

Figure 1.29 displays the template you will be using for this exercise. Open the document **wd01Internet.doc** and save the document as **Internet1.doc**. Use the Internet, or any other resources you have, to research the three questions that Gus has asked you to answer. Question number three is the one that Gus is most interested in reviewing. Fill in the answers to each question in the spaces provided. After completing the memo, save your work and print a copy of it for Gus to review.

FIGURE 1.29

What's this thing called the Internet?

01/01/04

To: Gus Marmer

From: <<Your Name>>

Re: What is this thing called the Internet?

What is the Internet?
[Type a brief description of the Internet here]

Internet features
[Type a few of the different features of the Internet here]

How the Internet will help the business
[Type a few ways the Internet can help the business here]

2. Choosing the Right ISP

An Internet service provider (ISP) is a company that provides individuals, organizations, and businesses access to the Internet. If you want to access the World Wide Web, you must use an ISP. ISPs offer a number of other services including e-mail, chat rooms, instant messaging, and Web space. Web space is a storage area where you keep your Web site. ISPs typically charge a monthly fee in order to use their services. AOL, Microsoft (MSN), and AT&T WorldNet are a few of the popular worldwide ISPs.

You are starting your own coffee bean export business. Your company is called BeansRUs and you want to purchase and sell exotic coffee beans worldwide. The first thing you need to do is set up a company e-mail account and a Web site. You have decided to join an ISP so you can have e-mail and Web space for your Web site. Realizing that there are many different ISPs avail-able, you are going to have to do some research prior to making your decision on which ISP to join. Using the Internet, research two different ISPs for the following information:

1. ISP name

2. Price per month

3. Services available

4. Features available

Figure 1.30 is an example of how you might want to organize your document. Open the document **wd01ISP.doc** and save it as **ISP1.doc**. Feel free to add any additional categories you think are valuable for making your final ISP decision. Once you have completed your document, make the final decision on which ISP you are going to use. Type the name of your final choice at the bottom of the document.

FIGURE 1.30

My ISP Comparison Report

Your name
01/01/04
ISP Comparison Report

ISP1 - Name
Type information here about the ISP including prices, services, and features

ISP2 - Name
Type information here about the ISP including prices, services, and features

Type your ISP choice here

1. Finding Training on the Web

The Internet is a great place for you to learn about all different kinds of topics. Did you know that you can find all sorts of free training on the Web? The Web offers training on just about any topic you can imagine including computers, cooking, writing, remote control cars, car engines, Christmas tree lights, airplanes, and even the human body.

You have decided that in addition to taking this course, you are also going to perform some self-training on the Internet. Search the Web for an e-business that specializes in training individuals to use word-processing software (see Figure 1.31 for an example of a training Web site). There are many different sites available, so be sure to carefully review two or three different sites.

Once you have had a chance to review several different Web sites, make a decision on which training you want to perform. Open a new document and save it as **Training1.doc**. In a paragraph, briefly describe the business offering the training including the business name, location, and purpose. Next, describe the training they offer including important items such as cost, schedule, and topics covered in the training. In the final paragraph, describe why this particular training Web site was better than the other training Web sites you reviewed.

2. Describing Cars for Sale on the Web

Search the Web for three automobiles of the same make and model but different years that are for sale. Many of these cars can be found by searching for "autos for sale." Write a brief description of these automobiles in a document named **Auto1.doc**. Save the document and be sure to add your name and address at the bottom of the document.

FIGURE 1.31

Training Web site

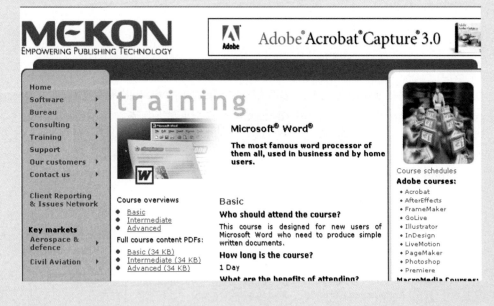

around the world

1. Your Dream Vacation

Traveling to different countries is a great way to spend a summer vacation. Where would you go if you could go anywhere in the world? China, Germany, Japan, Hawaii, Europe, or Tahiti might be a few options. You could head to France and visit the Eiffel Tower or head to Toronto and visit the CN Tower. You could relax on a beach in Maui, climb Mt. Everest, walk the Great Wall in China, and take a boat down the Amazon in South America. The options for your dream summer vacation are limitless.

Let's have some fun and plan your dream international summer vacation. Using the Internet, develop an itinerary for your vacation. Figure 1.32 displays the World Airport Guide Web site. This Web site can help you find out all kinds of information on every airport in the world and will be helpful when you begin planning your vacation.

You have one month to travel anywhere you want in the world. Your agenda should include such things as:

- Travel dates
- Travel arrangements
- Hotel accommodations
- Restaurants
- Entertainment
- Activities

Open the document **wd01Vacation.doc** and save it as **Vacation1.doc**. If you want to be creative and don't want to use the vacation template, feel free to develop your own vacation document by opening a new document and saving it as **Vacation1.doc**. Enter your vacation agenda in the document. Don't worry about the cost because money is no object. Have some fun and stay in luxurious hotels, eat in the best restaurants, and take advantage of exciting activities.

2. Posting a Room for Rent for an International Student

You have a room for rent in your house or apartment that you would like to rent to an international student. Compose a short paragraph describing the room you have for rent, its location, and the monthly rental fee. Make up a phone number for yourself and describe how you should be contacted. Save the file as **MyRental1.doc** and be sure to add your name on a separate line after the rental description.

FIGURE 1.32

Finding international airports on the Internet

running project

Developing a Mission Statement for the Kasota United School District

The Kasota United School District (KUSD) provides a kindergarten through twelfth grade (K-12) education for an average of 4,000 students each year. The district employs over 200 classroom teachers in four grade schools, two middle schools, and one high school. Each school building has a principal, a secretary, a librarian, two teachers' aides, and one or two custodians. In the central office a superintendent, assistant superintendent, and three secretaries administer the district. Many of the offices and teachers use student aides. Like many school districts, KUSD is struggling with its reputation, credibility, and teacher morale.

In an effort to improve the overall image of the district, the new superintendent, Greg Provenzo, made a commitment that all form letters, forms, handbooks, handouts, signs, notices, and memos will be created using word-processing software and printed with a high-quality printer. Besides improving the appearance of these documents, the spelling and grammar can be double-checked before any publication is released to the public.

Greg's number one priority is to reestablish the pride, reputation, and credibility of the district. To begin the process, he asks Emily Regan to draft two versions of a mission statement for the next board meeting. Emily is a new employee who seems to progress rapidly with her use and knowledge of word processing. First, Greg explains to Emily that a mission statement is a written statement of their school district's purpose. A mission statement for KUSD will help the community relate to the district, and the employees will know what to expect from the district. The mission statement for KUSD will keep everyone on track, in focus, and motivated. Work along with Emily and create two drafts of the mission statement. Greg asks that the following ideas and phrases be used:

- Educational standards
- Quality education
- Parental involvement
- Importance of an education
- Qualified and knowledgeable faculty and staff
- Fiscally responsible

Since mission statements are developed as a collaborative effort, the drafts of the KUSD mission statements will be shared at the board meeting and distributed to all faculty and staff within the district.

When you write your two draft versions of the mission statements, remember that the writing should be clear and concise. Individuals outside the district should easily understand the district's primary purpose. Refer to the two versions as **DraftA.doc** and **DraftB.doc**. Be sure to include your name on a separate line two lines below the last line of text in the mission statement drafts. When you have completed your work, be sure to save and print a copy of your document.

1. Insert and Overtype Modes

Practice using the insert and overtype modes. Once you are familiar with each, discuss why you think Word offers these two different ways to insert text. Also discuss what considerations, if any, you would use to determine which mode you prefer to work in.

2. Multiple Ways to Accomplish the Same Task—Menu Bar, Standard Toolbar, Formatting Toolbar, Keyboard, Mouse

Word offers several different ways to accomplish the same task. For example, you can use the menu bar to invoke the Save command, you can use the Standard toolbar to invoke the Save command, and you can use the keyboard (Ctrl + S) to invoke the Save command. Explain why Word offers so many different ways to accomplish similar tasks.

2

Editing and Formatting Documents

did you know?

the *best-known landmark in France is the Eiffel Tower, constructed in 1889 and only suppose to last 20 years.*

if *the entire world consumed fossil fuel at the same rate as the United States, the resources of five earths would be required to support the population.*

Alexander Graham Bell *invented the telephone in 1876 as a spin-off from his main research on deafness.*

there *are more than 1,000 chemicals in a cup of coffee and 13 of these caused cancer in rats.*

tropical *rain forests cover only 8 percent of the earth's land surface but contain 40 percent of all species of animals and plants and about 50 percent of all growing wood.*

your *eyes are always the same size from birth, but your nose and ears never stop growing.*

Chapter Objectives

- Insert and edit text, symbols, and special characters—MOS WW03S-1-1

- Insert frequently used and pre-defined text—MOS WW03S-1-2

- Navigate to specific content—MOS WW03S-1-3

- Locate, select, and insert supporting information—MOS WW03S-1-6

- Format text—MOS WW03S-3-1

- Format paragraphs—MOS WW03S-3-2

- Change and organize document views and windows—MOS WW03S-5-7

Developing a Promotional Letter for Magic Slopes Ski Resort

Documents create the all-important first impression. You and your ideas will be taken seriously when professionally presented. Of course, the contents of a document are the most important factor, but the quality of the document is also influenced by its appearance. A document's success impacts a business and individual goals. Professional documents drive results. Word allows you to easily integrate other information, including graphics, and modify the appearance to create rich, professional-looking documents that are read and get results.

Jamie Ash works in the front office of Magic Slopes, a small ski resort in Utah. The resort competes with two larger nearby ski resorts. Although

smaller, Magic Slopes always seems to have the most and best snow. Additionally, Magic Slopes has some of the hardest runs in the state, it provides advanced skiing and snowboarding lessons, and a day pass at Magic Slopes is considerably less than at the larger resorts.

Jamie has been asked to revise an old promotional letter to develop this year's promotion letter that will be sent to all local sports shops, high school students, college students, and season pass holders. Figure 2.1 shows what the letter looked like when Jamie received it—complete with the yellow sticky note.

FIGURE 2.1

Last year's promotional letter with sticky note of instructions

Last year's promotional letter with sticky note of instructions:

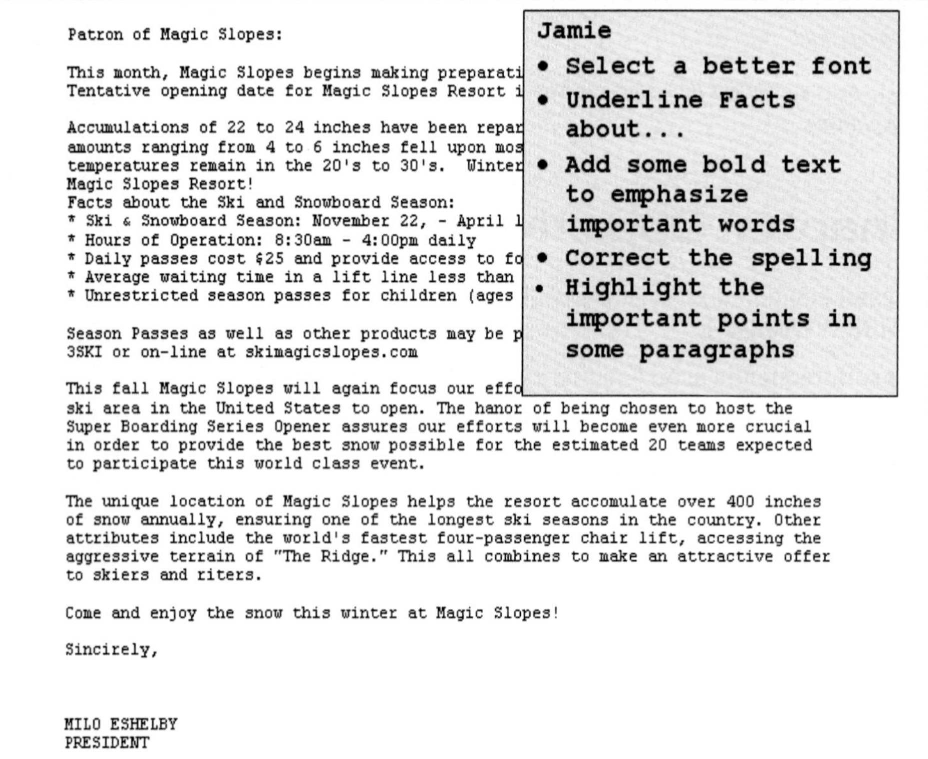

```
Patron of Magic Slopes:

This month, Magic Slopes begins making preparati
Tentative opening date for Magic Slopes Resort i

Accumulations of 22 to 24 inches have been repar
amounts ranging from 4 to 6 inches fell upon mos
temperatures remain in the 20's to 30's.  Winter
Magic Slopes Resort!
Facts about the Ski and Snowboard Season:
* Ski & Snowboard Season: November 22, - April 1
* Hours of Operation: 8:30am - 4:00pm daily
* Daily passes cost $25 and provide access to fo
* Average waiting time in a lift line less than
* Unrestricted season passes for children (ages

Season Passes as well as other products may be p
3SKI or on-line at skimagicslopes.com

This fall Magic Slopes will again focus our effo
ski area in the United States to open. The hanor of being chosen to host the
Super Boarding Series Opener assures our efforts will become even more crucial
in order to provide the best snow possible for the estimated 20 teams expected
to participate this world class event.

The unique location of Magic Slopes helps the resort accomulate over 400 inches
of snow annually, ensuring one of the longest ski seasons in the country. Other
attributes include the world's fastest four-passenger chair lift, accessing the
aggressive terrain of "The Ridge." This all combines to make an attractive offer
to skiers and riters.

Come and enjoy the snow this winter at Magic Slopes!

Sincirely,


MILO ESHELBY
PRESIDENT
```

Sticky note:

Jamie
- Select a better font
- Underline Facts about...
- Add some bold text to emphasize important words
- Correct the spelling
- Highlight the important points in some paragraphs

The yellow sticky note on the old letter suggests that Jamie do the following to the old version of the letter:

- Select a better font (original in Courier)
- Underline "Facts about . . ."
- Add some bold to emphasize words
- Correct the spelling
- Highlight the important points in some paragraphs

Features of word processing will allow Jamie to modify the old promotional letter and create a new, more attractive, and easy-to-read letter. Figure 2.2 shows the final promotional letter after Jamie made the suggested changes plus a few of her own to enhance the appearance of the letter.

FIGURE 2.2
This year's revised promotional letter

Patron of *Magic Slopes*:

This month, *Magic Slopes* begins making preparations for the 2003-2004 seasons. Tentative opening date for *Magic Slopes* Resort is set for October 27.

Accumulations of 22 to 24 inches have been reported at *Magic Slopes* but lighter amounts ranging from 4 to 6 inches fell upon most of the valley. The temperatures remain in the 20's to 30's. Winter is here—how we love it here at *Magic Slopes* Resort!

Facts about the ski and snowboard season:
   * Ski & snowboard season: November 22 - April 15

   * Hours of Operation: 8:30am - 4:00pm daily

   * Daily passes cost $25 and provide access to four chairlifts

   * Average waiting time in a lift line less than 5 minutes

   * Unrestricted season passes for children (ages 6-14): $100 and adults: $249

Season Passes as well as other products may be purchased by calling 1-800-333-3SKI or on-line at skimagicslopes.com

The unique location of *Magic Slopes* helps the resort accumulate over 400 inches of snow annually, ensuring one of the longest ski seasons in the country. Other attributes include the world's fastest four-passenger chair lift, accessing the aggressive terrain of "The Ridge." This all combines to make an attractive offer to skiers and riders.

This fall *Magic Slopes* will again focus our efforts on being the first seasonal ski area in the United States to open. The honor of being chosen to host the Super Boarding Series Opener assures our efforts will become even more crucial in order to provide the best snow possible for the estimated 20 teams expected to participate in this world class event.

Come and enjoy the snow this winter at *Magic Slopes*!

Sincerely,

Milo Eshelby
President

INTRODUCTION

Have you ever received a document that was full of spelling and grammatical errors? I bet you were not very impressed with the person who created the document. Creating documents that are error-free and professional-looking is an important skill to build. In this session, you are going to learn how to accomplish all of the following:

- Edit documents
- Spell-check and grammar-check documents
- Format text
- Format paragraphs
- Format documents

SESSION 2.1 EDITING DOCUMENTS

Text Editing Options

All writing becomes better with each revision. Chances are you'll find yourself quickly writing letters, reports, and messages. Once you have had a chance to go back and review your work, you might discover that the document contains a number of errors including spelling mistakes, grammatical errors, and the improper placement of words and sentences. In the days of the old typewriters, revising the rough draft meant you had to retype the entire document or retype parts of the document. You then had to literally use scissors, tape, or whiteout to cut and paste the final version together.

Cutting, pasting, and moving text are easy tasks to perform when you are using Word. If you make a mistake, you can simply undo your mistake with Word's Undo Typing feature. You can also use the AutoCorrect, spell-check, and grammar-check features of Word to help you produce an error-free document.

---

another*word*   **. . . on Cutting and Copying**

It's important to understand the difference between cutting and copying text. Cutting text is similar to deleting text; unless you paste the text somewhere else, the text is gone forever. Copying text simply creates a copy of the text, which you can then paste. When you are first starting to use these functions, it is safer for you to use the copy function than the cut function

---

Cut, Copy, and Paste

Text can be cut, or copied, from one location in a document and pasted to another location in the same document. Cutting, copying, and pasting text are some of the most useful features in Word. You can use the Standard toolbar, menu bar, keyboard, or mouse to perform all of these tasks. Figure 2.3 displays the Cut, Copy, and Paste buttons on the Standard toolbar. To use your keyboard shortcuts to cut, copy, and paste text simply highlight the text and press Ctrl+X to cut, Ctrl+C to copy, and Ctrl+V to paste. To use the menu bar to cut, copy, and paste text simply click on the Edit menu and select the corresponding task (see Figure 2.4). Finally, you can cut, copy, and paste text with a right-click of the mouse, which evokes the context sensitive shortcut menu (see Figure 2.5). The ***shortcut menu*** displays a list of commands relevant to a particular item, evoked with the right-click of a mouse button.

F I G U R E   2.3

Cut, Copy, and Paste icons on the Standard toolbar

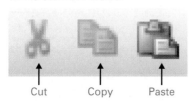

Cut   Copy   Paste

FIGURE 2.4

Cut, copy, and paste on the menu bar

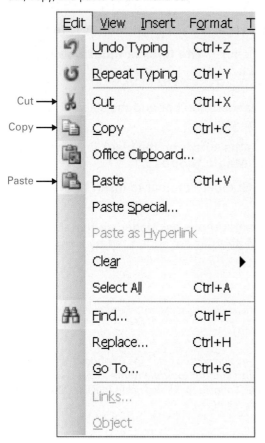

FIGURE 2.5

Cut, copy, and paste using the right-click on the mouse

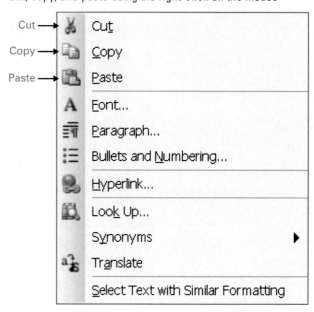

task reference Cutting, Copying, and Moving Text

- Select the item you want to move or copy
- To move the item, click **Cut** on the Standard toolbar
- Click where you want the item to appear
- Click **Paste** on the Standard toolbar

or

- To copy the item, click **Copy** on the Standard toolbar
- Click where you want the item to appear
- Click **Paste** on the Standard toolbar

After reading the Magic Slopes promotional letter, Jamie decides to switch the location of two paragraphs. Jamie is going to use the cut-and-paste feature of Word to put the paragraph that begins "The unique location of …" before the paragraph that begins "This fall Magic Slopes…"

Cutting and pasting text:

1. Open **wd02MagicSlopes.doc** and save it as **MagicSlopes1.doc**

2. Select the entire paragraph that begins **"The unique location of..."**

tip: *You can either use the mouse pointer or click in the left margin twice*

3. Click the **Cut** button on the Standard toolbar and the selected paragraph is removed from the document

4. Using the mouse pointer, position the cursor on the blank line above the paragraph that begins **"This fall Magic Slopes..."**

5. Click the **Paste** button on the Standard toolbar to insert the paragraph

6. Add or delete any lines between paragraphs as needed so that the end of each paragraph and the start of another are separated by a single blank line

7. Save your document

tip: *Once an item is copied, or cut, it can be pasted multiple times into multiple locations*

help yourself *Click the Ask a Question combo box, type **Clipboard**, and press* ***Enter***. *Click the hyperlink **About collecting and pasting multiple items** to display information on how you can use the Microsoft Office Clipboard to cut and paste multiple items. Click the Help screen **Close** button when you are finished*

Find and Replace

The *Find* command allows you to find any particular word or phrase in a document. The *Replace* command allows you to replace any particular word or phrase in a document with a new word or phrase. These features are particularly useful when you realize that a common term throughout your document is incorrect. For example, assume you used the word *internet* and forgot to capitalize the *I*. You could use the Find and Replace commands to quickly find all occurrences of the word *internet* and replace it with the word *Internet*.

---

task reference   Finding Text

- On the Edit menu, click **Find** to open the Find and Replace dialog box (see Figure 2.6)

- In the Find what box, enter the text you want to search for

- Select any other options that you want

- Click **Find Next**

- To cancel a search in progress, press **Esc**

- To close the Find and Replace dialog box, click the **Cancel** button or the **Close** button

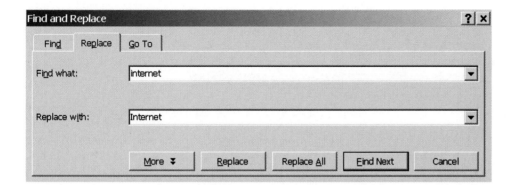

---

task reference — Replacing Text

- On the Edit menu, click **Replace**
- In the Find what box, enter the text that you want to search for
- In the Replace with box, enter the replacement text
- Select any other options that you want
- Click **Find Next**, **Replace**, or **Replace All**
- To cancel a search in progress, press **Esc**
- To close the Find and Replace dialog box, click the **Cancel** button or the **Close** button

---

Using find and replace:

1. Be sure **MagicSlopes1.doc** is opened
2. Select the **Edit** menu
3. Click **Replace**
4. In the Find and Replace dialog box type **2000-2001** in the Find what field
5. Type the **<current year-next year>** in the Replace with field
6. Click **Find Next**
7. Click **Replace** until all occurrences of the years have been updated

tip: *Click **Replace All** for Word to replace all occurrences of the word or phrase. Use caution when working with this command since it will replace all occurrences at once and you might find text you did not want reformatted changed. If this occurs, you need to click Undo right away*

8. Click **OK** on the information dialog box informing you that all occurrences have been found
9. Click the **Close** button
10. Save your document

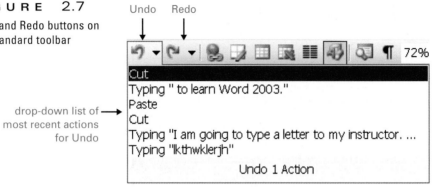

drop-down list of →
most recent actions
for Undo

Undo and Redo

Often you make a mistake or change your mind while you're editing your work. The *Undo* Typing button on the Standard toolbar, or Undo option in the Edit menu, cancels your last editing changes. Clicking on the Undo button will undo the last change you made to your document. Actually, Undo stores a number of previous editing changes. These can be seen by clicking on the down arrow next to the Undo typing button (see Figure 2.7).

A related feature to the Undo button is the Redo button, or Redo option in the Edit menu. *Redo* repeats recent actions, such as typing and formatting. Like Undo, Redo selected from the Edit menu only repeats the most recent action, while the Redo button repeats the most recent action or allows you to select from a list of recent actions when the drop-down arrow next to it is used.

Practicing Undo and Redo:

1. Using the mouse pointer highlight the first paragraph in the letter

2. Press the **Delete** key

3. The paragraph disappears

4. After you hit the Delete key, you realize that you didn't want to delete this paragraph

5. Press the **Undo** button

6. The paragraph returns

7. Find the phrase **Accumulations of 22 to 24 inches** in the next paragraph

8. Change **22** to **65**

9. Click the first word in the first sentence **Patrons**

10. Click the **Undo** button—notice the text changes from 65 back to 22

11. Save your document

The unique location. of Magic Slopes helps the resort accumulate over 400 inches of snow annually, ensuring one of the longest ski seasons in the country. Other attributes include the world's fastest four-passenger chair lift, accessing the aggressive terrain of "The Ridge." This all combines to make an attractive offer to skiers and riters.

Come and enjoy the snow this winter at Magic Slopes!

Correcting Your Documents

Spell Check and Grammar Check

Word underlines misspelled words with red wavy lines and grammatical errors with green wavy lines (see Figure 2.8). To correct a misspelled word or a grammatical error simply right-click on your mouse to display the shortcut menu and select the correct word (see Figure 2.9). If you want to wait until you have finished typing your document to make corrections, you can simply click on the Spelling and Grammar ![button] button on your Standard toolbar. This will start the spell-check function that will check all of the spelling and grammar in your entire document.

FIGURE 2.8

Text marked with wavy red lines indicates spelling errors and wavy green lines indicate grammatical errors

FIGURE 2.9

Fixing a spelling error using the right-click on a word underlined with a wavy red line

---

task reference   Checking Spelling

- Choose the error you want to correct by right-clicking a word with a wavy red underline
- Click the correct word or spelling from the list (see Figure 2.9)

or

- Click on the **Spelling and Grammar** ![button] button in the Standard toolbar to check the spelling and grammar in the entire document
- Choose the correct spelling of the word, or correct the word in the **Spelling and Grammar** dialog box (see Figure 2.10)
- Click **Ignore** to ignore any words that are spelled correctly and just not recognized by Word

---

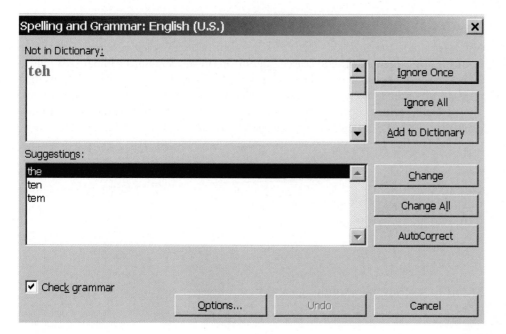

FIGURE 2.10

Correct spelling errors with the Spelling and Grammar dialog box

Jamie needs to correct the spelling in the Magic Slopes promotional letter. To learn more about the spell checker she decides to try spell checking two different ways.

*another*way

. . . to Check Spelling and Grammar All at Once

Pressing **F7** on your keyboard runs the spell check and grammar check. You can also click on the **Tools** menu and select **Spelling and Grammar**. When Word finds a possible spelling or grammatical error, you can make the changes in the Spelling and Grammar dialog box

Checking spelling in a document:

1. Move the mouse pointer over the word **reparted**, the first word in the document with a red wavy line underneath
2. Right-click on the mouse
3. Click to choose the word **reported** from the list of possible words
4. Click the **Spelling and Grammar** 🔤 button in the Standard toolbar to finish checking the spelling in the rest of the document
5. As the Spelling and Grammar dialog box appears for each misspelled word, you will accept suggestions for **purchased**, **accumulate**, **riders**, **honor**, and **Sincerely**, respectively
6. Click anywhere in the document when the spelling check is done
7. Save your document

tip: *A word of caution: While Word will suggest grammatical changes in your document, they might not be what you want, and they might not be correct. Be careful about accepting changes in grammar. Exercise your judgment and your grammatical knowledge*

Thesaurus

A thesaurus is a book of synonyms, or words having the same or nearly the same meaning as another word. Sometimes it can be difficult to find just the right word for a particular sentence. Word can help you find synonyms for words by using the thesaurus. If you move the cursor over a word, right-click the mouse, and click on synonyms, a list of alternative words is displayed (see Figure 2.11). For example, Word provides these synonyms for the word *move*: go, shift, budge, stir, be in motion, move about, travel, or progress. You can also access the thesaurus from this menu to research additional words. Again, you must exercise your good judgment and knowledge of words if you choose a synonym provided by Word.

Research

A new feature to Word 2003 is the research feature. The Research task pane is available from the Tools menu or the Research 📖 button on the Standard toolbar (see Figure 2.12). The Research task pane allows you to find information—a word, a definition, a translation—immediately, without having to stop working on your current document. The Research feature comes with an extensive Research Library that includes a multilanguage thesaurus and dictionary, automatic translation utility, and an Internet encyclopedia. The following research services are also available from the Research task pane:

- Dictionary
- Thesaurus
- Encyclopedia
- Translation
- Stock quotes and company information
- Web search

Be sure to take advantage of this great feature whenever you are preparing a report or paper.

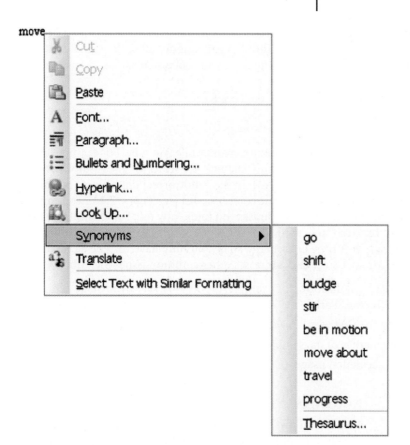

F I G U R E   2.11
Synonyms provided by
right-clicking on the word
move

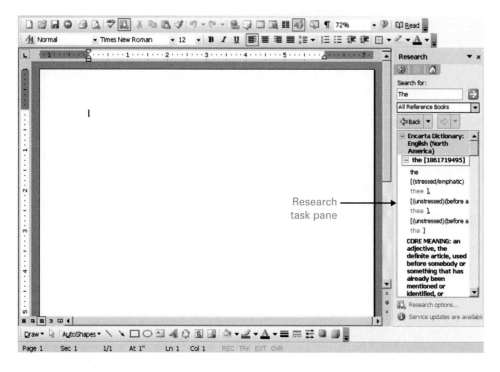

Proofreading Your Document

Spell check and grammar check are great features you can use to help ensure your documents are error-free. However, the spell check and grammar check features cannot replace the important task of proofreading your documents. For example, you might have the following sentence in your document: Remove all off the text. This sentence passed the spell check and grammar check; however, the sentence is incorrect because the word *off* should be *of*. The sentence should read: Remove all of the text. Be sure not to skip the important task of proofreading all of your documents.

Using AutoCorrect and AutoText

AutoCorrect

AutoCorrect automatically corrects common errors while you type. For example, if you type "teh" by mistake, Word automatically changes the word to "the." AutoCorrect is found on the Tools menu (see Figure 2.13). In the AutoCorrect dialog box you can see all of the words included in the automatic correction list (see Figure 2.14). You can add to this list words you often misspell or phrases you frequently use. For example, you can add an entry to replace "ac" with "ABC Corporation." Adding this phrase to AutoCorrect will save you time and energy since you only have to type ac instead of ABC Corporation. AutoCorrect also addresses other common issues including:

- Mixed initial capitalization, for example, typing "PArker" by mistake, when you meant to type "Parker"
- Capitalizing the first word in a sentence if you use lowercase
- Capitalizing names of days
- Correcting accidental usage of the Caps Lock key

FIGURE 2.13

Menu bar showing AutoCorrect options under Tools

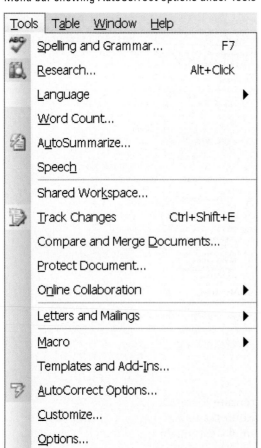

AutoText

AutoText allows you to insert text or graphics into documents quickly and with a minimum of keystrokes (see Figure 2.15). The AutoText and AutoCorrect features are similar because they both replace text. However, the AutoCorrect feature automatically replaces text, whereas you must tell the AutoText feature to replace text.

Word offers a number of predefined AutoText entries including one called signature. Signature can be used to insert a signature containing a person's name, address, and phone number. To insert the signature all you have to do is begin typing the first several letters of the word *Signature* and press the Enter key as soon as Word displays the text of the signature. Using the AutoText feature can save you time since you don't have to type in the person's name, address, and phone number. All you have to type is the word *Signature*. Once a signature is created, it can be used in any Word document.

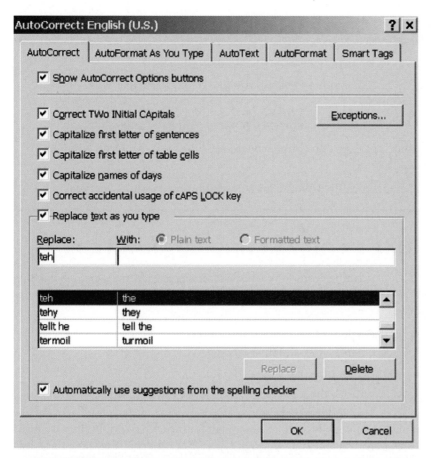

FIGURE 2.14
AutoCorrect dialog box

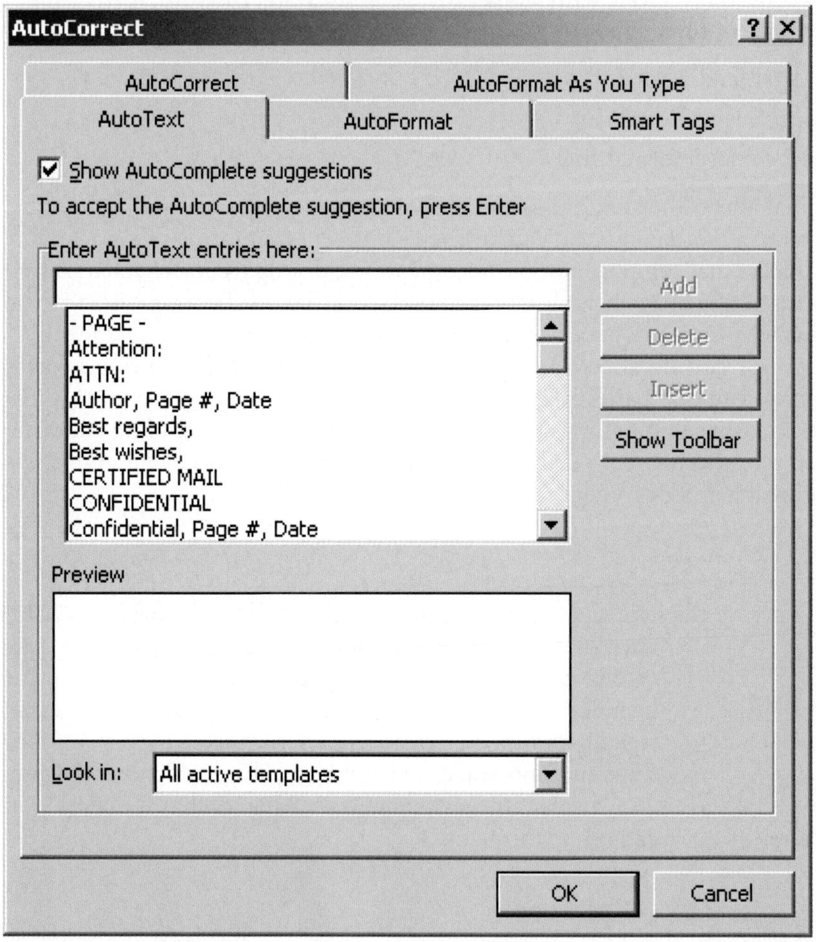

FIGURE 2.15
AutoText dialog box

SESSION 2.1

making *the grade*

1. _____ is the keyboard function used to copy text.

2. The _____ command allows you to find any particular word or phrase in a document.

3. The _____ button allows you to undo your last change.

4. Pressing _____ on your keyboard runs the spell check and grammar check.

5. What automatically corrects common spelling errors while you type?

SESSION 2.2 FORMATTING CHARACTERS

One of the most basic things you do in word processing is to format text. ***Formatting*** changes the look of a single letter, word, or a whole series of words. Formatting includes such things as:

- Changing the type, size, and appearance of text
- Applying bold, underline, and italics to text
- Changing the color of text

Formatting text can make reading more enjoyable and the message being relayed by the author easier to understand. Formatting can also help a reader find important information since many people simply scan a document for formatted text. In the past, most of these features were available only through typesetting and printing. Now these features are available to everyone with word-processing software. In Word, formatting is classified into one of three types:

- Character level formatting
- Paragraph level formatting
- Document level formatting

Formatting that affects the look of individual characters is called character formatting. Each character in a Word document can be given a different font format. Characters are the building blocks that compose a whole document. The distinguishing characteristic of character formatting is that you apply it only to selected strings of characters. That is, you can apply character formatting to as little as one individual character in a document.

Paragraph formatting affects a whole paragraph. Paragraph formatting encompasses the things you do to affect the blocks of text called paragraphs. Document formatting encompasses all the things you do to affect a document, including character and paragraph formatting. Let's take a closer look at character formatting in this session and paragraph and document formatting in Session 2.3.

Text Formatting

FIGURE   2.16
Four fonts

This is the Times New Roman font.
This is the Arial font.
This is the Comic Sans MS font.
This is the Book Antiqua font.

Typography refers to the style and appearance of printed text. Since the overall appearance of a document is critical to its success, you must take careful consideration of the appearance of text. A ***font*** is the overall design for a set of characters. Fonts describe the size, weight, and spacing of a character. Figure 2.16 displays four different fonts you can use when creating a document. Figure 2.17 displays the six main Formatting toolbar functions you can use to format text.

F I G U R E   2.17

Six Formatting toolbar
buttons

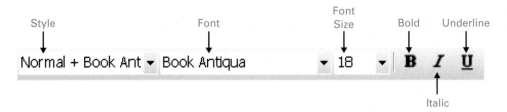

Font Type

There are numerous fonts you can choose from when creating a document. Two general categories of fonts include serif and sans serif. The serif font uses small decorative marks to embellish characters and make them easier to read. Fonts without these little marks are called sans serif (*sans* is French for "without"). Arial is a sans serif font and Times New Roman is a serif font. Word comes with many different fonts. If you require additional fonts, you can easily download them from the Internet or purchase them from a store. The following is a list of commonly used fonts and their general purpose.

- Times New Roman works in many situations and it's neutral, easy on the eye, and best for printed material
- Bookman (Goudy) Old Style is conservative and it reads larger than Times New Roman at the same point size
- Book Antiqua is easy to read, neutral, and appropriate for reports and magazine text
- Arial is a narrow legible font used in headings and often on Web pages
- Comic Sans is a more creative and fanciful font reserved for special uses

Font Size

The size of the font can easily be changed by clicking on the font size drop-down list on the Formatting toolbar. To change the size of a font simply highlight the text and click on the new font size in the list. The following displays several different font sizes.

- This is font 12
- This is font 14
- This is font 20

---

task reference   Changing the Font and Size

- To apply text formatting to a single character, word, or several words select the text you want to change

- Click on a font name in the Font ⟨Arial ▾⟩ box on the Formatting toolbar

or

- To change the size of text or numbers select the text you want to change

- Click a point size in the Font size ⟨16 ▾⟩ box on the Formatting toolbar

---

Jamie recognizes that the use of the old Courier font on the original promotional letter for Magic Slopes looks unprofessional and she is ready to change the font in the entire letter. Since she is unfamiliar with fonts, she decides to stick to a safe choice—Times New Roman with the 12-point size.

Changing font and font size:

1. Select all of the text in the **MagicSlopes1.doc** document by clicking **Edit**, **Select All** on the **menu bar** or pressing **Ctrl+A**

2. Click the **Font** list arrow on the Formatting toolbar

tip: *A list of available fonts appears in alphabetical order. The name of the current font is highlighted in the Font box and the Font text box. Fonts that have been used recently appear above the double line. In addition, the name of each font appears formatted in that font*

3. Click **Times New Roman** from the list of fonts

4. Click the **Font Size** arrow to see a list of available point sizes for the Times New Roman font

5. Click the **12** for a 12-point Times New Roman font

6. Click anywhere outside of the selected text to deselect it

7. Save your document

Font Appearance

Besides changing the font and size you can also change how the font appears using bold, italics, and underlines. **Bold** darkens the color of the letters, *italics* slants the letters to the right, and <u>underline</u> places a line under the text. You can also use these three features together and have text that is **bolded**, *italicized*, and <u>**underlined**</u> or just ***bolded and italicized***, or just <u>*italicized and underlined.*</u>

Now that Jamie's document is formatted with the correct font and size, she will continue making the rest of the changes suggested by her supervisor. First, Jamie needs to underline the phrase: "Facts about the Ski and Snowboard Season:"

---

task reference   Adding a Basic Underline

- Select the text you want to underline
- Click the **Underline** [U] button on the Formatting toolbar

or

- Select the text you want to underline
- Select **Ctrl+U** on the keyboard

Underlining selected text:

1. Place the cursor at the end of the second paragraph after the word **Resort!**

2. Press **Enter** to insert a blank line

3. Using the mouse pointer select these words **Facts about the Ski and Snowboard Season:**

4. Click on the **Underline** button in the Formatting toolbar

5. Click anywhere in the document outside the text to remove the highlight (deselect) on the selected text

6. Save your document

After some thought, Jamie decides to draw the reader's attention to several words in the letter. In order to do this Jamie must bold the following words:

- October 27
- $25
- 5 minutes
- season passes
- 1-800-333-3SKI
- skiMagicSlopes.com
- Super Boarding Series Opener
- 400

---

task reference   Making Text Bold

- Select the text you want to bold
- Click the **Bold** **B** button on the Formatting toolbar

or

- Select the text you want to bold
- Select **Ctrl+B** on the keyboard

Bolding selected text and numbers:

1. Using the mouse pointer, select the text **October 27** in the **MagicSlopes1.doc** document

2. Click the **Bold** button in the Formatting toolbar or press **Ctrl+B**

3. Select **$25** and click **Bold**

4. Select **5 minutes** and click **Bold**

5. Select **season passes** on the next line and click **Bold**

6. Select **1-800-333-3SKI** and click **Bold**

7. Select **skimagicslopes.com** and click **Bold**

8. Select **400** and click the **Bold** button

9. Select **Super Boarding Series Opener** and click **Bold**

10. Save your document

Finally, Jamie has to italicize every occurrence of the resort name, Magic Slopes. Since she has already used the Underline button and the Bold button on the Formatting toolbar, this will be an easy task. Adding italics simply requires selecting the text and then clicking on the Italic button on the Formatting toolbar.

---

task reference   Applying Italic Formatting
                                                    to Text or Numbers

- Select the text you want to italicize
- Click the **Italic** _I_ button on the Formatting toolbar

or

- Select the text you want to italicize
- Select **Ctrl+I** on the keyboard

Applying italics:

1. Find the first occurrence of **Magic Slopes**
2. Using the mouse pointer select **Magic Slopes**
3. Click the **Italic** button in the Formatting toolbar or press **Ctrl+I**
4. Select the next occurrence of Magic Slopes (in the next paragraph)
5. Click the **Italic** button in the Formatting toolbar
6. Repeat this process until all of the occurrences of Magic Slopes have been italicized

tip: _You can also use the Find and Replace dialog box to locate and change all occurrences of the words Magic Slopes_

7. Save your document

_another_word

. . . on Changing Bolded, Underlined, and Italicized Text Back to Normal Text

Many features of Word operate like an on/off or toggle switch. You can un-bold, un-underline, or un-italicized text by selecting it and then clicking on the appropriate button in the Formatting toolbar. Alternatively, you can press the Ctrl+B, Ctrl+I, or Ctrl+U keys on the keyboard

---

Font Style

Microsoft was the first to combine several different formatting options into one function. Word calls this collection of individual items a style. A style is a group of formats in one simple task. For example, you may want to format the title of a report to make it stand out. Instead of taking three separate steps to format your title as 16 pt, Arial, and bold, you can achieve the same result in one step by applying the Title style. On the left of the Formatting toolbar is a field called the Style Heading 1 ▼ box that shows all the styles available for an opened document. You'll learn more about styles in Chapter 3.

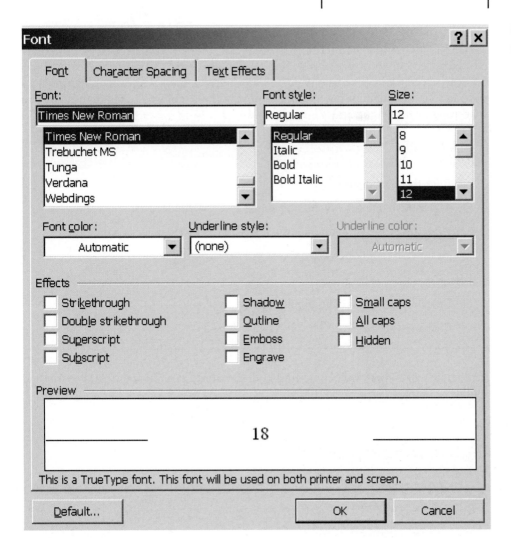

Format Font Window

The Format Font window offers an easy way to change all of the characteristics associated with a font at the same time (see Figure 2.18). The Format Font window is displayed when you click on the Format menu and select Font.

help yourself *Click the Ask a Question combo box, type **Font**, and press **Enter**. Click the hyperlink **Set the default font** to display information on how you can set a default font for all of your documents. Click the Help screen **Close** button when you are finished*

task reference   Opening the Format Font Window

- Select the **Format** menu
- Select **Font**
- The Format Font window is displayed
- Select the Font type, size, or style you want

*another***way**
. . . to Enhance Text

You can also enhance text with other effects found in the Format Font window including ~~strikethrough~~, shadow, and outline effects

Highlighting Text

Sometimes it's useful to be able to mark selected text for emphasis, revisions, or to draw the readers' attention to a certain section. *Highlighting* puts a transparent colored bar over the selected text (like using a highlighter in a textbook). After highlighting text, you can hide the highlighting without removing it, or remove the highlighting if you are through with editing and want a clean copy.

---

task reference   **Highlighting Text**

- Click the **Highlight** [icon] button on the Formatting toolbar
- The mouse pointer will change shape to a highlighter-marking pen
- Drag the mouse I-beam over the text and the active color is applied
- To turn off highlight, click on the **Highlight** button again

or

- Select the text you want highlighted
- Click on the **Highlight** button

Next Jamie will add yellow highlighting to all the words, numbers, and phrases that she applied bold to earlier.

Highlighting text:

1. Using the mouse pointer select the text **October 27**
2. Click the **Highlight** button list arrow, and click the **yellow** color square in the Formatting toolbar
3. Select **$25** and click **Highlight**
4. Select **5 minutes** and click **Highlight**
5. Select **season passes** on the next line and click **Highlight**
6. Select **1-800-333-3SKI** and click **Highlight**
7. Select **skiMagicSlopes.com** and click **Highlight**
8. Select the number **400** and click **Highlight**
9. Select **Super Boarding Series Opener** and click **Highlight**
10. Save your document

tip: *To pick a different color for highlighting click on the down arrow next to the Highlight button and select a color from the drop-down list. The small rectangle below the highlight pen on the Highlight button indicates which color is currently selected (see Figure 2.19). Be sure not to use a dark color with black text or you will have difficulties reading the text*

Changing the Text Color

The default text color in Word is black. If you want to change the text color, you simply click on the Font Color button on the Formatting toolbar and select the color you want for your text (see Figure 2.20).

FIGURE 2.19

Highlight button showing selection of colors

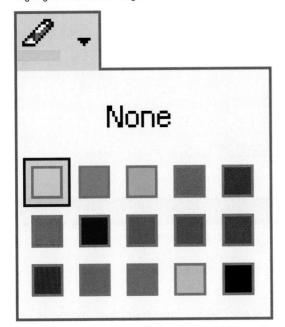

FIGURE 2.20

Font Color button showing selection of colors for fonts

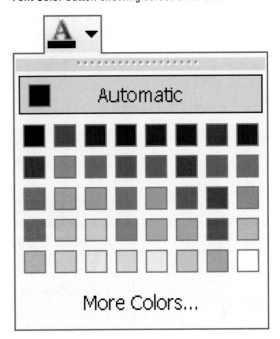

task reference   Changing Text Color

- Click the **Font Color** button on the Formatting toolbar

- Start typing in the new color

- To turn off the color click on the Font Color button and select a different color or Automatic for black

or

- Select the text you want colored

- Click on the **Font Color** button

Changing Case

Case refers to whether the text is in uppercase (all capital letters), lowercase (all small letters), or a mix of the two. For example, you might type an entire paragraph with the Caps Lock key engaged only to look up and see the screen filled with all uppercase letters. You now need to change the case of the text without having to retype all of your text. Word provides the ability to easily change the case on text already typed. In fact, Word offers you several choices when changing the case of text including:

- Sentence case (required by sentence structure)
- Lowercase (all small letters)
- Uppercase (ALL CAPITAL LETTERS)
- Title Case (As in a Title with Important Words Capitalized)
- Toggle case (changes any uppercase letters to lowercase and vice versa)

Like many of the functions in Word, to change the case of a word or words, first select the word or words and then select the Change Case feature in the Format menu.

F I G U R E   2.21
Change Case dialog box

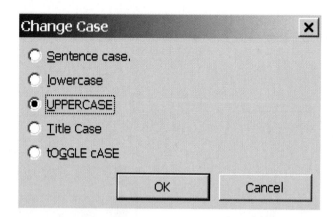

task reference   Changing Case

- Select the text requiring the case change
- Click on the **Format** menu
- Click **Change Case**
- Select the type of case change you are making—sentence case, lowercase, uppercase, title case, or toggle case (see Figure 2.21)

Jamie has three places where she wants to change the case from uppercase to lowercase in her letter. Jamie is going to use the Change Case feature to perform this task.

Changing case:

1. Select **Ski and Snowboard Season** from the line that states <u>Facts about the Ski and Snowboard Season:</u>
2. Click the **Format** menu
3. Click **Change Case**
4. Select **lowercase** and click **OK**
5. Use the mouse pointer to select **Snowboard Season** on the next line
6. Repeat steps 2 thru 4
7. In the next line select the word **Operation**
8. Repeat steps 2 thru 4
9. Select **MILO ESHELBY PRESIDENT** at the bottom of the letter
10. Repeat steps 2 and 3
11. Select **Title Case** and click **OK**
12. Save your document

SESSION 2.3 FORMATTING PARAGRAPHS AND DOCUMENTS

Paragraph Formatting

Some formatting affects the entire document or larger sections of the entire document. These formatting changes include setting margins, line spacing, alignments, indents, and tabs. In this session, you will learn how to apply all of these formatting techniques.

Margins

Margins are the blank spaces around the edges of a document. Each document has a top, bottom, left, and right margin. You typically insert text and graphics in the printable area of a document or inside the margins. However, you can position some items outside the printable area of a document or in the margins. These items usually include headers, footers, and page numbers.

---

another**word**

. . . on Left and Right Margins for Part of a Document

Word allows you to change the margins for part of a document. To do this, select the text, click **Page Setup** on the **File** Menu, and click the **Margins** tab. Set the margins you want and in the Apply to box click **Selected** text

---

task reference — Changing Left and Right Page Margins

- Switch to Print Layout view ▣ button
- Point to a margin boundary on the horizontal ruler or vertical ruler. When the pointer changes to a double-headed arrow, drag the margin boundary (see Figure 2.22)
- To specify exact margin measurements, hold down **Alt** as you drag the margin boundary; the ruler displays the measurements of the margins

or

- On the **File menu** click **Page Setup** and click the **Margins** tab
- Enter the settings you want
- Click **Default** to have Word save the new default settings in the template on which the document is based

FIGURE 2.22

Double-headed arrow on the margin boundaries of the vertical and horizontal margins

Setting the left margin:

1. Click **View** on the menu bar and select the **Print Layout**
2. Position the mouse pointer in the horizontal ruler until you see a double-headed arrow for the left margin
3. Hold down on the **Alt** key
4. Hold down on the left mouse button
5. Watching the dark gray area, drag the left margin to exactly 1.5 inches
6. Release the left mouse button
7. Save your document

Setting the bottom margin using Page Setup:

1. Click **View** on the menu bar and select the **Normal** view
2. Click on the **File** menu
3. Click **Page Setup**
4. Select the **Margins** tab
5. Select the **Bottom** margin box
6. Use the arrows beside the box to change the margin from 1 inch to **.5**

tip: *Some printers require more than .5 inches. If a message comes up regarding fixing the margin, you should select Fix*

7. Click **OK** in the lower right of the Page Setup dialog box
8. Save your document

tip: *Clicking on the small up and down arrows across from the top, bottom, left, and right margin settings in the Page Setup dialog box increases (up arrow) or decreases (down arrow) the margin settings in 0.1-inch increments*

Line Spacing

Line spacing determines the amount of vertical space between lines of text. Word uses single-line spacing by default. The line spacing you select will affect all lines of text in the selected paragraph or in the paragraph that contains the insertion point. You set line spacing on the Indents and Spacing tab under the Format menu, Paragraph command (see Figure 2.23). Types of line spacing available include:

- *Single* spacing accommodates the largest font in that line, plus a small amount of extra space—shortcut keys are Ctrl+1
- *1.5 lines* spacing is one-and-one-half times that of single line spacing—shortcut keys are Ctrl+5

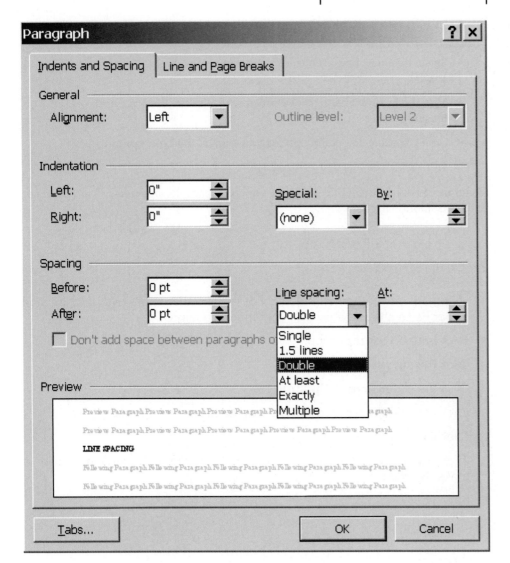

F I G U R E　2.23

Paragraph dialog box
showing line spacing
setting

- **Double** spacing is twice that of single line spacing—shortcut keys are Ctrl+2
- **At least** line spacing is defined as the minimum line spacing that Word can adjust to accommodate larger font sizes or graphics that would not otherwise fit within the specified spacing
- **Exactly** is fixed-line spacing that Word does not adjust. This option spaces all lines evenly
- **Multiple** line spacing is increased or decreased by a percentage that you specify
- **At** line spacing is the amount of line spacing you select. This option is available only if you select At Least, Exactly, or Multiple in the Line spacing box

help yourself *Click the Ask a Question combo box, type **Line spacing**, and press **Enter**. Click the hyperlink **Adjust line or paragraph spacing** to display information on how to change the spacing before and after each paragraph. Click the Help screen **Close** button when you are finished*

---

task reference   Adjusting Line Spacing

- Select the lines, paragraphs, or pages where you want to set the line spacing
- Click the **Format** menu, click **Paragraph**, click the **Indents and Spacing** tab
- Under Spacing select the options you want in the **Line spacing** box

---

To improve readability, Jamie decides to double-space the bulleted list in the Magic Slopes promotional letter.

Double spacing lines:

1. Using the mouse pointer select all of the text that starts with an * located under <u>Facts about the ski and snowboard season</u>
2. Click on the **Format** menu
3. Click **Paragraph**
4. Click the **Indents and Spacing** tab
5. Click the **down arrow** to the right of the Line spacing box
6. Click **Double**
7. Click **OK** at the bottom right of the Paragraph dialog box to close and make the change
8. Save your document

Alignment

Alignment of text refers to the horizontal position of text in relation to the right and left margins. Text flush with the left margin is left aligned. Text flush with the right margin is right aligned. Text positioned exactly in the middle of the left and right margin is centered. Text flush with both the right and the left margin is justified. Figure 2.24 provides illustrations of each type of alignment.

FIGURE 2.24

Left, right, centered, and justified text

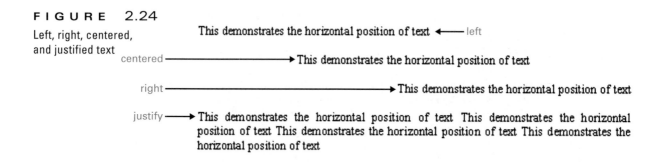

task reference   Aligning Text Left, Right, Centered, and Justified

- Select the text you want to align left
- Click the **Align Left** ▤ button on the Formatting toolbar or use **Ctrl+L** from the keyboard

or

- Select the text you want to align right
- Click the **Align Right** ▤ button on the Formatting toolbar or use **Ctrl+R** from the keyboard

or

- Select the text you want to center
- Click the **Center** ▤ button on the Formatting toolbar or use **Ctrl+E** from the keyboard

or

- Select the text you want to justify
- Click the **Justify** ▤ button on the Formatting toolbar or use **Ctrl+J** from the keyboard

anotherway
. . . to Start Typing Left, Right, or Centered Text

You can use *Click and Type* to add a left, right, or center aligned paragraph. Switch to Print Layout view or Web Layout view. At the start of a new paragraph, move the I-beam pointer across the page from the left margin to the right margin. When you see the Align Left, Center, or Right icon, double-click and then start typing your text

Centering text:

1. Using the mouse pointer locate the cursor anywhere on the first line that contains **Patrons of *Magic Slopes***

2. On the Formatting toolbar click the **Center** ▤ button or use **Ctrl+E** from the keyboard

3. Save your document

Indents

Word-processing software uses three types of indenting including first line indent, hanging indent, and negative indent. *First line indent* is often used to indicate the first line of a new paragraph. *Hanging indents* occur when the first line or phrase is against the left margin and the remaining text is indented a set amount from the left margin. Hanging indents are frequently used for bulleted and numbered lists, bibliographic entries, glossary terms, and resumes. Text with a *negative indent* extends beyond the horizontal margin set for the rest of the text. Figure 2.25 provides thumbnail sketches that illustrate the three types of indents.

F I G U R E 2.25

Thumbnails of the three
types of indents

Examples of paragraph indentation

The paragraph looks like this

← ——————————— first line indent

← ——————————— hanging indent

← ——————————— negative indent

---

task reference — Changing the Indent

- Select the paragraph where you want to create a first line indent
- If you don't see the horizontal ruler click **Ruler** on the **View** menu
- On the horizontal ruler drag the First Line Indent marker (Figure 2.26) to the position where you want the text to start

or

- Select the paragraph where you want to increase or decrease the left indent of an entire paragraph
- On the Formatting toolbar click the **Increase Indent** 📑 button or **Decrease Indent** 📑 button

or

- Select the paragraph where you want to create a hanging indent
- On the horizontal ruler drag the **Hanging Indent** marker (Figure 2.26) to the position where you want the text to start

or

- Select the paragraph you want to out-dent or extend into the left margin
- If you don't see the horizontal ruler click **Ruler** on the **View** menu
- On the horizontal ruler drag the **Left Indent** marker to the position where you want the paragraph to start

F I G U R E   2.26

First Line Indent and Hanging Indent marker

Indenting practice:

1. Select the entire List of Facts about the ski and snowboard season
2. Click the **Increase Indent** button on the Formatting toolbar
3. Save your document

Tabs

In the days of the typewriter, fonts were mono-space characters—spaces between characters were equal. In other words, each character was given the same amount of space, so a skinny letter like an *i* had more white space around it than a wide letter like an *m*.

F I G U R E   2.27

Format Tabs command

Now computers use proportional space fonts—characters and spaces use only the amount of space that they need. With mono-space fonts you could press the space bar to align text, although your typing teacher would object! When you try this with proportional space fonts, you often end up with uneven spacing in the printed document, even if it looks good on the screen.

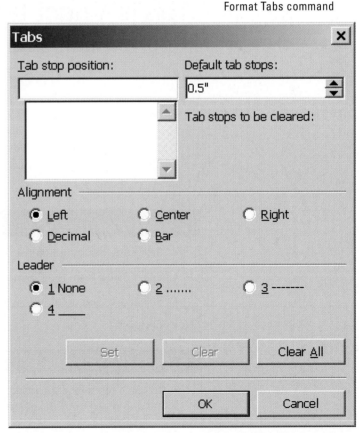

To avoid problems with text lining up, Word uses tab stops instead of spaces, just like your typing teacher would have insisted even with the old typewriters! *Tab stops* insert a space for formatting text, as in indenting a line or block of text. The default tab settings for Word are every half-inch. If you do not like the Word settings, you can set your own tabs using the Format Tabs command (see Figure 2.27).

Tab Types

Tabs come in different types that are defined by the way text lines up with the tab. The table in Figure 2.28 explains the different tab types. Figure 2.29 provides an example of left (normal), right, center, and decimal tabs.

F I G U R E   2.28

Different tab types

Tab Type	Icon	Purpose
Left Tab (Normal)	⌊	The left tab is similar to the typewriter tab. Text will begin at the tab position and continue to the right of the tab.
Right	⌋	With the right tab, text will end at the tab and flow to the left.
Center	⊥	The center tab works similar to centering a line of text but instead of centering between margins, text is centered at the tab location.
Decimal	⊥.	The decimal tab is used to line up numbers and text with a period. This is useful for a group of numbers or a list of instructions.
Bar	▮	The bar tab is used to add a vertical line at the position. This could be used when you want to set off some text. Set this tab in the Tabs dialog box, found under the Format menu.
First Line Indent	▽	The First Line Indent tab will only move the first line of your paragraph.
Hanging Indent	⊔	The Hanging Indent tab will move all the text in your paragraph except the first line.

F I G U R E   2.29

Examples of left, right, center, and decimal tabs

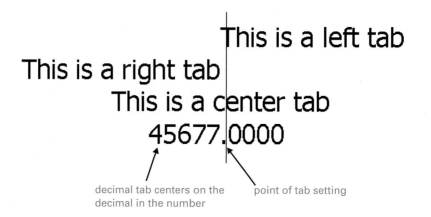

decimal tab centers on the   point of tab setting
decimal in the number

---

task reference   **Setting Tabs**

• Select the paragraph(s) that will receive a new tab setting

• Select **Tabs** from the **Format** menu

• Select the type of tab you want

• Click **OK**

task reference   **Using Tabs**

• To use a tab, place the insertion point where you want text to align with the tab and press the Tab key on your keyboard

task reference	Moving Tabs

- Click the tab you want to move and drag the tab to the new location and release the mouse button

task reference	Deleting Tabs

- Click the tab you want to delete on the gray bar under the horizontal ruler and drag the tab into the document area of the screen and release the mouse button

Setting tabs in a document:

1. **Select** the whole document
2. Click the **Format** menu
3. Click **Tabs**
4. Ensure Alignment **Left** is selected
5. Set the Default tab stops to **.3**
6. Click **Set**
7. Click **OK**
8. Insert the cursor before the first word in the first paragraph
9. Press the **Tab** key on the keyboard
10. Repeat steps 8 and 9 for each paragraph in the letter
11. Save your document

Document Formatting

Displaying Formatting Marks

When typing in a Word document you insert nonprinting characters. *Nonprinting characters* are text that is not visible in a document such as spaces, tabs, and paragraph marks. At times you need to be able to display these nonprinting characters to see where each paragraph ends or to find extra spaces or tabs. When you display these nonprinting characters, they show as the following on your screen:

- Space: dot (·)
- Paragraph: paragraph symbol (¶)
- Tab: right arrow (→)

Showing or hiding these formatting marks is a simple task. Let's display the formatting marks on Jamie's promotional letter (see Figure 2.30).

F I G U R E   2.30

Jamie's document with
formatting marks showing

October·2002¶

¶

Patron·of·*Magic·Slopes*:¶

¶

This·month,·*Magic·Slopes*·begins·making·preparations·for·the·2000-2001·season.· Tentative·opening·date·for·*Magic·Slopes*·Resort·is·set·for·October·27.¶

·¶

Accumulations·of·22·to·24·inches·have·been·reported·at·*Magic·Slopes*·but·lighter· amounts·ranging·from·4·to·6·inches·fell·upon·most·of·the·valley.·The·temperatures· remain·in·the·20's·to·30's.··Winter·is·here·how·we·love·it·here·at·*Magic·Slopes*· Resort!¶

¶

Facts·about·the·ski·and·snowboard·season:¶

        *Ski·&·snowboard·season:·November·22,··April·15¶

        *Hours·of·operation:·8:30am··4:00pm·daily·¶

        *Daily·passes·cost·$25·and·provide·access·to·four·chairlifts¶

        *Average·waiting·time·in·a·lift·line·less·than·5·minutes¶

        *Unrestricted·season·passes·for·children·(ages·6-14):·$100·and·adults:·$249¶

¶

Season·passes·as·well·as·other·products·may·be·purchased·by·calling·1-800-333-3SKI· or·on-line·at·skimagicslopes.com.¶

¶

The·unique·location·of·*Magic·Slopes*·helps·the·resort·accumulate·over·400·inches·of· snow·annually,·ensuring·one·of·the·longest·ski·seasons·in·the·country.·Other·attributes· include·the·world's·fastest·four-passenger·chair·lift,·accessing·the·aggressive·terrain·of·

Show or hide formatting marks:

1. To show the formatting marks, use the Standard toolbar and click on the **Show/Hide** button represented by the paragraph symbol (¶)

2. Click on the **Show/Hide** button again to hide the formatting marks

or

1. Click the **Tools** menu

2. Click **Options**

3. Click on the **View** tab

4. Under **Formatting marks**, select the check boxes next to the characters you want to display

5. Click **OK**

tip: *To display all formatting marks, select the All check box instead of selecting each individual check box*

making *the grade*

1. What are the blank spaces around the edge of a document?
2. The four types of margins include top, bottom, left, and _____.
3. What determines the amount of vertical space between lines of text?
4. Double-spacing is twice that of _____ line spacing.
5. _____ indents are frequently used for bulleted and numbered lists, bibliographic entries, glossary terms, and resumes.

SESSION 2.4 SUMMARY

Being able to cut, copy, and paste selected text makes the transition from a draft copy to a final copy effortless—allowing the writer to focus on content and get all of the parts of a document in the right order. Word provides a variety of features to format and edit your documents. Numerous fonts and font sizes are available and these fonts can be enhanced by bold, italic, and underline formatting. Any text in a document can by highlighted with a color, similar to how people use highlight markers. Word even makes it easy to change the case of selected text or recover from a mistake by using the Undo and Redo features.

Word also allows for various changes that affect the placement of text on the page. Top, bottom, right, and left margins can be set to whatever is needed to accommodate the text. Further, the alignment of text can be modified from left, centered, right, or justified and the line spacing can be set to whatever looks the best.

MICROSOFT OFFICE SPECIALIST OBJECTIVES SUMMARY

- Insert and edit text, symbols, and special characters—MOS WW03S-1-1
- Insert frequently used and pre-defined text—MOS WW03S-1-2
- Navigate to specific content—MOS WW03S-1-3
- Locate, select, and insert supporting information—MOS WW03S-1-6
- Format text—MOS WW03S-3-1
- Format paragraphs—MOS WW03S-3-2
- Change and organize document views and windows—MOS WW03S-5-7

making the grade *answers*

SESSION 2.1
1. Ctrl+C
2. Find
3. Undo
4. F7
5. AutoCorrect

SESSION 2.2
1. Formatting
2. Nonprinting characters

3. Typography
4. Font
5. Italic

SESSION 2.3
1. Margins
2. Right
3. Line spacing
4. Single
5. Hanging

task reference *summary*

Task	Page #	Preferred Method
Cutting, copying, and moving text	WD 2.5	• Select the item you want to move or copy; to move the item, click **Cut** on the Standard toolbar, click where you want the item to appear, click **Paste** on the Standard toolbar or • To copy the item, click **Copy** on the Standard toolbar, click where you want the item to appear
Finding text	WD 2.6	• On the Edit menu, click **Find** to open the Find and Replace dialog box; in the Find what box, enter the text you want to search for, select any other options that you want, click **Find Next**; to cancel a search in progress, press **Esc**; to close the Find and Replace dialog box, click the **Cancel** button or the **Close** button
Replacing text	WD 2.7	• On the Edit menu, click **Replace**; in the Find what box, enter the text that you want to search for; in the Replace with box, enter the replacement text, select any other options that you want, click Find Next, Replace, or Replace All; to cancel a search in progress, press Esc; to close the Find and Replace dialog box, click the Cancel button or the Close button
Checking spelling	WD 2.9	• Choose the error you want to correct by right-clicking a word with a wavy red underline, click the correct word or spelling from the list or • Click on the **Spelling and Grammar** button in the Standard toolbar to check the spelling and grammar in the entire document, choose the correct spelling of the word; or correct the word in the **Spelling and Grammar** dialog box, click **Ignore** to ignore any words that are spelled correctly and just not recognized by Word
Changing the font and size	WD 2.15	• To apply text formatting to a single character, word, or several words, select the text you want to change, click on a font name in the Font box on the Formatting toolbar or • To change the size of text or numbers, select the text you want to change, click a point size in the Font size box on the Formatting toolbar
Adding a basic underline	WD 2.16	• Select the text you want to underline, click the **Underline** button on the Formatting toolbar or • Select the text you want to underline, select **Ctrl+U** on the keyboard
Making text bold	WD 2.17	• Select the text you want to bold, click the **Bold** button on the Formatting toolbar or • Select the text you want to bold, select **Ctrl+B** on the keyboard
Applying italic formatting to text or numbers	WD 2.18	• Select the text you want to italicize, click the **Italic** button on the Formatting toolbar or • Select the text you want to italicize, select **Ctrl+I** on the keyboard
Opening the Format Font window	WD 2.19	• Select the **Format** menu, select **Font**; the Format Font window is displayed; select the Font type, size, or style you want
Highlighting text	WD 2.20	• Click the **Highlight** button on the Formatting toolbar; the mouse pointer will change shape to a highlighter-marking pen; drag the mouse I-beam over the text and the active color is applied; to turn off highlight, click on the **Highlight** button again or • Select the text you want highlighted, click on the **Highlight** button

task reference **summary**

Task	Page #	Preferred Method
Changing text color	WD 2.21	• Click the **Font Color** $\boxed{\text{A} \blacktriangledown}$ button on the Formatting toolbar, start typing in the new color; to turn off the color, click on the Font Color button and select a different color or Automatic for black or • Select the text you want colored, click on the **Font Color** button
Changing case	WD 2.22	• Select the text requiring the case change, click on the **Format** menu, click **Change Case**, select the type of case change you are making—sentence case, lower-case, uppercase, title case, or toggle case
Changing left and right page margins	WD 2.23	• Switch to Print Layout view $\boxed{\blacksquare}$ button, point to a margin boundary on the horizontal ruler or vertical ruler. When the pointer changes to a double-headed arrow, drag the margin boundary, to specify exact margin measurements, hold down **Alt** as you drag the margin boundary; the ruler displays the measurements of the margins or • On the **File menu** click **Page Setup** and click the **Margins** tab, enter the settings you want, click **Default** to have Word save the new default settings in the template on which the document is based
Adjusting line spacing	WD 2.26	• Select the lines, paragraphs, or pages where you want to set the line spacing, click the **Format** menu, click **Paragraph**, click the **Indents and Spacing** tab; under Spacing select the options you want in the **Line spacing** box
Aligning text left, right, centered, and justified	WD 2.27	• Select the text you want to align left, click the **Align Left** $\boxed{\equiv}$ button on the Formatting toolbar or use **Ctrl+L** from the keyboard or • Select the text you want to align right, click the **Align Right** $\boxed{\equiv}$ button on the Formatting toolbar or use **Ctrl+R** from the keyboard or • Select the text you want to center, click the **Center** $\boxed{\equiv}$ button on the Formatting toolbar or use **Ctrl+E** from the keyboard or • Select the text you want to justify, click the **Justify** $\boxed{\equiv}$ button on the Formatting toolbar or use **Ctrl+J** from the keyboard
Changing the indent	WD 2.28	• Select the paragraph where you want to create a first line indent; if you don't see the horizontal ruler, click **Ruler** on the **View** menu; on the horizontal ruler drag the First Line Indent marker to the position where you want the text to start or • Select the paragraph where you want to increase or decrease the left indent of an entire paragraph; on the Formatting toolbar click the **Increase Indent** $\boxed{\equiv}$ button or **Decrease Indent** $\boxed{\equiv}$ button or • Select the paragraph where you want to create a hanging indent; on the horizontal ruler drag the **Hanging Indent** marker to the position where you want the text to start or • Select the paragraph you want to out-dent or extend into the left margin; if you don't see the horizontal ruler click **Ruler** on the **View** menu; on the horizontal ruler drag the **Left Indent** marker to the position where you want the paragraph to start
Setting tabs	WD 2.30	• Select the paragraph(s) that will receive a new tab setting, select **Tabs** from the **Format** menu, select the type of tab you want, click **OK** **Using Tabs** • To use a tab, place the insertion point where you want text to align with the tab and press the Tab key on your keyboard

task reference *summary*

Task	Page #	Preferred Method
		Moving Tabs
		• Click the tab you want to move and drag the tab to the new location and release the mouse button
		Deleting Tabs
		• Click the tab you want to delete on the gray bar under the horizontal ruler and drag the tab into the document area of the screen and release the mouse button

TRUE/FALSE

1. AutoCorrect automatically corrects common errors while you type.

2. Undo repeats recent actions, such as typing and formatting.

3. Tab stops insert a space for formatting text, as in indenting a line or block of text.

4. Redo allows you to undo your last change.

5. Line spacing determines the amount of vertical space between lines of text.

FILL-IN

1. Uppercase refers to text typed in all _____ letters.

2. The highlight button is found on the _____ toolbar.

3. _____ button on the Standard toolbar cancels your last editing changes.

4. Single line spacing accommodates the _____ font in a line, plus a small amount of extra space.

5. Each document has a _____, bottom, left, and right margin.

6. Bold, italics, and _____ are the three most common ways to format text.

MULTIPLE CHOICE

1. Which of the following is not a valid margin?
   a. Top
   b. Bottom
   c. Center
   d. Right

2. Which of the following is not a valid line spacing format?
   a. Single
   b. Double
   c. At
   d. Or

3. Which of the following allows you to replace any particular word or phrase in a document with a new word or phrase?
   a. Redo
   b. Undo
   c. Replace
   d. None of the above

4. Which of the following is a menu that shows a list of commands relevant to a particular item, evoked with the right-click of a mouse button?
   a. Formatting toolbar
   b. Standard toolbar
   c. Shortcut toolbar
   d. Shortcut menu

5. Which of the following items can be formatted?
   a. Single letter
   b. Word
   c. Series of words
   d. All of the above

review of concepts

REVIEW QUESTIONS

1. Name two different formats for line spacing.

2. List two different ways you can invoke the spell-check feature.

3. List two different ways you can change the case of text.

4. Describe the Find and Replace features.

5. Describe the Undo and Redo features.

CREATE THE QUESTION

For each of the following answers, create an appropriate, short question.

ANSWER	QUESTION
1. Change case	_____
2. Redo	_____
3. Replace	_____
4. Red wavy underline	_____
5. Highlight	_____
6. Indent	_____
7. Tab	_____

FACT OR FICTION

1. Line spacing determines the amount of vertical space between lines of text. The different types of line spacing available include single, 1.5 lines, double, at least, exactly, multiple, and at.

2. Text can only be cut from one location in a document and pasted to another location in the same document or pasted into an entirely different document. Once text is cut, or copied, it can only be pasted once into the same document.

3. The Find command allows you to find any particular word or phrase in a document and the Replace command allows you to replace any particular word or phrase in a document.

4. Spell check and grammar check are great features you can use to help ensure your documents are error-free. There is no need to proofread your documents if you used both of these features.

5. Formatting changes the look of a single letter, word, or a whole series of words. Formatting includes such things as changing the text type, text size, text appearance, and the color of text.

1. Adding to the Magic Slopes Promotional Letter

The Magic Slopes promotional letter is almost ready for Jamie to distribute. The letter has to be perfect in order to help generate additional season pass sales. Let's take one final look at the letter, make some last-minute changes, and ensure everything is perfect before Jamie sends it to her customers.

1. Open **MagicSlopes1.doc**

2. Save MagicSlopes1.doc as **MagicSlopes2.doc**

3. Add all capital letters to **Facts about the ski and snowboard season**

FIGURE 2.31

Modified Magic Slopes promotional letter

4. Add bold to **Facts about the ski and snowboard season**

5. Remove the underline on **Facts about the ski and snowboard season**

6. Center **Facts about the ski and snowboard season**

7. Change the font to Arial 12 for the entire letter

8. Change the first Magic Slopes to green text

9. Run spell check and grammar check to ensure everything is correct; ignore the spell check if it catches *Eshelby*.

10. Use the Thesaurus to find another word for **Preparations** in the first paragraph and underline the word you choose

11. At the bottom of the letter, center **Sincerely**, **Milo Eshelby**, and **President**

12. Replace Milo Eshelby with **your name**

13. Proofread your document

14. Save your document

15. Compare your work to Figure 2.31

Patron of Magic Slopes:

This month, *Magic Slopes* begins making arrangements for the 2003-2004 seasons. Tentative opening date for *Magic Slopes* Resort is set for October 27.

Accumulations of 22 to 24 inches have been reported at *Magic Slopes* but lighter amounts ranging from 4 to 6 inches fell upon most of the valley. The temperatures remain in the 20's to 30's. Winter is here—how we love it here at *Magic Slopes* Resort!

FACTS ABOUT THE SKI AND SNOWBOARD SEASON:
* Ski & snowboard season: November 22 - April 15

* Hours of Operation: 8:30am - 4:00pm daily

* Daily passes cost $25 and provide access to four chairlifts

* Average waiting time in a lift line less than 5 minutes

* Unrestricted season passes for children (ages 6-14): $100 and adults:

$249

Season Passes as well as other products may be purchased by calling 1-800-333-3SKI or on-line at skimagicslopes.com

The unique location of *Magic Slopes* helps the resort accumulate over 400 inches of snow annually, ensuring one of the longest ski seasons in the country. Other attributes include the world's fastest four-passenger chair lift, accessing the aggressive terrain of "The Ridge." This all combines to make an attractive offer to skiers and riders.

This fall *Magic Slopes* will again focus our efforts on being the first seasonal ski area in the United States to open. The honor of being chosen to host the Super Boarding Series Opener assures our efforts will become even more crucial in order to provide the best snow possible for the estimated 20 teams expected to participate in this world class event.

Come and enjoy the snow this winter at *Magic Slopes*!

Sincerely,

Your Name
President

2. Producing an Attractive Memo

Which articles do you read when you look at a newspaper or a magazine? Chances are you read the articles that catch your eye or have an attractive appearance. The contents of a document are the most important factor, but the appearance of the document is just as important. Professional looking documents tend to achieve better results, so your ideas have a better chance of being taken seriously when they are presented in a professional manner.

John Rath is a new employee at the Wolfe Research and Rescue Foundation. His boss, Judith Lightfoot, has asked him to put together a memorandum describing important tips and techniques for writing memos. John has done an excellent job gathering all of the important tips and techniques for writing memos; however, his document needs some serious formatting help. John has asked you to help him format his memo in a professional manner.

1. Open the document **wd02Memo.doc**

2. Save the document as **Memo1.doc**

FIGURE 2.32

John Rath's final memo

MEMORANDUM

TO: Judith Lightfoot

FROM: John Rath

DATE: 01/01/04

RE: How to write a memo

     Throughout your professional career, you will be asked to write memos. Following these guidelines should help you with this task. While writing a memo, you should keep in mind six simple questions:
     (1) Why are you writing this memo?
     (2) Who is supposed to read it?
     (3) What do you expect them to do after they read it?
     (4) How will you know they have done it?
     (5) What impact will it have on the company?
     (6) How will you measure that impact?

The title **MEMORANDUM** should be bold, uppercase, 12 point, Times New Roman, and centered. The titles **TO:**, **FROM:**, **DATE:**, and **RE:** should be left aligned, uppercase, bold, 12 point, and Times New Roman. A blank line should be inserted between **MEMORANDUM** and **TO:**. In addition, a blank line should exist between each of the four titles.

The information to the right of these four titles should be aligned using tabs. If the person whom the memo is addressed to has a title, it is acceptable to place the title either directly after their name, separated by a comma, or on the following line. You should sign your initials next to your name. The date should be spelled out (not 11/11/02). Replacing **RE:** with **SUBJECT:** is acceptable.

Memos should be concise. Don't state the obvious unless trying to emphasize a point. Furthermore, when referring to individuals that the reader already knows, state only as much information as is needed to uniquely identify the person you are referring to. You should establish the purpose for the communication in the subject line. A concluding statement of some sort is often needed. For the best impression correct grammar and spelling are very important.

Following these guidelines will produce memos with a professional look.

---

3. Change the document Font to **Times New Roman**

4. Change the Font size to **12**

5. Center and bold the word **MEMORANDUM**

6. Change the TO: FROM: DATE: and RE: to left aligned

7. After the colon next to the word TO press **Tab** once and type **Judith Lightfoot**

8. After the colon next to the word FROM press **Tab** once and type **John Rath**

9. After the colon next to the word DATE press **Tab** once and type **today's date**

10. Double-space the lines containing TO: FROM: DATE: and RE:

11. Place each of the six simple questions in the first paragraph on separate lines, remove the commas, and at the end of the fifth question, add extra spaces

12. Underline the sentence **The date should be spelled out (not 11/11/02)** in the third paragraph

13. Underline the sentence **You should establish the purpose for the communication in the subject line** in the fourth paragraph

14. Remove the tabs on each paragraph

15. Compare the overall look of your finished memo to Figure 2.32

16. Save your document

1. Formatting a Letter of Recommendation

Often people are asked to write a letter of recommendation in order to recommend someone for a new job or entrance into a program such as a university. These are difficult letters to write and they can make or break a person's chances of being accepted. The letters must highlight the person's skills and abilities. It is critical that these letters are professional looking and error-free. Letters of recommendation reflect on the application as well as on the author of the letter.

You currently work for Telstar Data as a senior manager in the Technical Communications Department. One of your employees, Jodi Walton, has asked you to write her a letter of recommendation. Jodi has worked for you for the past six years and is an excellent employee. Jodi has recently been asked to apply for the senior manager position at Arco Computer and Software. Although you are sad to see Jodi go, you understand that the job opportunity at Arco is one that can't be missed.

From the data files, retrieve a copy of the file **wd02Recommendation.doc**. This file contains the draft of Jodi's letter of recommendation. Using your expertise in formatting and editing improve the appearance of the document. Figure 2.33 provides an example of how the document might be formatted. Feel free to format the document any way you want. Just ensure the document is professional looking and error-free.

FIGURE 2.33

Jodi's recommendation letter

Roger Greener
Arco Computer and Software
456 West Blue
Twin City, ID 83304

01/01/04

Mr. Greener:

I've been Jodi Walton's manager for over six years. While I wish her only the best and fully understand that she must advance her career, I'm truly sorry to see her go. It has been a pleasure having her on my team.

Jodi is a professional technical writer of the highest caliber, who meticulously researches, formats, edits, and proofs her documents. I've received many compliments from customers who rely on Jodi's documentation. Jodi's managers in tech support, engineering, technical training, and other departments PRAISE her work.

Jodi is an innovative self-starter, who rarely needs supervision. She is punctual and typically exceeds expectations. She handles pressure well, and will voluntarily work overtime and take work home to meet a deadline.

For example, we received a rush order from one of our customers for a complex product modification, including critical user documentation. Jodi not only made the extremely tight deadline, but beat it; yet she still produced a stellar, technically accurate addendum for the standard user manual. Sales, marketing, training, and engineering were quite pleased with Jodi's performance in this crunch. Even our CEO was impressed, and our customer was ecstatic. This is just one example among many of Jodi's superior skills and admirable work ethics.

Jodi is an INVALUABLE ASSET to any technical communications department, and I highly recommend hiring her. If you'd like to discuss her attributes in more detail, please contact me.

Sincerely,
Howard Weiss, Manager, Telstar Data, Ext. 245, hweiss@xyzco.com

2. Creating a Personal Resume

The first thing you do when applying for a job is send the future employer your resume. A resume is a summary of your education, work experience, and qualifications, often submitted with an employment application. Your resume should reflect who you are and what you've accomplished.

The average employer spends only 10 seconds looking at each resume. That's right, only 10 seconds. This doesn't seem like much time to make a great impression, yet it is the only chance you have to make a great impression on your potential future employer. In order to stand out among the other job applicants you must have a professional looking, flawlessly accurate resume.

Create your resume using your Word expertise. Ensure the resume is professional looking and error-free. Make your resume easy to read by using different fonts, font sizes, highlights, and appearances. Use Figure 2.34 as a guide when you are creating your resume. You can also use the sample resume provided in the student data files under the name **wd02Resume.doc**.

FIGURE 2.34

Example resume

RESUME
Susan Smith

Current Address
PO Box 1238
Anywhere, ID 00000

Telephone: 000/888-8888
E-mail address: sasmith3@micron.com

Education
*Local High School, Anywhere, ID: Graduated 1999
*College of Southern Idaho, Twin Falls, ID, 1999-2001: A.S. Food Science

Career Objective
Obtain satisfying job in the food science industry that provides advancement opportunities during my career.

Activities and Honors
*Active member of 4-H Club for three years. Learned food preparation
*Member FFA for four years and was elected president during senior year
*Member Postsecondary Agricultural Student (PAS) organization 2000-2001
*Advisor to local 4-H Club 2000 to present

Employment and Work Experiences
*January 2001 to Present: Sunrise Bakery, Arco, ID; general help; prepare breads and donuts, some work in sales
*July 2000 to December 2000: ABC Grocery, McCall, ID; restocked shelves; boxed groceries; worked into checker position

References
Available on request

1. Creating a Cover Letter

You should send a cover letter along with your resume as an informal introduction to your future employer. Sending a cover letter is also a great way to have another chance to emphasize your skills and abilities. Your cover letter should informally outline how you can help the company. Your resume will address the specifics of your skills and abilities.

Each time you send out your cover letter, you must customize it for that company. It should highlight the skills you have that will best help that particular company. It can be regarded as a sign of laziness if you send out a cover letter that is not tailored to the specific company. According to Jobstar Central, the following are the top five criteria that make a good cover letter:

1. No spelling or typing errors
2. Address it to the person who can hire you
3. Write it in your own words
4. Show that you know something about the company and the industry
5. Use terms and phrases that are meaningful to the employer

You are applying for a job as a word-processing expert for the Electronic Age Book Publisher. Create a cover letter to accompany your resume. You can create one on your own or use the document titled **wd02CoverLetter.doc** in your student data files. Save the document as **Cover1.doc**. Use Figure 2.35 as a sample guide for creating your cover letter.

FIGURE 2.35

Caylie O'Connell's cover letter

Caylie O'Connell
P.O. Box 99
Kiowa, Colorado 80017
(303) 555-1222

January 01, 2004

Attn: Human Resources

To Whom It May Concern:

I would like to introduce myself as a candidate for the accounts receivable position you are seeking to fill. I have many years of accounting and business experience that may fit who you are looking for.

Please review my attached resume. I have worked various aspects of accounting including personnel, payroll, employee health insurance, and worker's compensation. I have also been in the purchasing department as an estimator for home building for the last three years. My professional skills are vast and well rounded.

I would like to request an opportunity to speak with you and let you know more about how I could do an exceptional job for you.

Thank you for your consideration.

Sincerely,

Caylie O'Connell

enclosure

2. Typing an Agenda

You are the Executive Administrative Assistant at your college. There is an upcoming meeting for the Computer Information Technology Advisory Committee to discuss e-commerce. The chair of the committee, Sam Smith, has asked you to type his hand- written agenda (see Figure 2.36). Use your word processing skills to enhance the agenda found in **wd02Agenda.doc**. Ensure the document is easy to read, professional looking, and error-free.

FIGURE 2.36

Handwritten agenda

Agenda
Computer Information Technology Advisory Committee
1:00 p.m. Friday, March 6, 2001
Vice President's Office Conference Room

Approval of Minutes from February 6 Meeting
Approval of Agenda
Chairs Announcements; Introduction of New Member

Standing Reports
System Data Center - L. Neredith
Distance Learning - K. Massey & B. Gilla
Compressed Video - B. Miller
System Technology Plan - D. Tapid
Institutional Research - C. Durnwell
DP Council - E. Bigsby
Committee on Computer Access and Use Policy.
Webpage Advisory Committee - B. Douglas

Old Business
Academic Computing Conference - K. Daria, M. Schittzelhoffe
Consultant's List - B. Douglass, E Toleski
Professional Ethics
Database Connection to Washington State University - C. Roti
April 15 Statewide Meeting

New Business
Teaching Learning Round Table - K. Massolo
Campus Distance Learning Issues - E. Moleski
Soft Skillkey for distance education students - M. Winters
NWREAS accreditation guidelines for distance education issued
Jackpot/Hospitality project - C.Roti

1. The Food and Agriculture Organization of the United Nations (FAO)

Founded in 1945, the Food and Agriculture Organization of the United Nations is helping to build a world without hunger. FAO is one of the largest specialized agencies in the United Nations system and has worked to alleviate poverty and hunger around the world. Figure 2.37 displays the Web site for FAO (www.fao.org). Visit FAO's Web site and develop a short one-page report on your findings. Title the report Food and Agriculture Organization Web site. Use 18-point Arial font for this title and center it at the top of the page. Develop your report around these three headings:

- Statistical Databases at the FAO
- News Highlights and Current Issues
- Current Special Initiatives

Place these headings against the left margin and type them in 12-point, bold, italic, Arial font. Type the body of the report (what you supply) in 12-point Times New Roman font. Use first line indent for the paragraphs and single-space the paragraphs. Set all margins to 1-inch. Type your name and the date on two separate lines aligned right at the bottom of the page. Use 9-point Arial for your name and the date. Save your report as **FAO1.doc**.

2. Enhancing a Mission Statement

Webster E-Books, an electronic publishing firm, is dedicated to seeking out and electronically printing and distributing reference books. Webster E-Books is currently working on developing a company mission statement. Open the document **wd02Mission.doc** and save it as **Mission1.doc**. Review the four different mission statements and add some enhancements to the document. Make all the headings 14-point Arial bold. Center the top heading. Underline the headings Draft A, Draft B, Draft C, and Draft D.

FIGURE 2.37

The FAO Web site

around the world

1. Creating a Poster

WorldMax is an international real estate company, with offices in six locations worldwide. WorldMax posters need to be developed for an upcoming international conference. The posters should include the company name, locations, mission, main office, Web site address, and e-mail address. Use different fonts, font sizes, font appearances, and font colors to make an attractive poster. Save your poster as **Poster1.doc**. Use the following information to create a draft copy of the poster:

- WorldMax
- Nobody sells the world more real estate than WorldMax
- Offices in Edmonton, Canada; Paris, France; Mexico City, Mexico; Sidney, Australia; London, England; Moscow, Russia
- Web address: property.worldmax.com
- E-mail: sell_real@worldmax.com
- Phone: 511-678-1116
- Fax: 511-678-0476
- Main office in Seattle, Washington, 1200 Overland Avenue

2. International Recipes

Your Aunt Inga from Sweden has started sending you handwritten copies of all her favorite recipes. You want to type these so you can save the recipes electronically on your computer. You also want to be able to send the recipes to friends via e-mail. Retype Aunt Inga's recipe for fudge (Figure 2.38) and save the document as **Recipe1.doc**.

FIGURE 2.38

Aunt Inga's handwritten recipe for fudge

Old-fashioned Fudge
2/3 C milk
1/3 C cocoa
2 C sugar
dash of salt
1/4 tsp. cream of tartar
1 tsp vanilla
Mix milk and cocoa in pan over low heat until cocoa is dissolved. Add sugar, salt and cream of tartar. Cook and stir over medium heat till soft ball stage. Remove from heat. Add 2-3 Tbls butter or margarine. Let cool till butter is melted (or a little longer if you want). Add vanilla. Beat with electric mixer until it starts to set up. Pour into buttered pan and let cool.

running project

Producing an Attractive Guideline Series

Faced with a lack of uniform expectations and an influx of new teachers, the Kasota United School District (KUSD) wants to provide a series of guidelines that represent the best practices in teaching. Dr. Greg Provenzo, superintendent, meets on a weekly basis with six of the top teachers in the district to discuss the best practices and to formulate a series of guidelines. Each of these guidelines must be simple, straightforward, and fit on one page with lots of white space on the page.

This committee decided that the first guideline to be issued should be one on how to write a lesson plan. Peter Snapp, one of the teachers on the committee, was given the assignment to produce the final document that will be photocopied and distributed across the district. To project the image of quality he will need to put all of his word-processing skills to work. To look at the first draft of their work and to begin working on this first guideline, open the file **wd02LessonPlan.doc** and save it as **Lessonplan1.doc**.

The draft of the first guideline is in Courier font. Change the font to Times New Roman 12-point for the entire document. Center the first three lines of the document, and use the Arial font and bold to improve this heading. Use bold, italic, and underlining on the sub-headings in the document. Set the left and right margins each to 0.5 inch. Change the top and bottom margins so that the document fits on one page. Finally, check the spelling and grammar, proofread, and save your document. Compare your finished product with Figure 2.39.

FIGURE 2.39

Finished Lesson Plan Guidelines

KUSD
Kasota United School District
Lesson Plan Guidelines

Basic Description
The lesson plan is a short (1 to 2 pages) description of a lesson. Follow the technical requirements listed below. Each lesson plan will incorporate the following:

- A statement of the topic
- A description of the learners
- The objectives
- A sequence of instructional activities for presenting the lesson
- A means of evaluating learning

Content and Technical Requirements
To be complete the lesson plan should also meet these 14 educational content and technical requirements:

1. Learner analysis addresses age and general characteristics
2. Contains at least six objectives per lesson
3. Content/Activities/Materials (CAM) Table included
4. CAM table addresses objectives of instruction
5. Evaluation activity measures achievement of objectives
6. Title of lesson plan is Arial 14-point font centered
7. Body text is Times New Roman 12-point font
8. Titles in table are bold
9. Sub-heads in Lesson Plan are italic
10. Sub-heads in Evaluation activity are underlined
11. Margins: 1" top, 0.75" bottom, 1" right, 1" left
12. Analysis section is bullet list
13. Objectives section is numbered list
14. No spelling errors

Five Common Mistakes
A lesson plan that contains one or more of these five common mistakes needs rethinking and revision:

1. Objective of the lesson does not specify what the student will actually do that can be observed.
2. Lesson assessment is disconnected from the behavior indicated in the objective.
3. Materials specified in the lesson are extraneous to the actual described learning activities.
4. Instruction in which the teacher will engage is not efficient for the level of intended student learning.
5. Student activities described in the lesson plan do not contribute in a direct and effective way to the lesson objective.

1. Cutting and Copying Text

Discuss the differences between cutting and deleting text. Provide an example of a situation when you would cut text and a situation when you would delete text. Also, provide an overview of the Clipboard and an example of a situation when you might use the Clipboard.

2. Indents and Tabs

You can use either indents or tabs to move text. Create a document describing the primary difference between using indents and using tabs. Provide an example of a situation when you would use indents and a situation when you would use tabs.

3. Create a Study Schedule

Word can create many different types of documents. One of the most useful documents you can create is a study schedule. Create a study schedule for this course. Be sure the document is professional looking, easy to read, and error-free.

3

Advanced Editing and Formatting

did you know?

ENIAC, *the first electronic computer, appeared more than 50 years ago. The original ENIAC was about 80 feet long, and weighed 30 tons.*

orthorhombic *perskovite is the predominant mineral found in Earth's lower mantle and the most abundant mineral on Earth.*

every *day, about 30 trillion gallons of water falls on land.*

when *a police officer uses a laser gun, the light rebounds and is detected about a millionth of a second after it was sent.*

the *Chunnel links Britain and France with a 31-mile railway tunnel, 23 miles of which are under water at an average depth of 150 feet below the seabed.*

Jane Crouch *made history when she received the first female professional boxing license by the British Boxing Board of Control in June 1998.*

Chapter Objectives

- Insert frequently used and predefined text—MOS WW03S-1-2
- Create bulleted lists, numbered lists, and outlines—MOS WW03S-2-2
- Modify document layout and page setup—MOS WW03S-3-5
- Format text—MOS WW03S-3-1
- Create new documents using templates—MOS WW03S-5-1
- Insert and modify content in headers and footers—MOS WW03S-3-4
- Modify document layout and page setup—MOS WW03S-3-5
- Create custom styles for text, tables, and lists—MOS WW03E-1-1
- Create and modify document background—MOS WW03E-3-2
- Control pagination—MOS WW03E-1-2

Creating a Movie Listing for Bill's Videos

Bill Schultz owns Bill's Videos, the most popular video store in Saskatoon, Saskatchewan. The store has been in business since 1985 and has over 5,000 videos on VHS and DVD. Bill's Videos also has the largest selection of foreign films in the city. Bill is interested in attracting additional customers and has decided to compile a listing of the top 300 videos rented in 2004, along with other store facts, which he will distribute to all of the homes within a 10-mile radius. The document will include such things as a store overview, location, hours of operation, rental policy, late fees, membership costs, and employment opportunities. If the advertising campaign is successful, Bill will use the same campaign every year updated with the current top 300 video picks.

Bill has put together the initial document (see Figure 3.1). Bill understands that the appearance of the document is critical to its success. Currently, Bill's document does not look very professional and Bill needs your help to format the document properly. Bill wants to add a table of contents, an index, numbering, footers, and borders and shading to help make the document look professional. Bill's final document should look similar to Figures 3.2 and 3.3.

FIGURE 3.1

Bill's initial document

Bill's Video Store Overview
Bill's Video Store has been in business since 1985. The store has over 5,000 movies available for you to rent. Bill's video has the largest selection of foreign films in the city. Bill guarantees all videos to be in stock or you'll receive a free rental.

Location
The store is located at 101 Talley Street, Saskatoon, Saskatchewan. Phone (360) 555 - 5555

Hours of Operation
The store is open every day from 9:00 a.m. to 12:00 p.m.

Rental Policy
Each rental costs $2.95 and is due five days after the rental date.

Late Fees
There is a $2.00 late fee charged for each day a video is late.

Membership Costs
A membership costs $9.95 a year. Along with the purchase of a membership you receive a free two liter bottle of soda and two bags of microwave popcorn.

Employment Opportunities
Please contact Bill Schultz directly at 555-1212 for employment opportunities.

Top 300 Video List
12 Angry Men (1957) - Henry Fonda VHS / DVD
2001: A Space Odyssey (1968) - Keir Dullea VHS / DVD

FIGURE 3.2

The Table of Contents and first page of Bill's final document

TABLE OF CONTENTS

Bill's Video Store Overview

Bill's Video Store has been in business since 1985. The store has over 5,000 movies available for you to rent. Bill's video has the largest selection of foreign films in the city. Bill guarantees all videos to be in stock or you'll receive a free rental.

Location

The store is located at 101 Talley Street, Saskatoon, Saskatchewan. Phone (360) 555 – 5555

Hours of Operation

The store is open every day from 9:00 a.m. to 12:00 p.m.

Rental Policy

Each rental costs $2.95 and is due five days after the rental date.

FIGURE 3.3

The last page and Index of Bill's final document

294.   What's Up, Doc? (1972) - Barbra Streisand VHS
295.   When Harry Met Sally (1989) - Billy Crystal VHS / DVD
296.   Who's Afraid of Virginia Woolf? (1966) - Elizabeth Taylor VHS / DVD
297.   Witness (1985) - Harrison Ford VHS / DVD
298.   Woman of the Year (1942) - Spencer Tracy VHS / DVD
299.   Working Girl (1988) - Melanie Griffith VHS / DVD
300.   Young Frankenstein (1974) - Gene Wilder VHS / DVD

Satisfaction Guarantee

Bill personally guarantees the satisfaction of every customer. For all movie questions please contact Bill Schultz directly at 555-1212.

INDEX

INTRODUCTION

Formatting the text of a document changes the appearance of a document to enhance readability. In the last chapter, you were introduced to several text formatting options such as font, font size, font appearance, and changing the color of text. In this section, you'll learn some advanced formatting options such as controlling hyphenation and preventing paragraph breaks. You'll also learn how to use templates and format multiple-page documents.

CHAPTER OUTLINE

3.1 Advanced Editing and Formatting WD 3.4

3.2 Using Templates WD 3.13

3.3 Formatting Reports WD 3.22

3.4 Summary WD 3.34

SESSION 3.1 ADVANCED EDITING AND FORMATTING

Hyphenation

The hyphenation feature gives documents a polished and professional look. Hyphenation helps eliminate gaps or "rivers of white" in justified text. It also helps maintain even line lengths in narrow columns. Figure 3.4 shows how using hyphenation can eliminate the gaps in justified text.

Word provides several ways to hyphenate all or part of your text including:

- Automatically hyphenate text as you type
- Hyphenate text all at once
- Fine-tune hyphenation
- Postpone hyphenation until after editing

When you turn on automatic hyphenation, Word automatically inserts hyphens where they are needed in the document. If you later edit the document and change line breaks, then Word rehyphenates the document.

An *optional hyphen* is used to control where a word or phrase breaks if it falls at the end of a line, for example, to specify that the word "nonprinting" breaks as "non-printing" rather than "nonprint-ing." When you choose manual hyphenation, Word searches for text to hyphenate, asks you to confirm each proposed optional hyphen, and then inserts the optional hyphens. If you later edit the document and change line breaks, then Word displays and prints only the optional hyphens that still fall at the ends of lines. Word doesn't rehyphenate the document.

To control where a word breaks if it falls at the end of a line, you can manually insert an optional hyphen. To prevent a hyphenated word from breaking if it falls at the end of a line, insert a nonbreaking hyphen. A *nonbreaking space* prevents a line break between two words. A *nonbreaking hyphen* prevents a hyphenated word from breaking if it falls at the end of a line.

If you plan to use manual hyphenation, it's a good idea to postpone hyphenation until after you've finished editing. Otherwise, you may need to rehyphenate the document if you've made changes that affect line breaks. If you plan to use automatic hyphenation, you can also postpone hyphenation if you find it distracting to watch Word automatically insert hyphens and adjust line breaks.

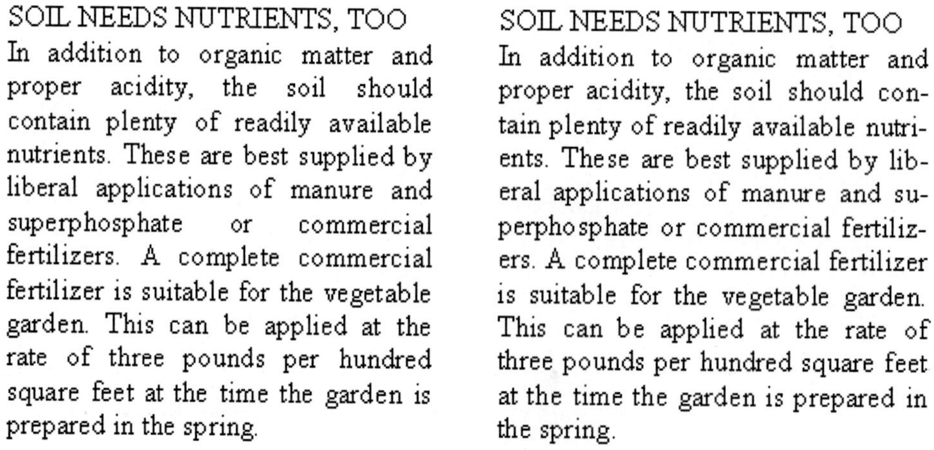

FIGURE 3.4
Justified text on the left without hyphenation and justified text with hyphenation on the right

SOIL NEEDS NUTRIENTS, TOO
In addition to organic matter and proper acidity, the soil should contain plenty of readily available nutrients. These are best supplied by liberal applications of manure and superphosphate or commercial fertilizers. A complete commercial fertilizer is suitable for the vegetable garden. This can be applied at the rate of three pounds per hundred square feet at the time the garden is prepared in the spring.

SOIL NEEDS NUTRIENTS, TOO
In addition to organic matter and proper acidity, the soil should contain plenty of readily available nutrients. These are best supplied by liberal applications of manure and superphosphate or commercial fertilizers. A complete commercial fertilizer is suitable for the vegetable garden. This can be applied at the rate of three pounds per hundred square feet at the time the garden is prepared in the spring.

task reference — Hyphenating Text with Three Different Methods

- On the **Tools** menu, point to **Language**, and then click **Hyphenation** (Figure 3.5)
- Select the **Automatically hyphenate document** check box
- In the **Hyphenation zone box**, enter the amount of space to leave between the end of the last word in a line and the right margin
- To reduce the number of hyphens, make the hyphenation zone wider
- To reduce the raggedness of the right margin, make the hyphenation zone narrower
- In the **Limit consecutive hyphens** to box, enter the number of consecutive lines that can be hyphenated

or

- On the **Tools** menu, point to **Language**, and then click **Hyphenation**
- Click **Manual**
- If Word identifies a word or phrase to hyphenate, do one of the following:
- To insert an **optional hyphen** in the location Word proposes, click **Yes**
- To insert an optional hyphen in another part of the word, use the arrow keys or mouse to move the insertion point to that location, and then click **Yes**

or

- Click where you want to insert the optional hyphen
- Press **Ctrl+- (hyphen)**

anotherway

. . . to Remove Hyphenation

You can remove hyphenation by clearing the **Automatically hyphenate document** check box in the Hyphenation dialog box and click **OK**. You can also manually remove hyphens by using the Find and Replace feature to find optional hyphens, which you can then remove

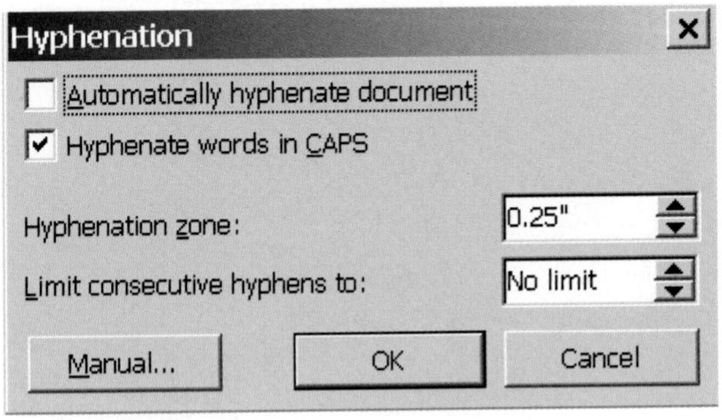

FIGURE 3.5

Hyphenation dialog box

Automatically hyphenating text:

1. Open the document **wd03Videos.doc**
2. Save the document as **Videos1.doc**
3. On the **Tools** menu, point to **Language**, and then click **Hyphenation**

WORD

4. Select the **Automatically hyphenate** document check box

5. Select **Hyphenate words in CAPS** check box

6. In the **Hyphenation zone box** enter **.20**

7. In the Limit consecutive hyphens to box enter **No Limit**

8. Click **OK**

9. Save your document

Inserting the Date and Time

Most of the time you will need to place the document creation date somewhere on the document. You can use the Insert Date and Time command on the Insert menu to have Word automatically insert the date and time for you (see Figure 3.6).

Some documents need to have the date updated every time the document is opened. It is a waste of your time and energy to have to manually update the date every time you open the document. You can use Word to insert a date field that is automatically updated every time the document is opened. Simply click on the check box to Update automatically in the Insert Date and Time command window to have Word automatically update the date and time every time the document is opened.

---

*another*word

. . . Automatic Update of the Date and Time

Only use the Update Automatic Date feature when you want the date to change every time you open the document. Do not use the Update Automatic Date feature if you want to keep the original creation date of the document

---

FIGURE 3.6

Date and Time dialog box

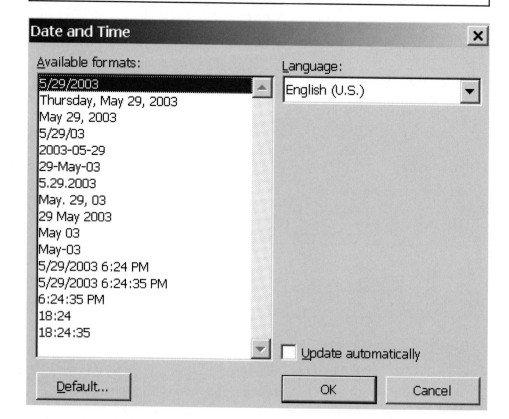

task reference   Inserting the Date and Time

- Insert the cursor where you want the date and time to be located
- Click on the **Insert** menu and choose **Date and Time**
- Click on the date and time format you require
- Check **Update Automatically** if you require the date and time to be updated every time the document is opened
- Click **OK**

Bill decides to put the date on the top of the movie listing. Bill does not want the date to change automatically because he needs the date to reflect the creation date of the document.

Inserting the date automatically:

1. Make sure **Videos1.doc** is open
2. Insert two blank lines at the top of the first page
3. Insert the cursor on the first blank line
4. Click on the **Insert** menu and choose **Date and Time**
5. Click on the first month/day/year format option
6. Click **OK**
7. Save your document

Inserting Bullets and Numbered Lists

Bullet or numbered lists are especially effective for helping the reader of your document identify the important points or steps. With Word you can quickly add bullets or numbers to existing lines of text, or you can automatically create bulleted and numbered lists as you type. The two buttons on the Formatting toolbar displayed in Figure 3.7 insert or convert selected text to bullet or number lists.

FIGURE 3.7

Bullet and Numbering buttons on the Formatting toolbar

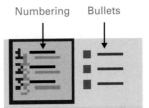

Numbering   Bullets

task reference   Adding Bullets or Numbers

- **Select** the items you want to add bullets or numbers
- On the Formatting toolbar, do one of the following:
- To add bullets, click **Bullets** button

or

- To add numbering, click **Numbering** button

Bill decides to add numbers beside all the videos in the list. This will allow his customers to reference a video by number and by name. Bill is going to use the Numbering button on the Formatting toolbar to insert numbers beside each video.

Adding numbers:

1. Make sure **Videos1.doc** is open
2. Select all the videos in the document
3. Click on the **Numbering** button on the Formatting toolbar
4. Save your document

help yourself *Click the Ask a Question combo box, type **Bullets**, and press **Enter**. Click the hyperlink Modify bulleted or numbered list formats to display information on how you can customize bullets and add in symbols, pictures, or graphics. Click the Help screen **Close** button when you are finished*

Borders and Shading

Borders and shading can be used to help separate text in a document. You can use borders to create boxed text, shaded text, horizontal lines, and vertical lines. A border can be applied to any line, paragraph, page, or entire document. Use the Borders and Shading command in the Format menu to apply a border or shading (see Figure 3.8 and Figure 3.9).

The borders tab allows you to control the style, color, and width of a border around selected text. The page border tab allows you to control the style, color, and width of a border around an entire page. The shading tab allows you to shade selected areas of text.

F I G U R E   3.8
Borders Command box

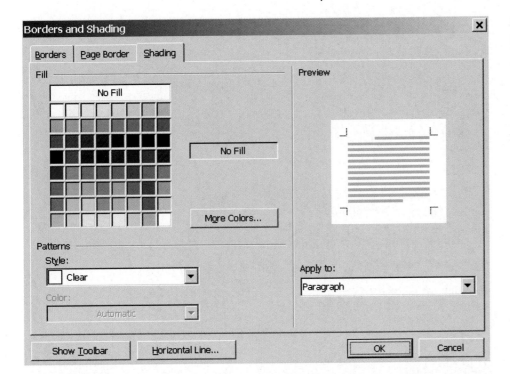

FIGURE 3.9
Shading Command box

---

task reference — Creating a Border

- Select the paragraph where you want the border
- Click on the **Format** menu and choose **Borders and Shading**
- Select the **Borders** tab and set the border style, color, and width
- Click **OK**

Bill decides to add a title to his movie listing document. Bill wants to place a border around the title and add grey shading inside the border to help the title stand out. Bill is going to use the Borders and Shading command box to create his new title.

Creating a border:

1. Insert two blank lines before the date at the top of the page

2. Move the cursor to the top of the page

3. Type **BILL'S VIDEOS** in bold, all caps, Times New Roman, 36-point, centered

4. Press **Enter** key

5. Type **TOP 300 MOVIE RENTALS 2004** in bold, all caps, Times New Roman, 36-point, centered

6. Highlight **BILL'S VIDEOS TOP 300 MOVIE RENTALS 2004**

7. Click on **Format**, **Borders and Shading**, **Borders** tab

8. Click on **Box** in the Setting area

9. Click on a **black solid line** in the Style area

10. Set the Width to **1 1/2** pt

11. Click **OK**

12. Save your document

Creating a shaded area:

1. Make sure **BILL'S VIDEOS TOP 300 MOVIE RENTALS 2004** is highlighted

2. Click on Format, Borders and Shading, Shading tab

3. Click on a color of your choice for the shading; make sure it is not too dark for your text

4. Check to see that **Paragraph** is selected in Apply to text box

5. Click **OK**

6. Save and close your document

Changing Page Size and Orientation

Page Size

Word offers several ways to print a document on different sizes of paper. Use the Page Setup dialog box on the File menu to adjust paper sizes. No matter what paper size you select for your documents in the Page Setup dialog box, you can specify a different paper size for the printed output. For example, you can specify that a letter-size document (8.5×11 inches) print on legal-size paper (8.5×14 inches). Word increases the sizes of the fonts, graphics, tables, and so on, without changing line breaks and page margins.

To better see the layout of a two-page document, you can print both pages on one sheet of paper. For example, if a letter-size document's orientation is portrait, Word shrinks the two pages by 64 percent, and then turns the pages so that they print sideways on the sheet (landscape). In addition to 2 pages, Word can print 4, 6, 8, and 16 pages on one sheet. To do this, Word shrinks the pages to the appropriate sizes and groups them on the sheet. Word decreases the font size of each font used, the size of pictures and tables, and so on. You can print a multiple-page document on one sheet of paper.

---

task reference   **Printing Multiple Pages on a Document**

- On the **File** menu, click **Print**

- Under Zoom, click **2, 4, 6, 8, or 16** pages in the Pages per sheet box (see Figure 3.10)

- Click **OK**

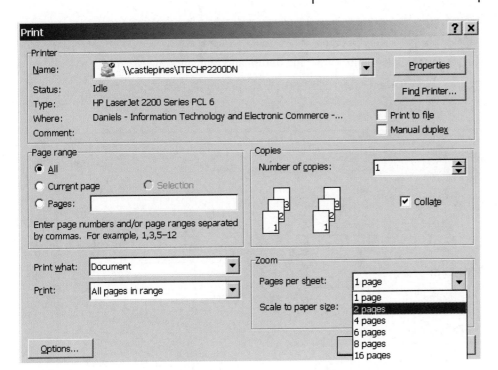

FIGURE   3.10

Print dialog box with two pages selected

Page Orientation

The *orientation* of a page refers to the flow of text and graphics across the width or length of a page. Word can change the orientation of a page from portrait to landscape or vice versa. This is called changing page orientation. *Portrait* refers to the orientation of text and graphics on the length of a page. *Landscape* refers to the orientation of text and graphics on the width of a page (see Figure 3.11).

Default page orientation for Word is portrait. Depending on the type of document being produced or printed you might want to change the orientation to landscape. For example, a threefold brochure and some tables will print better in landscape orientation.

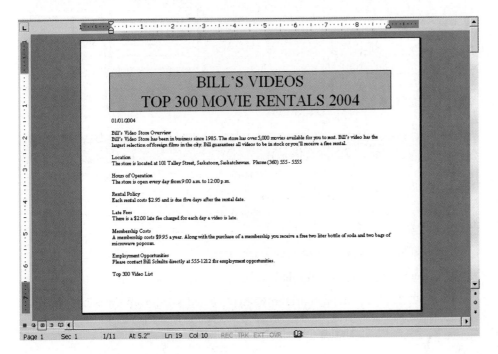

FIGURE   3.11

Document printed in landscape orientation

task reference Changing Page Orientation

- On the **File** menu, click **Page Setup**, and then click the **Margins** tab
- Under **Orientation**, click **Portrait** or **Landscape** (see Figure 3.12)
- Click **OK**

FIGURE 3.12

Page Setup dialog box showing Margins tab and Orientation

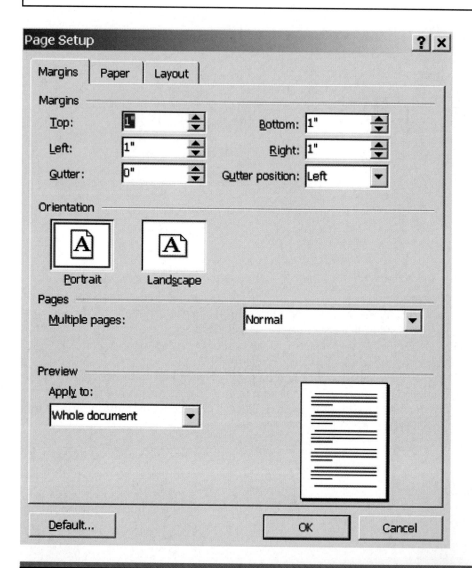

SESSION 3.1

making *the grade*

1. The _____ hyphen is used to control where a word or phrase breaks if it falls at the end of a line.

2. Portrait refers to the orientation of text and graphics on the _____ of a page.

3. What are the two types of page orientation?

4. Where can you apply a border?

5. The _____ hyphen prevents a hyphenated word from breaking if it falls at the end of a line.

SESSION 3.2 USING TEMPLATES

Styles

A *style* is a set of formatting characteristics identified by name that you can apply to text in your document to quickly change its appearance. In Word, there are two main types of styles that you can create and apply: character styles and paragraph styles. *Character styles* include any of the options available from the Font dialog box, such as bold, italic, and small caps. Character styles store only character formatting and apply to selected text or to the word containing the insertion point. *Paragraph styles* include character and paragraph formatting, tab settings, paragraph positioning, borders, and shading. Paragraph styles store both character and paragraph formatting and apply to selected paragraphs or the paragraph containing the insertion point.

When you open a new document, the standard styles of Normal, Heading 1, Heading 2, and Heading 3 are associated with the blank document, and you can see these by clicking on the arrow on the right edge of the Style box on the Formatting toolbar (see Figure 3.13).

help yourself *With so many ways to format, manipulate, and otherwise transform text in Word, you might forget exactly what you've done. Fortunately, it's easy to see exactly what formatting has been applied to a specific section of text. Select Help, What's This? and click the text that you're curious about. A **task pane** appears detailing every last bit of formatting information about the text in question*

Applying a Style

You can apply a paragraph or a character style by selecting a style name from the Style box on the Formatting toolbar or by accessing Styles and Formatting in the task pane.

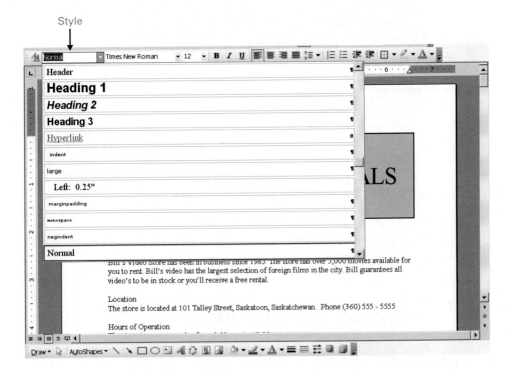

FIGURE 3.13

Style box

CHAPTER 3 **WORD** | **3.2** Using Templates

---

task reference	Applying a Style with the Formatting Toolbar

- Position the insertion point anywhere in the paragraph or select any amount of text in the paragraph

- On the Formatting toolbar, from the **Style** pull-down listing, select the paragraph or character style you want to apply

or

- From the Format menu, select **Styles and Formatting**

or

- Click on the **Styles and Formatting** button on the Formatting toolbar

and

- Select the style(s) you want to apply (see Figure 3.14)

- If the style you want is not listed in the Style task pane, select another category of styles from the Show pull-down listing at the bottom of the task pane

---

FIGURE 3.14

Applying styles through the task pane

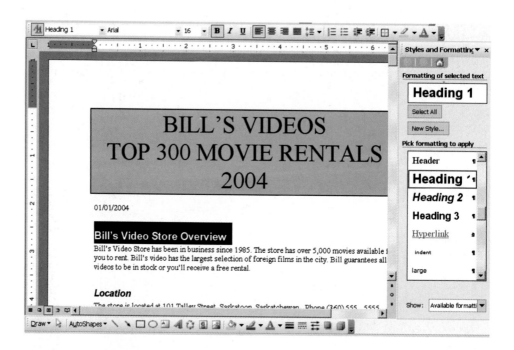

Bill decides that it would be easier to add styles to his document than to format each line. Bill is going to add Heading 1 and 2 styles to his document.

Learning to apply a default style:

1. Select **Bill's Video Store Overview** and on the Formatting toolbar from the Style pull-down listing select the **Heading 1** paragraph style

2. Select **Location** and click **Heading 2** from the Style pull-down listing

3. Select **Hours of Operation** and click on Heading 2

4. Select **Rental Policy** and click on Heading 2

5. Select **Late Fees** and click on Heading 2

6. Select **Membership Costs** and click on Heading 2

7. Select **Employment Opportunities** and click on Heading 2

8. Select **Top 300 Video List** and click on Heading 1

9. Select **Satisfaction Guaranteed** and click on Heading 1

10. Save your document

tip: *Now when you click in any of the lines that have been formatted, the Style pull-down listing on the Formatting toolbar shows the style for that line or paragraph*

Occasionally, the formatting adjustments you make are not exactly what you intended and you want to reapply the original formatting. If you have multiple styles in your document, Select All will not work. You will have to select text manually to change styles.

task reference	Reapplying Original Formatting to a Style

- Select the section of document you want to revert to the default style
- On the Formatting toolbar, from the Style pull-down listing, select the original style—the style you wish to reapply

or

- Select Clear Formatting to restore the formatting to the normal style for your document

Using Word's Predefined Styles

Each document you create is based on a template. New blank documents are based on the Normal template even though no template is actively selected. When you create a new document, the styles that are part of the template you select are copied into that document. Each template contains a set of standard styles, most of which are available with all Word templates. Styles created in one template may differ from those in another.

task reference	Using Word's Predefined Styles

- Click **Styles and Formatting** from the Format menu
- Highlight the paragraph you want to add the style to
- Click on the style

anotherway
. . . to View Styles Applied to Paragraphs

To see which paragraph styles are applied to text, you can display style names at the left side of the document window. Word displays the style names in Normal and Outline view only. To use this feature, click on Tools, Options, and View tab and change the size of the Style area width to 1 inch

Using Style Gallery

The *Style Gallery* allows copying of the style formatting from the new template into the active document, only replacing the style definitions. You can use the Style Gallery command to preview and then change the appearance of a document by switching the style definition. When you change the styles in the Style Gallery you are copying the style formatting from the new template into the active document. You are not replacing the template; you are only replacing the style definitions.

You can use the Style Gallery command to preview and change the overall appearance of a document by switching the style definitions to those of another template. When you change the styles in the Style Gallery, you are copying the style formatting from the new template into the active document. You are not replacing the template; you are only replacing the style definitions.

Once you have applied styles to text in a document, you can use the Style Gallery command to preview and change the overall appearance of a document. When you preview a document, you can select different templates and see how the document would look if you used styles from those templates.

---

task reference   **Previewing Styles**

- On the Format menu, click **Theme**

- Click **Style Gallery**

- In the Template box, select the template that contains styles you want to use

- To preview how your document will look with the different styles, click **Document** under Preview (see Figure 3.15)

- To see a sample document with styles from the selected template, click **Example**

- To see a list of the styles used in the selected template, click **Style samples**

F I G U R E   3.15

Document preview in the Style Gallery

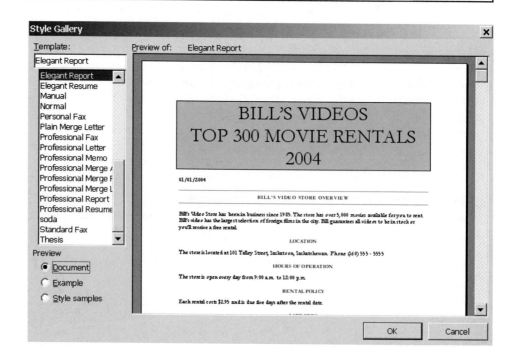

Learning to use the Style Gallery:

1. On the Format menu, click **Theme**
2. Click **Style Gallery**
3. In the Template box, select the template that contains the style you want to use. You can choose any style you want but you might want to preview the document before you choose a style
4. Click **OK**
5. Save your document

Creating a Style by Example

To create a style by example, you first format a paragraph the way you want it and then create a style based on the formatting in that paragraph. As you format a paragraph used as an example to create a style, remember that paragraph styles also contain character formatting. Character formatting includes the font, size, and so on. If your example paragraph contains left and right indents, a border, and shading, those formatting choices will also be part of your style.

Make sure your character formatting is consistent. For example, if one word in your paragraph is bold, every word in your new style will be bolded.

---

task reference   Creating a Paragraph Style by Example

- Place your cursor within the newly formatted example paragraph
- On the Formatting toolbar, in the Style text box, click the name of the existing style (often Normal)
- Type a new name for the style you want to create (see Figure 3.16)
- To create the style, press **Enter**

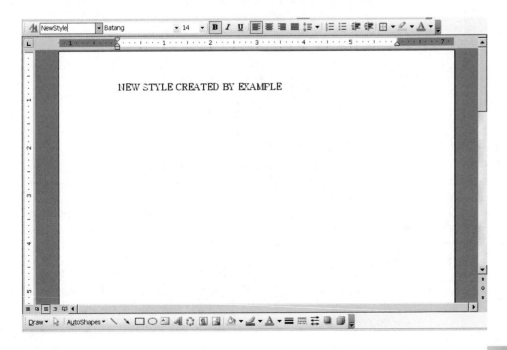

FIGURE 3.16

Naming a new style created by example

F I G U R E   3.17
Task pane showing styles
and button for New Style

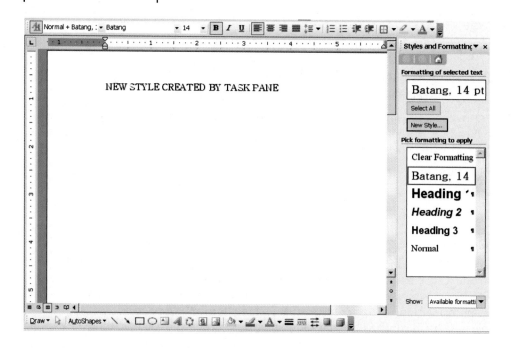

F I G U R E   3.18
New Style dialog box

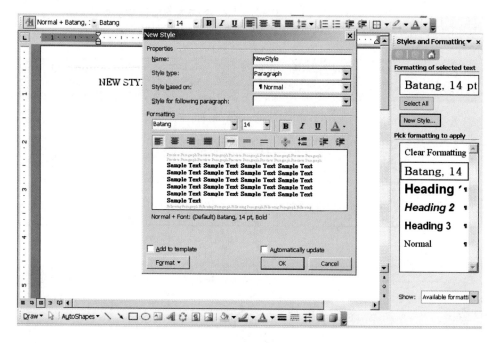

Creating a Style Using the Task Pane

Using the task pane, you define formatting characteristics and select options such as whether to base the style on another style, whether to follow it with another style, and whether to add the style to the current template.

When you create a style by using the task pane, you have the option to apply that style to the currently selected paragraph or simply add it to the list of styles you created for your document or for your template.

When naming styles, remember all names are case sensitive, so be sure to type it just as you want it. Also, notice that the Paragraph preview and Character preview boxes display the formatting of the currently selected paragraph. The Description section indicates the characteristics of the formatting, including font name and size.

FIGURE 3.19
Pull-down listing after
clicking Format

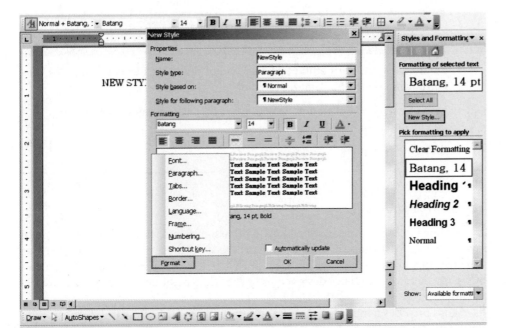

task reference — Creating a Paragraph Style Using the Task Pane

- From the Formatting toolbar, click on **Styles and Formatting** button and the task pane appears (see Figure 3.17)
- To create a new style, click **New Style**
- The New Style dialog box appears (see Figure 3.18)
- In the Name text box, type a name for the new style
- In the Style type pull-down list, to create a character style select **Character**; to create a paragraph style select **Paragraph**
- From the Style based on pull-down list, select an existing style to base the new style on
- Click **Format** to show a pull-down listing (see Figure 3.19)
- Select the attribute you want to change, and the Font dialog or Paragraph dialog box appears
- Fill out the corresponding dialog box
- Click **OK**
- To do more formatting or to create additional styles, repeat the steps
- To apply your new style to the selected text, in the task pane, click on the formatting you wish to apply
- Close the **task pane**

Deleting a Style

You can delete styles that you no longer wish to use from a document or template. A style can be deleted using the Styles and Formatting task pane. If you delete a paragraph style that you created, Word applies the Normal style to all paragraphs that were formatted with that style and removes the style definition from the task pane. You can delete any style except Word built-in styles that are a part of any new blank document.

---

task reference   Deleting Styles from a
                                         Document or Template

- If the Styles and Formatting task pane is not open, click **Styles and Formatting** on the Formatting toolbar

- In the Styles and Formatting task pane, right-click the style you want to delete, and then click **Delete**

- Close the **task pane**

Templates

A *template* is a collection of styles, keyboard assignments, and toolbar assignments saved to a file. By storing styles in a template, the styles are available for use whenever you are using that template. You can save time and effort when creating new documents by basing them on templates designed for a specific type of document you create frequently.

Word provides templates for several common types of documents like memos, reports, and business letters. You can use these templates just as they are, you can modify them, or you can create your own templates. Word automatically bases new documents on the Normal template unless you specify another template. Some useful templates include Agenda, Calendar, Letter, Newsletter, Memo, Resume, Report, and Thesis (see Figure 3.20)

Templates are special files that have a .dot extension. The special templates called Wizards have a .wiz extension. Both are stored in particular folders.

Furthermore, templates have been divided into several categories that are listed by subdirectory: General, Legal Pleadings, Mail Merge, Letters & Faxes, Memos, Reports, Other Documents, and Publications. Picking one of these folder areas takes you to a list of only those template and Wizard files in that category.

F I G U R E   3.20

Templates available in Word

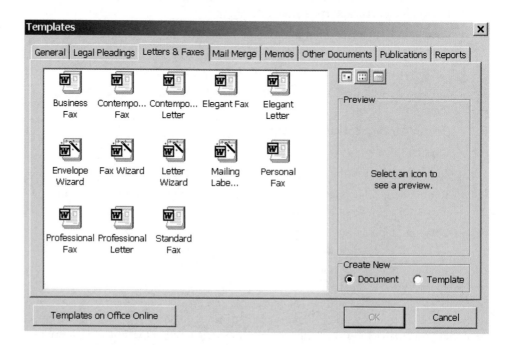

Creating a Template

The advantage of using a template, over just retrieving an existing document with the layout you want, is that the template will prompt you for the needed information and place it in the correct place. Also, the original master template is protected. When you save the resulting document, you cannot overwrite the master template by mistake. Templates can be created from scratch, based on an existing document, or based on another template.

The template file type will already be selected if you are saving a file that you created as a template. When a template is saved, you will need to give it a different filename if it is based on a template. Even if a template is based on a document saved as a template, you might want to give it a different filename. The Save As adds the .dot extension to the filename.

Bill decides to save the Videos1 document as a template. This will allow him to open the template next year and simply update the date and movie listing instead of having to create a new document. After saving the document as a template, Bill will be able to open a new document and select the VideoTemplate in the General Template category.

Creating a template for Videos1.doc:

1. On the File menu, click **Save As**

2. Retype the document name as **VideosTemplate.dot**

3. In the Save as type box, click **Document Template**

4. Click **Save**

5. Click **File, Close** to close your template

---

anotherword   ...**on the Relationship of Styles and Templates**

All documents in Word are based on a template. Templates contain styles, but templates are a special kind of document that provides basic tools for shaping a final document. Templates allow you to use preformatted styles, toolbars, menus, and so forth, and apply them to a document

---

SESSION 3.2

making *the grade*

1. _____ styles include any of the options available from the Font dialog box, such as bold, italic, and small caps.

2. The two types of styles include character and _____.

3. Paragraph styles include character and paragraph formatting, tab settings, paragraph positioning, borders, and _____.

4. The _____ command is used to preview and change the appearance of a document by switching the style definitions to those of another template.

5. What is a collection of styles, keyboard assignments, and toolbar assignments saved to a file?

SESSION 3.3 FORMATTING REPORTS

Page Numbers

Page numbers act as a guide for readers letting them easily locate specific pieces of information. (They are also a great help if anyone accidentally drops a large report that is not bound and the pages all scatter!) Word provides a quick and easy method of adding page numbers. On the menu bar under the Insert button item, you can choose the Page Numbers command. Page numbers then appear left, right, or centered at the top or bottom of the page (see Figure 3.21).

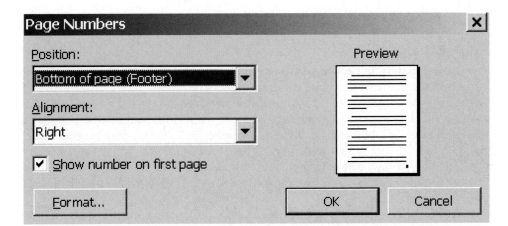

---

task reference   **Inserting Page Numbers**

- On the **Insert** menu, click **Page Numbers**

- In the **Position box**, specify whether to print page numbers in the header at the top of the page or in the footer at the bottom of the page

- **Select** any other options you want, for example, to show or hide the page number on the first page or other format options

- Click **OK**

Inserting page numbers on the bottom center of a page:

1. Open **Videos1.doc**

2. Click **Insert**, **Page Numbers**

3. On the Page Numbers dialog box in the Position box **select Bottom of page** (Footer)

4. In the Alignment box select **Center**

5. Click **OK**

6. Check the bottoms of the pages to verify that you have page numbers

7. Save your document

---

anotherword   **. . . on Page Number Format**

You can change the font or size of page numbers, switch to roman numerals (i, ii, iii), or specify how to start or restart page numbering. These options are in the Page Number Format dialog box obtained by clicking Insert, Page Numbers

WORD

Page Breaks and Section Breaks

Page Break

A page break is the point at which one page ends and another begins. A *soft page break* is inserted automatically at a point determined by Word. When you fill a page with text or graphics, Word inserts a soft page break automatically and starts a new page. With a soft page break, if you change the font or margins, the text will automatically adjust. A *hard page break* is inserted manually at a specific point. To force a page break at a specific location, you can insert a manual hard page break. However, if you insert manual page breaks, you might have to frequently rebreak pages as you edit the document. Instead, you might want to set pagination options to control where Word positions automatic page breaks.

In Print Layout view, in Print Preview, and in a printed document, text after a page break appears on a new page. In Normal view, an automatic page break appears as a single dotted line across the page, and a manual page break appears as a single dotted line marked "Page Break."

---

task reference   Inserting Page Breaks

- Click where you want to insert a page break
- On the **Insert** menu, click **Break**
- Under Section break types, click **Page Break**
- Click **OK**

Bill decides to add hard page breaks in his document to help make the document easier to read. He wants the title to be on a title page, the movie list to be on a separate page, and the satisfaction guarantee section to be on its own page. Bill is going to use his page breaking skills to insert the three page breaks.

Inserting page breaks:

1. Insert the cursor directly before the **date**
2. Click **Break** on the **Insert** menu
3. Click on **Page break**, click **OK**
4. Insert the cursor directly before the **Top 300 Movie List** heading
5. Click **Break** on the **Insert** menu
6. Click on **Page break**, click **OK**
7. Insert the cursor directly before **Satisfaction Guarantee**
8. Click **Break** on the **Insert** menu
9. Click on **Page break**, click **OK**
10. Save your document

Preventing Text from Separating between Pages

Depending on the view you have selected, page breaks are indicated by a dotted line in the Normal view and what looks like the edge of a piece of paper in the Print Layout view. Word arbitrarily decides where to put page breaks. Occasionally, these page breaks occur at inconvenient locations, for example, leaving a single line or word of a paragraph at the top or bottom of a column or page, or in the middle of a table or between a heading and the first lines of a paragraph. An *orphan* occurs when you leave a single line or word of a paragraph at the top or bottom of a column or page. A *widow* occurs when the last line of a paragraph prints by itself at the top of a page. The default setting in Microsoft Word prevents widows and orphans. You can change this default setting. Keeping lines of a paragraph together or preventing tables from splitting is a function found on the menu bar under the Format button.

---

task reference   Keeping Lines Together

- Select the paragraphs that contain lines you want to keep together

- On the **Format** menu, click **Paragraph**

- Click the **Line and Page Breaks** tab

- Select the **Keep lines together** check box (see Figure 3.22)

- Click **OK**

or

- Select **Keep with next** (depending on whether you are dealing with lines or paragraphs or both)

- Click **OK**

Section Break

Another type of break is a section break. This is a mark you insert to show the end of a section. If your document is divided into sections, you can click in a section or select multiple sections, and then perform such tasks as changing the paper orientation or formatting for that particular section. A *section break* stores the formatting elements, such as margins, page orientation, headers and footers, and sequence of page numbers for a specific area of a document. A section break appears as a double dotted line that contains the words "Section Break." For example, a section break could be used to include a table that needs to be printed in landscape orientation in the middle of a document that is otherwise all portrait oriented.

A section break controls the section formatting of the text that precedes it. For example, if you delete a section break, the preceding text becomes part of the following section and assumes its section formatting. Note that the last paragraph mark (¶) in the document controls the section formatting of the last section in the document or of the entire document if it doesn't contain sections. Four types of section breaks include (see Figure 3.23):

1. *Next page*—inserts a section break and starts the new section on the next page

2. *Continuous*—inserts a section break and starts the new section on the same page

3. *Even page*—inserts a section break and starts the new section on the next even-numbered page

4. *Odd page*—inserts a section break and starts the new section on the next odd-numbered page

WORD

FIGURE 3.22
Paragraph dialog box
showing Line and Page
Breaks tab

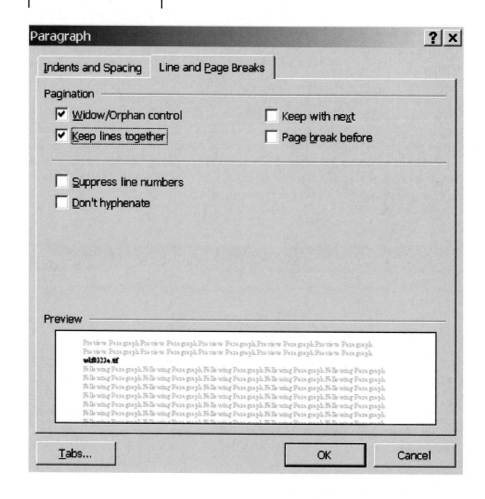

FIGURE 3.23
Examples of different
section breaks

next-page section break   continuous section break   even- or odd-page section break

help yourself *Click the Ask a Question combo box, type Section break, and press Enter. Click the hyperlink About Sections and Section breaks to display information on the different types of formats you can set for section breaks. Click the Help screen Close button when you are finished*

task reference   **Inserting Section Break**

- Click where you want to insert a section break
- On the **Insert** menu, click **Break**
- Under Section break types, **click** the option that describes where you want the new section to begin (see Figure 3.24)
- Click **OK**

Headers and Footers

Headers are displayed and printed in the margin at the top of a page. *Footers* are displayed and printed in the margin at the bottom of a page. Headers and footers allow you to print information on each page or specified pages regarding page number, volume number, title, subject matter, and so on. Both headers and footers are in the margin area and do not reduce the text area of your document (Figure 3.25). Although most people will put text in a header or footer, you can also use other elements like small graphic images (company logo) for special documents.

You can use the same header and footer throughout a document or change the header and footer for part of the document. For example, use a unique header or footer on the first page, or leave the header or footer off the first page. You can also use different headers and footers on odd and even pages. You can even have different headers and footers for each different section in your document.

The text or graphics you enter in a header or footer are automatically left aligned. You may want to center the item instead or include multiple items, for example, a left-

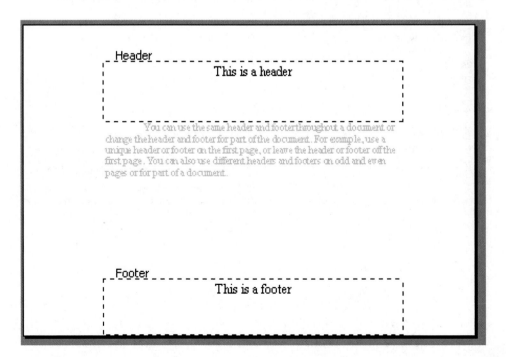

aligned date and a right-aligned page number. To center an item, press Tab; to right align an item, press Tab twice. If margins are changed, however, you will need to adjust the center and right-aligned tab accordingly.

You can change the horizontal position of headers and footers—for example, center a header or footer, or align it with the left or right margin. You can also change the vertical position of headers and footers by adjusting the distance from the top or bottom edge of the page, as well as the amount of space that appears between the document text and the header or footer.

---

task reference   Adding a Header

- On the **View** menu, click **Header and Footer**

- To create a header, enter text or graphics in the header area

- Or click a button on the Header and Footer toolbar (see Figure 3.26)

- When you finish, click **Close**

FIGURE 3.26

Header and Footer toolbar with table explaining the function of buttons on the Header and Footer toolbar

	Explanation of buttons on the Header and Footer toolbar	
	Button	**Function**
	[Switch Between Header and Footer]	Flip-flops between the page's header and footer
	[Show Previous]	Shows the previous page's header or footer
	[Show Next]	Shows the next page's header or footer
	[Same as Previous]	Tells Word to make this page's header or footer the same as the previous one
	[Page Numbers]	Adds a page number to a header or footer
	[Date]	Adds a date to a header or footer
	[Time]	Adds the system time to a header or footer
	[Page Setup]	Displays the "Page Setup" dialog box
	[Show/Hide Document Text]	Hides and unhides the document text
	[Close]	Closes the Header box or Footer box, removes the toolbar, and returns you to normal view

---

task reference   Adding a Footer

- On the **View** menu, click **Header and Footer**

- Click Header and Footer button to switch between the header and the footer

- To create a footer, enter text or graphics or page options in the footer area

- When you finish, click **Close**

---

anotherway
. . . to Insert Page Numbers

Using the header and footer you can insert running-total page numbers, such as "Page 3 of 12." On the View menu, click Header and Footer. Decide where you want the page numbers—header or footer. On the Header and Footer toolbar, click Insert AutoText, and then click Page X of Y

To view a header or footer, switch to Print Layout view. To edit or format a header or footer, you need to display the header or footer you want. In Print Layout view, you can quickly switch between the header or footer and the document text by double-clicking the dimmed header or footer or the dimmed document text.

When you change a header or footer, Word automatically changes the same header or footer throughout the entire document. To change a header or footer for part of a document, divide the document into sections and break the connection between them.

Bill decides to add a footer on his document displaying the words "Property of Bill's Video." Bill has also decided to place the date in the footer instead of on the second page of the document.

Adding a footer:

1. On the menu bar, click **View**, click **Header and Footer** to open a rectangle for the header outlined with a dashed line

2. Click on the **Switch Between Header and Footer** button to place the cursor in the footer section (see Figure 3.26)

3. In Times New Roman 12-point font type **Property of Bill's Video** on the far left of the footer

4. Press tab twice to enter the date by clicking on the date button in the Header and Footer toolbar (see Figure 3.26)

5. Click **Close** on the Header and Footer toolbar

6. Remove the date from the top of the document

7. Save your document

Footnotes and Endnotes

Footnotes are references or explanations that usually appear at the bottom of a page in a document. *Endnotes* are references or explanations that typically appear at the end of a document. Normally, footnotes and endnotes are used in printed documents to explain, comment on, or provide references for text in a document. You can include both footnotes and endnotes in the same document. For example, you might use footnotes for detailed comments and endnotes for citation of sources.

A footnote or an endnote consists of two linked parts—the note reference mark and the corresponding note text (see Figure 3.27). You can automatically number marks or create your own custom marks. Word renumbers footnotes and endnotes every time you add, delete, or move notes.

F I G U R E   3.27
Two linked parts of a
footnote or endnote

part of footnote appearing in text

Kasota United School District[1] hosts a
"Welcome to Wednesday" opportunity

[1] Dr. Alex Trexell, superintendent

part of footnote appearing at bottom of page

A footnote or endnote can be of any length and format. You can change the placement of footnotes so that they appear directly below the text. Similarly, you can change
the placement of endnotes so that they appear at the end of each section.

> **task reference**   Inserting a Footnote or an Endnote
>
> - In Print Layout view, click where you want to insert the footnote or endnote
>   reference mark
> - On the **Insert** menu, click **Reference**, click **Footnote**
> - Select **Footnote** or **Endnote**
> - Under Numbering, **click** the option you want
> - Click **Insert** (Word inserts the note number and places the insertion point
>   next to the note number.)
> - Type the note text
> - Scroll to your place in the document and click to continue typing

Creating a Table of Contents

The two basic tasks to creating a table of contents include specifying the entries and
building these entries into a table of contents. You can base a table of contents on predefined headings, user-defined styles, or table of contents entries (TC fields). For now
we will focus on a table of contents based on predefined headings. A one-to-one corre-
spondence exists between the heading level and the style assigned to it. For example,
Heading 1 entries will be assigned the TOC 1 style, Heading 2 entries are assigned the
TOC 2 style, and so on. You can change this if you wish.

To build a table of contents, Word searches for the predefined (built-in) headings,
user-defined styles, and table of contents entries you've specified to be included in your
table. Then Word collects these items and inserts them into your document as a TOC
field, and applies the table of contents styles (such as TOC 1, TOC 2, TOC 3) to the entries. It is important to note that a TOC can only be generated if there are styles applied
to the document to designate headings and subheadings.

task reference   Creating a Table of Contents

- Be certain that your document contains built-in heading styles (Heading 1 through Heading 9) to the headings you want to include in your table of contents

- Click where you want to insert the table of contents

- On the Insert menu, click **Reference**, **Index and Tables**, and then click the **Table of Contents** tab on the Index and Tables dialog box (see Figure 3.28)

- Click a design in the Formats box

or

- To specify a custom table of contents layout, choose the options you want

- Select any other table of contents options you want

- Click **OK**

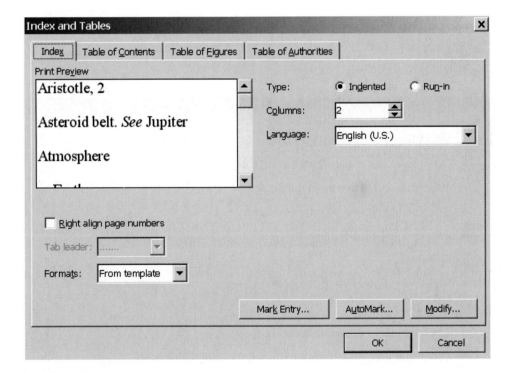

FIGURE 3.28

Index and Tables dialog box

Inserting a table of contents:

1. Insert a blank line before **Bill's Video Store Overview**

2. Insert the cursor directly before **Bill's Video Store Overview**

3. Insert a page break

4. Move the cursor to the top of the new page and type **TABLE OF CONTENTS** bold, all caps, 14-point, Times New Roman, centered

5. Place the cursor on the second line

6. Press the **Enter** key twice; make sure Show/Hide is off or the page numbering will be affected

7. Click **Insert, Reference, Index and Tables** on the menu bar

8. Click the **Table of Contents** tab

9. Click **OK**

10. Save your document

Creating an Index

An *index* is a listing of key word locations placed at the end of a long document. If a reader wants to look up a certain topic in a document, they can quickly refer to the index to find out what page the topic is on. Creating an index in Word is a two-step process.

Marking the Index

The first step is to mark the words and phrases in your document that you want to include in the index. Once that step is completed, you then build the actual index.

task reference	Marking an Index Entry

- Select the text you want to mark as an index entry
- Click **Insert, Reference, Index and Tables, Index** tab
- Click **Mark Entry** button in dialog box
- Selected text appears in the Main Entry field
- Edit the entry if necessary (for example, changing capitalization)
- Click **Mark**
- Mark Index Entry dialog box remains open
- Click **Close**
- The Mark Index Entry dialog box closes
- Click the **Show/Hide** button to hide nonprinting characters

Bill decides to place an index at the end of his document. This will allow his potential customers to quickly look up a topic on the last page of the document.

Marking words for the index:

1. Select **Video Store Overview** from Bill's Video Store Overview

2. Click **Insert, Reference, Index and Tables, Index** tab

3. Click the **Mark Entry** button on the Index and Tables dialog box

4. Selected word will appear in area next to Main Entry on the Mark Index Entry dialog box

5. Click the **Mark** button on the Mark Index Entry

6. Click **Close**

tip: *The Show/Hide formatting marks will display each time you mark an entry. Leave the formatting marks on until you have finished all entries and then turn off the formatting marks*

7. Repeat steps 2 through 6 for each of the following words: **Location, Hours of Operation, Rental Policy, Late Fees, Membership Costs, Employment Opportunities, Top 300 Video List,** and **Satisfaction Guarantee**

8. Turn off the formatting marks by clicking on the Show/Hide button on the Formatting toolbar

9. Save your document

Building the Index

After you've marked all the index entries, you choose an index design and build the finished index. Word then collects the index entries, sorts them alphabetically, references their page numbers, finds and removes duplicate entries from the same page, and displays the index in the document. Be sure not to alter the index entries themselves in the finished index, or the next time you rebuild the index, any changes will be lost. However, if you add, delete, move, or edit index entries or other text in a document, you should manually update the index. For example, if you edit an index entry and move it to a different page, you need to make sure that the index reflects the revised entry and page number.

---

task reference — Building an Index

- Mark all of the index entries in your document

- Insert the cursor where you want to place the index

- On the Insert menu, click **Reference, Index and Tables**, and then click the **Index** tab

- To use one of the available designs, click a design in the Formats box

or

- To design a custom index layout, choose the options you want

- Select any other index options that you want

- Click **OK**

Building an index:

1. Add a **page break** on the last page of the document after the Satisfaction Guarantee paragraph

2. Insert the cursor on the top of the new page

3. Type **INDEX** bold, all caps, 14-point, Times New Roman, centered

4. Press **Enter** twice, click on the align left button on the Formatting toolbar, and make sure Show/Hide is off

5. On the Insert menu, click **Reference, Index and Tables,** and then click the **Index** tab

6. Use the default setting

7. Click **OK**

8. Save your document

---

task reference   Updating an Index or
                                                       Table of Contents

- Click to the left of the index or table of contents
- Press F9

SESSION 3.3

making the grade

1. Page _____ acts as a guide for readers letting them easily locate specific pieces of information.

2. A _____ page break is inserted automatically at a point determined by Word.

3. A _____ page break is inserted manually at a specific point.

4. A _____ break stores the formatting elements, such as margins, page orientation, headers and footers, and sequence of page numbers for a specific area of a document.

5. _____ are displayed and printed in the margin at the bottom of a page.

SESSION 3.4 SUMMARY

Hyphenation is a tool that can improve the appearance of a document by eliminating the "rivers of white" on a line. With Word, documents can be automatically hyphenated, or automatic hyphenation can be turned off. Nonbreaking spaces and nonbreaking hyphens prevent phrases or numbers from breaking at the end of a line.

Paragraphs and lines can be formatted to prevent text from separating between pages in long documents. Word can also prevent a page break from occurring within a paragraph or within a table row, or ensure that a page break doesn't fall between two paragraphs, such as a heading and the following paragraph.

For multiple-page documents, Word easily inserts page numbers. Page numbers are automatically added each time Word inserts an automatic or soft page break, or when the user inserts a hard page break to force a new page.

Using the View menu, footnotes or endnotes and headers and footers are easily inserted to printed documents. Footnotes and endnotes explain, comment on, or provide references for text in a document. Headers and footers print in the top and bottom margins of a document. They allow you to print information on each page or specified pages regarding page number, volume number, title, subject matter, and so on.

MICROSOFT OFFICE SPECIALIST OBJECTIVES SUMMARY

- Insert frequently used and predefined text—MOS WW03S-1-2
- Create bulleted lists, numbered lists, and outlines—MOS WW03S-2-2
- Modify document layout and page setup—MOS WW03S-3-5
- Format text—MOS WW03S-3-1
- Create new documents using templates—MOS WW03S-5-1
- Insert and modify content in headers and footers—MOS WW03S-3-4
- Modify document layout and page setup—MOS WW03S-3-5
- Create custom styles for text, tables, and lists—MOS WW03E-1-1
- Create and modify document background—MOS WW03E-3-2
- Control pagination—MOS WW03E-1-2

making the grade answers

SESSION 3.1

1. Optional
2. Length
3. Landscape and portrait
4. Any line, paragraph, page, or entire document
5. Nonbreaking

SESSION 3.2

1. Character
2. Paragraph

3. Shading
4. Style Gallery
5. Template

SESSION 3.3

1. Numbers
2. Soft
3. Hard
4. Section
5. Footers

task reference summary

Task	Page #	Preferred Method
Hyphenating text with three different methods	WD 3.5	• On the **Tools** menu, point to **Language**, and then click **Hyphenation** • Select the **Automatically hyphenate document** check box • In the **Hyphenation zone box**, enter the amount of space to leave between the end of the last word in a line and the right margin • To reduce the number of hyphens, make the hyphenation zone wider • To reduce the raggedness of the right margin, make the hyphenation zone narrower • In the **Limit consecutive hyphens to** box, enter the number of consecutive lines that can be hyphenated or • On the **Tools** menu, point to **Language**, and then click **Hyphenation** • Click **Manual**

WORD

task reference *summary*

Task	Page #	Preferred Method
		• If Word identifies a word or phrase to hyphenate, do one of the following: • To insert an **optional hyphen** in the location Word proposes, click **Yes** • To insert an optional hyphen in another part of the word, use the arrow keys or mouse to move the insertion point to that location, and then click **Yes** or • Click where you want to insert the optional hyphen • Press **Ctrl+- (hyphen)**
Inserting the date and time	WD 3.7	• Insert the cursor where you want the date and time to be located • Click on the **Insert** menu and choose **Date and Time** • Click on the date and time format you require • Check **Update Automatically** if you require the date and time to be updated every time the document is opened • Click **OK**
Adding bullets or numbers	WD 3.7	• **Select** the items you want to add bullets or numbers • On the Formatting toolbar, do one of the following: • To add bullets, click **Bullets** button or • To add numbering, click **Numbering** button
Creating a border	WD 3.9	• Select the paragraph where you want the border • Click on the **Format** menu and choose **Borders and Shading** • Select the **Borders** tab and set the border style, color, and width • Click **OK**
Printing multiple pages on a document	WD 3.10	• On the **File** menu, click **Print** • Under Zoom, click **2, 4, 6, 8, or 16** pages in the Pages per sheet box • Click **OK**
Changing page orientation	WD 3.12	• On the **File** menu, click **Page Setup**, and then click the **Margins** tab • Under **Orientation**, click **Portrait** or **Landscape** • Click **OK**
Applying a style with the Formatting toolbar	WD 3.14	• Position the insertion point anywhere in the paragraph or select any amount of text in the paragraph • On the Formatting toolbar, from the **Style** pull-down listing, select the paragraph or character style you want to apply or • From the Format menu, select **Styles and Formatting** or • Click on the **Styles and Formatting** button on the Formatting toolbar and • Select the style(s) you want to apply • If the style you want is not listed in the Style task pane, select another category of styles from the Show pull-down listing at the bottom of the task pane
Reapplying original formatting to a style	WD 3.15	• Select the section of document you want to revert to the default style • On the Formatting toolbar, from the Style pull-down listing, select the original style—the style you wish to reapply or • Select Clear Formatting to restore the formatting to the normal style for your document
Using Word's predefined styles	WD 3.15	• Click **Styles and Formatting** from the Format menu • Highlight the paragraph you want to add the style to • Click on the style

task reference *summary*

Task	Page #	Preferred Method
Previewing styles	WD 3.16	• On the Format menu, click **Theme** • Click **Style Gallery** • In the Template box, select the template that contains styles you want to use • To preview how your document will look with the different styles, click **Document** under Preview • To see a sample document with styles from the selected template, click **Example** • To see a list of the styles used in the selected template, click **Style samples**
Creating a paragraph style by example	WD 3.17	• Place your cursor within the newly formatted example paragraph • On the Formatting toolbar, in the Style text box, click the name of the existing style (often Normal) • Type a new name for the style you want to create • To create the style, press **Enter**
Creating a paragraph style using the task pane	WD 3.19	• From the Formatting toolbar, click on **Styles and Formatting** button and the task pane appears • To create a new style, click **New Style** • The New Style dialog box appears • In the Name text box, type a name for the new style • In the Style type pull-down list, to create a character style select **Character**; to create a paragraph style select **Paragraph** • From the Style based on pull-down list, select an existing style to base the new style on • Click **Format** to show a pull-down listing • Select the attribute you want to change and the Font dialog or Paragraph dialog box appears • Fill out the corresponding dialog box • Click **OK** • To do more formatting or to create additional styles, repeat the steps • To apply your new style to the selected text, in the task pane, click on the formatting you wish to apply • Close the **task pane**
Deleting styles from a document or template	WD 3.20	• If the Styles and Formatting task pane is not open, click **Styles and Formatting** on the Formatting toolbar • In the Styles and Formatting task pane, right-click the style you want to delete, and then click **Delete** • Close the **task pane**
Selecting a template	WD 3.21	• Click **New** on the File menu • Click on **General Templates** on the task pane • Select a template
Creating templates two ways	WD 3.21	• To base a template on an existing document • On the File menu, click **Open** • Open the document you want or • To base a new template on an existing template • On the File menu, click **New** • In the New Document task pane under New from template, click **General Templates** • Click a template similar to the one you want to create • Click **Template** under Create New, and then click **OK** Or for a document • On the File menu, click **Save As** • In the Save as type box, click **Document Template** • Click **Save**

task reference *summary*

Task	Page #	Preferred Method
Inserting page numbers	WD 3.23	• On the **Insert** menu, click **Page Numbers** • In the **Position box**, specify whether to print page numbers in the header at the top of the page or in the footer at the bottom of the page • **Select** any other options you want, for example, to show or hide the page number on the first page or other format options • Click **OK**
Inserting page breaks	WD 3.24	• Click where you want to insert a page break • On the **Insert** menu, click **Break** • Under Section break types, click **Page Break** • Click **OK**
Keeping lines together	WD 3.25	• Select the paragraphs that contain lines you want to keep together • On the **Format** menu, click **Paragraph** • Click the **Line and Page Breaks** tab • Select the **Keep lines together** check box • Click **OK** or • Select **Keep with next** (depending on whether you are dealing with lines or paragraphs or both) • Click **OK**
Inserting section break	WD 3.26	• Click where you want to insert a section break • On the **Insert** menu, click **Break** • Under Section break types, **click** the option that describes where you want the new section to begin • Click **OK**
Adding a header	WD 3.28	• On the **View** menu, click **Header and Footer** • To create a header, enter text or graphics in the header area • Or click a button on the Header and Footer toolbar (see Figure 3.26) • When you finish, click **Close**
Adding a footer	WD 3.29	• On the **View** menu, click **Header and Footer** • Click Header and Footer button to switch between the header and the footer • To create a footer, enter text or graphics or page options in the footer area • When you finish, click **Close**
Inserting a footnote or an endnote	WD 3.30	• In Print Layout view, click where you want to insert the footnote or endnote reference mark • On the **Insert** menu, click **Reference**, click **Footnote** • Select **Footnote** or **Endnote** • Under Numbering, **click** the option you want • Click **Insert** (Word inserts the note number and places the insertion point next to the note number.) • Type the note text • Scroll to your place in the document and click to continue typing
Creating a table of contents	WD 3.31	• Be certain that your document contains built-in heading styles (Heading 1 through Heading 9) to the headings you want to include in your table of contents • Click where you want to insert the table of contents • On the Insert menu, click **Reference**, **Index and Tables**, and then click the **Table of Contents** tab on the Index and Tables dialog box • Click a design in the Formats box or • To specify a custom table of contents layout, choose the options you want • Select any other table of contents options you want • Click **OK**

task reference summary

Task	Page #	Preferred Method
Marking an index entry	WD 3.32	• Select the text you want to mark as an index entry • Click **Insert**, **Reference**, **Index and Tables**, **Index** tab • Click **Mark Entry** button in dialog box • Selected text appears in the Main Entry field • Edit the entry if necessary (for example, changing capitalization) • Click **Mark** • Mark Index Entry dialog box remains open • Click **Close** • The Mark Index Entry dialog box closes • Click the **Show/Hide** button to hide nonprinting characters
Building an index	WD 3.33	• Mark all of the index entries in your document • Insert the cursor where you want to place the index • On the Insert menu, click **Reference**, **Index and Tables**, and then click the **Index** tab • To use one of the available designs, click a design in the Formats box or • To design a custom index layout, choose the options you want • Select any other index options that you want • Click **OK**
Updating an index or table of contents	WD 3.34	• Click to the left of the index or table of contents • Press F9

TRUE/FALSE

1. A nonbreaking space prevents a line break between two words.

2. An orphan occurs when the first line of a paragraph is printed by itself at the bottom of a page.

3. A style is a set of formatting characteristics identified by name that you can apply to text in your document to quickly change its appearance.

4. Portrait is the orientation of text and graphics on the width of a page.

5. Footnotes are references or explanations at the end of a page in a document.

FILL-IN

1. _____ display and print in the margin at the bottom of a page.

2. A(n) _____ is a listing of key words placed at the end of a long document.

3. A _____ page break is inserted manually at a specific point.

4. A(n) _____ hyphen is used to control where a word or phrase breaks if it falls at the end of a line.

5. A soft page break is inserted automatically at a point determined by _____.

MULTIPLE CHOICE

1. Which of the following are included as options for character styles?
   a. Bold
   b. Italics
   c. Small caps
   d. All of the above

2. Which of the following prevents a hyphenated word from breaking if it falls at the end of a line?
   a. Nonbreaking space
   b. Optional hyphen
   c. Nonbreaking hyphen
   d. None of the above

3. What is displayed and printed in the margin at the bottom of a page?
   a. Footnotes
   b. Endnotes
   c. Footers
   d. None of the above

4. What is referenced or explained at the end of a page in a document?
   a. Footnotes
   b. Endnotes
   c. Footers
   d. None of the above

5. What is inserted manually at a specific point?
   a. Soft page break
   b. Hard page break
   c. All of the above
   d. None of the above

review of concepts

REVIEW QUESTIONS

1. Name two different types of page breaks.

2. Name two different types of paper orientation.

3. Describe a page break.

4. Describe the difference between a page break and a section break.

5. Name two different types of section breaks.

CREATE THE QUESTION

For each of the following answers, create an appropriate, short question.

ANSWER	QUESTION
1. Style Gallery	_____
2. Footer	_____
3. Index	_____
4. Orphan	_____
5. Widow	_____
6. Character style	_____
7. Endnote	_____

FACT OR FICTION

1. Character styles include character and paragraph formatting, tab settings, paragraph positioning, borders, and shading.

2. A section break stores the formatting elements, such as the margins, page orientation, headers and footers, and sequence of page numbers, for a specific area of a document.

3. Word allows you to copy the style formatting from one document into another document. However, Word does not allow you to create any new styles that are not already defined by Word.

4. An optional hyphen is used to control where a word or phrase breaks if it falls at the end of a line, for example, to specify that the word *nonprinting* breaks as "non-printing" rather than "nonprint-ing."

5. Endnotes are text, graphics, and file information that appear in the footnote at the beginning of a document.

practice

1. Adding to the Top 300 Video List

Bill has asked you to add your favorite movies to the Top 300 Video list. Bill would also like you to add another section called Future Expansion in the Bill's Video Store Overview section. The future expansion section will include information about the new store that Bill is building across town.

1. Save the document as **VideosFuture.doc**
2. Insert the cursor after the Employment Opportunities paragraph; press **Enter** twice
3. Type **Future Expansion**
4. Click on the Formatting toolbar from the Style pull-down listing and select the **Heading 2** paragraph style
5. Press **Enter** key
6. Ensure the heading for the new line is **Normal**
7. Type **Visit our new location at 1717 Market Street in the Twins Shopping Plaza.**
8. Insert your cursor after the last entry in the **TOP 300 VIDEO LIST**
9. Click on **Insert**, **Break**, **Page break**, **OK**
10. Type **<Your Name>'s Top Movie Listing**, ensure the style is Heading 1, press the **Enter** key
11. Type in your favorite movies, one movie per line, ensure the style is normal
12. **Select** all of your favorite movies
13. Click the numbering button on the Formatting toolbar
14. Move the cursor to the Table of Contents
15. Right-click on the **Table of Contents**
16. Click on **Update Field** select ToC F9
17. Select **Update Entire table**, click **OK**
18. Compare your updated table of contents with Figure 3.29. Note that the page numbers might be different depending on how many movies you entered
19. Save and close your document

TABLE OF CONTENTS

Bill's Video Store Overview 3
  Location 3
  Hours of Operation 3
  Rental Policy 3
  Late Fees 3
  Membership Costs 3
  Employment Opportunities 3
  Future Expansion 3
Top 300 Video List 4
Jim's Top Movie Listing 11
Satisfaction Guarantee 12

FIGURE 3.29
Updated Table of Contents

2. Printing Landscape

You are the owner of Green Tree Today, a highly successful Christmas ornament mail-order business. In your business you have found that sending legal-size letters along with your packages is an effective way to reach customers with news about new offerings or the status of an order.

1. Open a New Blank Document

2. Save the document as **Tree1.doc**

3. Click **File**, **Page Setup**, **Paper** tab

4. In the Paper size window, select **Statement**

5. Select the **Margin** tab

6. Under Orientation select **Landscape**

7. Set the top, bottom, left, and right margins at **0.5 inch**

8. Click **OK**

9. Click View, Header and Footer

10. Add the Company Name in the Header

11. Switch to the footer

12. Add the page number to the center of the footer

13. Add the date to the far right of the footer

14. Close the Header and Footer

15. Type the following text using a Times New Roman font size 12, single spacing

16. Preview your document and compare it with Figure 3.30

17. Save and close your document

FIGURE 3.30

Ms. Mink's letter

Green Tree Today

Ms. Jodi Mink
1338 West Maumee Road
Bedford #1134A
Adroan, MI 49921

Dear Ms. Mink:

We are unable to make delivery on the purchase order VOC1293 on June 10, 2006, as planned. We should have our merchandise ready to ship within 10 days of the original delivery date and we hope that you can hold off until that time.

We did want to inform you of this delay as soon as we were advised in order to give you as much time as possible to make alternate arrangements, if necessary. We can assure you, however, that if your order remains in force, we will expedite delivery to you as soon as we have received the merchandise.

Please accept our apology for this delay and thank you for your understanding.
Green Tree Today

Service Department

1   01/01/2004

1. Printing a Two-Page Distance Learning Survey on One Page

You are an analyst at E-Learn, a company that specializes in helping teachers get the most out of their students. You have been working hard developing a new course evaluation form (see Figure 3.31). You have decided to send the form to a few of your colleagues for their feedback prior to sharing it at the next company meeting. Here is the feedback you received from your colleagues.

- Change the bullets to numbers
- Add a footer with page numbers
- Change the document to print two pages per sheet
- Change the orientation to landscape

Open the document **wd03Evaluation.doc**. and save it as **Evaluation1.doc**. Make all of the above changes to the document and save the new changes.

FIGURE 3.31

E-Learn course evaluation

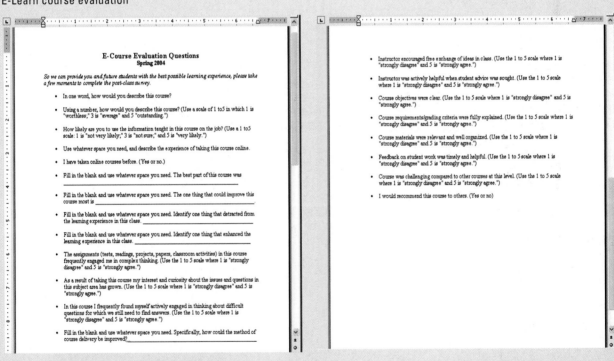

2. Applying Heading Levels to an Outline

You work for a local veterinarian as a veterinarian assistant. You are compiling a document on the nutrition and nutrients for animals. You have shown the document to your boss, Jamie Grammar, and he has requested the following changes:

- Apply Heading 1 to all topics that are flush against the left margin
- Apply Heading 2 to topics that are indented
- Add a title page containing **Applied Animal Nutrition** two lines down from the top

- Then press **Enter** twice, add the Current Date, center both lines, and set them at Times New Roman 26-point, all caps and bold
- Shade the title and date at 10 percent gray and add a 3-point box single line border
- Center the title in the middle of the title page
- Add a page for a table of contents
- Add a table of contents

Open the file **wd03Lecture.doc** and save it as **Lecture1.doc**. Compare your finished document with Figure 3.32.

FIGURE 3.32

Applied Animal Nutrition Table of Contents

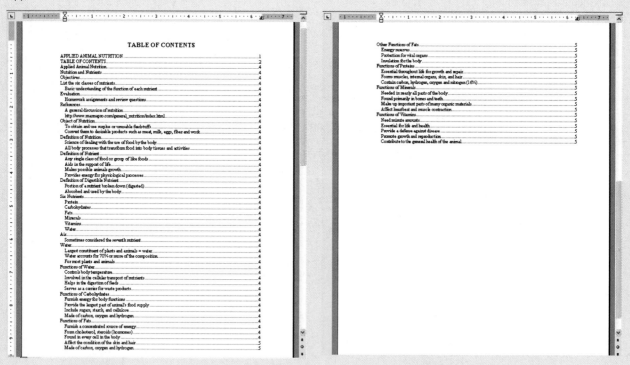

1. Formatting a Glossary of E-Commerce Terms

As part of the training for Learn E-Skills Now, the company wants to provide the participants with a glossary of e-commerce terms. Using Styles in Word format the e-commerce glossary that includes the following terms:

- ARPAnet
- Authentication
- Bandwidth
- Browser
- Cyberspace
- E-Money
- Encryption
- Extranet
- HMTL
- Intranet
- Internet
- ISDN
- Java
- NC
- Search Engine
- Secure Electronic Transaction (SET)
- SSL
- TCP/IP
- World Wide Web

Open the document **wd03Glossary.doc** and save it as **Glossary1.doc**. Format the document using styles. Figure 3.33 provides an example of how you might format the document.

FIGURE 3.33

Final Glossary for Learn E-Skills Now

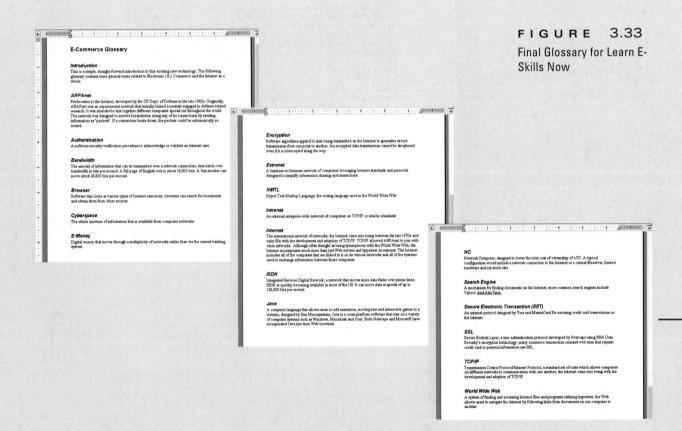

2. Finalizing a White Paper on E-Business

Prior to a conference on e-business at the community college where you teach, you wrote a white paper describing e-business and the need for rural America to become involved. To make a point about the potential of e-business you found some sales data that will be used in a footnote. Open the document **wd03Whitepaper.doc** and save it as **Whitepaper1.doc**.

Locate the year **2004** in the text and attach this footnote to that year:

Based on a survey during the 2004 holiday season the average consumer spent $300 each time they ordered online.

Delete Dr. Cole Parker as the author of the paper and add your name as the author. Compare your work to Figure 3.34. Save and close the file.

FIGURE 3.34

Completed white paper with footnote

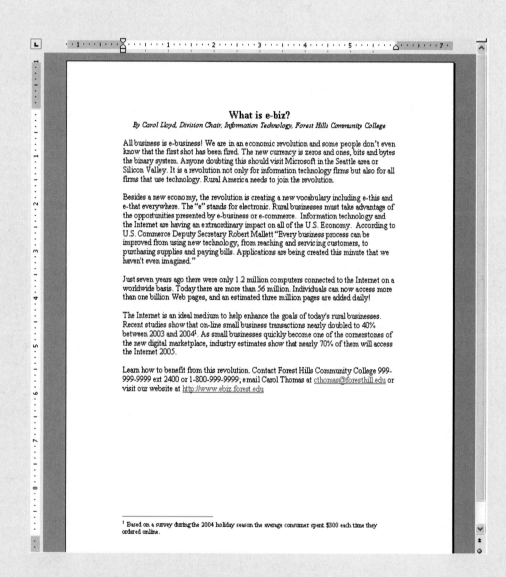

1. Finding and Reporting on Medical Information

You just started working for a small genetic engineering company. On your first day your boss asks you to search for information on genetic engineering, stem cell research, cancer cures, or some other topic of interest. You must produce a report highlighting all of the information you gathered by the end of the day. The report should be at least two pages long and include several bulleted or numbered lists of the different Web sites you visited. There are many sites available on the Web including:

- Mayo Clinic—Mayoclinic.com (see Figure 3.35)
- National Library of Medicine—www.nim.nih.gov
- Merck Manual—www.Merckhomeedition.com
- National Institutes of Health—www.nih.gov
- Centers for Disease Control and Prevention—www.cdc.gov
- World Health Organization—www.who.int/en/
- The United States Department of Health and Human Services—www.hhs.gov
- Health A-Z—www.healthatoz.com
- Health Web—www.healthweb.org

After you have finished your research, compile your information in one of Word's report templates—contemporary elegant or professional. Transfer your research information to this template and develop a report. Modify the report template as needed and then submit your report. Be sure to include headings and footers, page breaks where required, title page, table of contents, and an index. Save the report as **ResearchReport1.doc**.

2. Searching for Your Ancestors on the Web

Genealogy is fast becoming a hobby or pastime of many people. The World Wide Web is ideal for genealogical research. Many sites are available to help you find your ancestors and to find out information about them. Two excellent sites for starting your research are:

- American Family Immigration History Center (Ellis Island) www.ellisisland.org/default.asp
- Family Search www.familysearch.org

Visit these Web sites and search for your ancestors or at least for your family name. Also, follow the links at these sites to other sources of information. After you have some information about your ancestors or your family name, include this information in a letter to your instructor. Use one of the letter templates that come with Word to format your letter. Save your document as **Family1.doc**.

FIGURE 3.35
Mayo Clinic Web site

around the world

1. Creating a Letterhead Template for International Business

Letterhead is paper that is preprinted with company information such as the name, address, and logo of the company. Enviro-World Wide, Inc., outsource experts to governments that deal with environmental issues. Enviro-World Wide employees are outsourced anywhere in the world. The company has 10 offices in various locations. The head office is in East Lansing, Michigan. The company wants all letterhead to look alike, and to look like it came from the central office in East Lansing, Michigan. Using your Word skills develop a letterhead template for Enviro-World Wide, Inc. Use the following information in the header:

- Enviro-World Wide, Inc.
- 5483 Future Life Avenue
- East Lansing, Michigan 99999
- USA
- Phone: 000.999.9999

- Fax: 000.999.1111
- Web site: Enviro-ww.com
- E-mail: Earth@enviroww.com

Use what you know about fonts and styles to create this letterhead template. Figure 3.36 provides an example of what the template could look like. Save your work as **Letterhead1.dot**.

2. Developing a Style for a Resume

Your organization is seeking contract work with the government of a foreign country. To complete the application process, all the members of your organization must submit a one- to two-page resume. To make a good impression, you want all of the resumes to be consistent. Use the Contemporary Resume template to create a resume template for your organization that will reflect any international work an individual might have completed in the past. Save your revised template as **ForeignResume1.dot**.

FIGURE 3.36

Letterhead template for Enviro-World Wide, Inc.

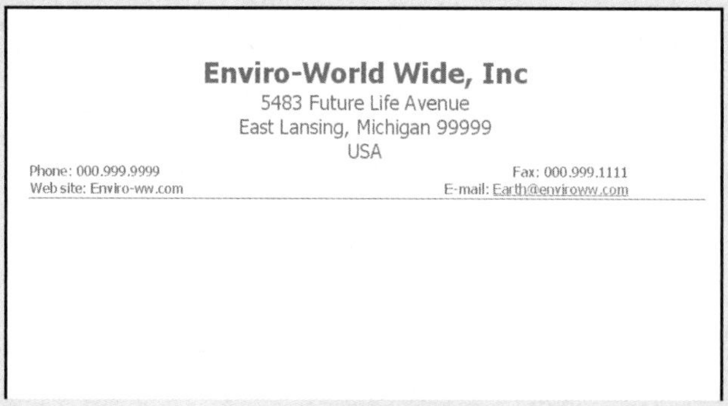

Enviro-World Wide, Inc
5483 Future Life Avenue
East Lansing, Michigan 99999
USA

Phone: 000.999.9999
Web site: Enviro-ww.com

Fax: 000.999.1111
E-mail: Earth@enviroww.com

Creating Styles and a Template for Syllabi

The superintendent of the Kasota United School District (KUSD), Greg Provenzo, announced that each high school class (grades 10, 11, and 12) would have its own syllabus. These syllabi are to be provided to the students on the first day of class, and they will provide the student and the teachers with consistent, useful information about the class, how it will be conducted, what will be learned, and how the students will be graded. A friend of Greg's, Dr. Libby Bair, did the same thing in her school district last year. Libby offered to share one of the syllabi she created in Word (Figure 3.37). After studying this syllabus format, Greg decided that KUSD can use it with a few minor changes. The file for doing this is saved as **wd03Syllabus.doc.**

Greg wants to make the following changes to the syllabus from his friend and then save it as a document template to be distributed at the high school:

- Delete the lines containing office location, hours, and phone number
- Delete Dr. Bair's name and e-mail address
- Add a line for **Grade Level** under the heading Semester, and apply the Part1 style
- Add footer with **"Kasota United School District High School"** and the **page number**
- Modify all of the Title, Part1, and Part2 styles so they are in **Arial** font but still the same size
- After making these changes, save the syllabus document as a **Syllabus1.dot.**

FIGURE 3.37

Syllabus with styles that Greg plans to modify and save as a template for KUSD

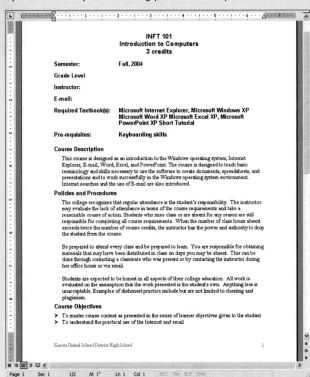
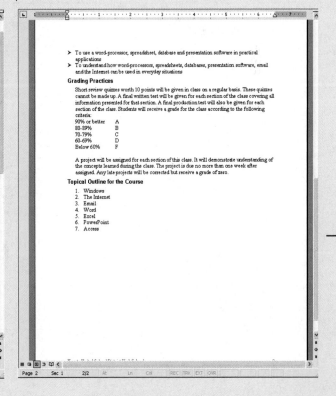

1. Creating a Report Template

Word offers several features you can use to create a report. Create a template for a generic long report called **MyReport1.doc**. Format the template for everything you would normally use in a report including automatic page numbering, page breaks, section breaks, table of contents, index, and headers and footers. Be sure to insert generic headings so you can create a table of contents. Once completed, discuss the value of using templates. Does it save time?

2. The Difference between Styles and Templates

This session discussed both styles and templates. Discuss the fundamental differences between styles and templates. Include a brief discussion about when you would use each different type.

4

Using Tables and Graphics

know? did you

in *1906, the Frank Fleer Corporation marketed Blibber-Blubber, the first bubble gum ever. It never caught on because it was brittle and the bubbles often burst into sticky fragments all over the chewer's face.*

during *the year 2000, each American worked an average of 47.1 hours per week.*

Charles F. Dowd, *a school principal in New York State, proposed a time zone system. At noon on Sunday, November 18, 1883, the new system went into effect. It became the basis for the international system of time zones.*

Mickey Mouse *made his debut in the cartoon* Steamboat Willie *in 1928.*

of *all the private residences in the United States, the one that receives the most guests every year is the White House, home of the President. About 6,000 visitors tour the White House every day.*

at *its height the Inca Empire stretched 4,000 km/2,500 miles north-south and 800 km/500 miles east-west. Population estimates vary from 3.5 million to 16 million.*

Chapter Objectives

- **Insert and modify tables—MOS WW03S-2-1**
- **Insert, position, and size graphics—MOS WW03S-1-4**
- **Sort content in lists and tables—MOS WW03E-2-1**
- **Perform calculations in tables—MOS WW03E-2-2**
- **Modify table formats—MOS WW03E-2-3**
- **Format, position, and resize graphics using advanced layout features —MOS WW03E-1-3**

Developing Promotional Material for Green Thumb Landscape and Garden Center

Word processing creates documents with a professional appearance. Presenting material in tables and the addition of graphics add to the professional appearance of documents. Moreover, information presented in a table format is easier to comprehend.

Taylor Scott manages the Green Thumb Landscape and Garden Center. Each spring customers ask her all kinds of questions including what to plant and when to plant. For the last few years, Taylor has been giving her customers a handwritten outline of general plant information. Although the information in the document is ex-

tremely useful, Taylor is disappointed in the appearance of the document. Taylor recently purchased a computer for her company and she wants to use Word to put all of this information into a professional looking document (see Figure 4.1). Taylor wants to be able to hand out the document to her customers at the Garden Center and at local trade shows. Since the document is representing her business, it must be attractive and professional looking. Taylor also wants to provide her customers with a one-page flyer of tips on planning their vegetable garden (see Figure 4.2).

FIGURE 4.1
Taylor's finished planting guide

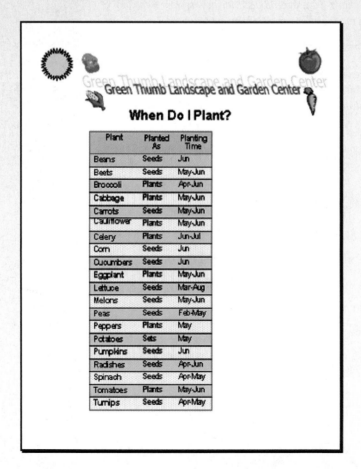

INTRODUCTION

The table feature in Word is extremely useful and easy to use. You'll find that when you present material in tables, your readers will have an easier time understanding the material. Word also offers many different ways that you can add graphics to your documents. Your documents will be very attractive and professional looking when they contain tables and graphics.

SESSION 4.1 CREATING TABLES

A table is made up of columns and rows of cells. A *cell* is the area at the intersection of a column and a row. Figure 4.3 illustrates the different parts of a table in Word. These parts include:

- *Border*—outside edges of a table
- *Gridlines*—lines separating columns and rows in a table
- *End mark*—used to indicate the end of a row or a cell and is viewable only when the Show/Hide button is clicked
- *Table move handle*—used to drag a table to another location by holding down the left mouse button
- *Table resize handle*—used to enlarge or reduce a table by clicking and holding down the left mouse button

By default, tables have a black ½-pt, single-line, solid-line border that will be printed. If you remove this border, you will still see the gridlines that form the cell boundaries. Gridlines are not printed. With Show/Hide turned on, end marks show up at the end of cells and end of rows. These marks are nonprinting characters that, like gridlines, appear only on the screen. The table move handle is located at the top left-hand of the table, and the table resize handle is located at the lower right corner of the table. The table move handle moves the table to another place on a page, and the table resize handle changes the size of the table.

Tables are useful for showing a large number of related facts or statistics in a small space. Tables can present data more concisely than text, and tables provide more accurate information than a graph. You can also use tables to create interesting page layouts. Creating tables, which was once a difficult task, is now easy when you use Word.

Creating a Table

You can use any of the following three methods to create a table:

1. Use the Insert Table button
2. Use the Draw Table tool
3. Convert existing text, data from a database, or data from a worksheet into a table

You can quickly create a simple table by using the Insert Table button on the Standard toolbar, or you can insert a table using the Table button on the menu bar. Using the Draw Table tool on the Standard toolbar quickly creates a more complex table—one that contains cells of different heights or a varying number of columns per row. Using the Draw Table tool is similar to drawing a rectangle on graph paper—first, draw a line from one corner of the table to the corner diagonally opposite in order to define the boundary of the entire table, and then draw the column and row lines inside (see Figure 4.4). You can convert existing paragraphs of text to a table. You can also create a table from an existing data source, such as a database or a worksheet.

F I G U R E   4.3

Rows, columns, cells, borders, gridlines, end marks, and table move and resize handles in a table

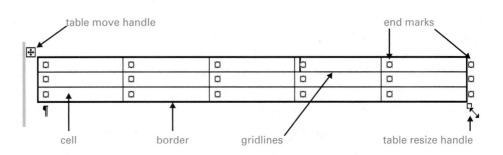

FIGURE 4.4
Illustration of drawing a table

First...   then...   or...   and so on...

FIGURE 4.5
Dragging to select the number of columns and rows in a table

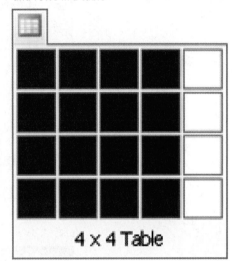

4 × 4 Table

task reference — Inserting an Empty Table

- Click where you want to create a table
- Click **Insert Table** button on the Standard toolbar
- Drag to select the number of columns and rows you want (see Figure 4.5)
- Release the mouse button to insert the blank table

anotherword . . . on Deleting Columns and Rows

Be careful when you delete columns or rows that are not blank. When you delete a column or row, everything is deleted, including the data. These are times when you should remember the value of the Undo typing button!

Deleting and Inserting Columns and Rows

The Insert Table button shows a five-column by four-row table. You can change that by clicking and dragging a cell to create any size table. You can also add additional columns or rows once a table is created.

task reference — Adding Columns or Rows to a Table

- Click the position in the table where you want to add columns or rows
- Drag to select the number of columns or rows to insert
- On the **Table** menu, click **Insert**
- Click **Columns to the Right** or **Columns to the Left**

or

- On the **Table** menu, click **Insert**
- Click **Rows Above** or **Rows Below** (see Figure 4.6)

anotherway
. . . to Add Rows to a Table

To insert a row at the end of a table, click the last cell of the last row and then press the **Tab** key

F I G U R E   4.6

Inserting columns or rows
by clicking Table, Insert

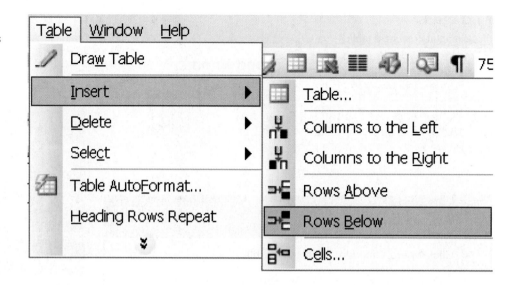

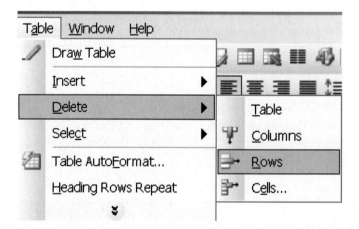

task reference   Deleting Columns or
Rows in a Table

- Click the position in the table where you want to delete columns or rows
- Click **Table, Delete**
- Choose Columns or Rows (see Figure 4.7)

F I G U R E   4.7

Deleting columns or rows
in a table using the Table
menu

Taylor will start with a simple table that she will use to display her planting guide. To complete her table Taylor needs to add more rows, since the table she inserted only contained four rows. Eventually, she will format the table and even add some graphics.

Creating a table and entering text into a table:

1. Open a new document and save it as **Plantguide1.doc**
2. Type **When Do I Plant?** in Arial 24-point bold, click the **Center** button, press **Enter** twice, and click the **Align Left** button. Change font to Times New Roman, 12-point, turn off bold.

3. Click **Insert Table** button on the Standard toolbar, and create a 3-column by 4-row table

4. Move the mouse pointer to the first row of the first column, click, and type **Plant** in Arial 14-point bold

5. Press **Tab** to move to the first row of the second column, and type **Planted As** in Arial 14-point bold

6. Press **Tab** to move to the first row of the third column, and type **Planting Time** in Arial 14-point bold

7. Press **Tab** to move to the second row of the first column, and type **Beans** in Arial 14-point

8. Press **Tab** and type **Seeds**

9. Press **Tab** and type **Jun**

10. Press **Tab** to move to the first column in the next row

11. Continue steps 8 through 11 until all the cells are filled with the information shown in Figure 4.8

tip: *When you get to the end of row 4, pressing tab will add a new row at the end of the table*

12. Save your document

FIGURE 4.8
Information to complete planting guide

When Do I Plant?

Plant	Planted As	Planting Time
Beans	Seeds	Jun
Beets	Seeds	May-Jun
Broccoli	Plants	Apr-Jun
Cabbage	Plants	May-Jun
Carrots	Seeds	May-Jun
Cauliflower	Plants	May-Jun
Celery	Plants	Jun-Jul
Corn	Seeds	Jun
Cucumbers	Seeds	Jun
Eggplant	Plants	May-Jun
Lettuce	Seeds	Mar-Aug
Melons	Seeds	May-Jun
Peas	Seeds	Feb-May
Peppers	Plants	May
Potatoes	Sets	May
Pumpkins	Seeds	Jun
Radishes	Seeds	Apr-Jun
Spinach	Seeds	Apr-May
Tomatoes	Plants	May-Jun
Turnips	Seeds	Apr-May

Adjusting Column Widths and Row Height

When you are creating tables, you will want to change the width of the columns and the height of the rows in order to make your table more attractive. You might want to add cell padding by changing the cell margin. *Cell padding* represents the spacing between the boundary of the cell and the text inside the cell.

If you use a table to lay out a page and you want to use another table to present information, you can insert a nested table. A *nested table* is a table within a table (see Figure 4.9). You can also use Draw Table to create nested tables. For example, if you use a table to lay out the Web page for your company's sales department, you might want to insert in the layout a nested table illustrating the department's quarterly earnings.

Text to Table

Sometimes it's easier to understand information in table rather than text form. Word allows you to convert text to a table and vice versa. When you convert text to a table, you use separator characters to indicate where a new column should begin. *Separator characters* are characters such as paragraph marks (¶), tabs (→), or commas you choose to indicate where you want text to separate when you convert a table to text, or where you want new columns or rows to begin when you convert text to a table.

When you convert text to a table, Word begins rows at paragraph marks. If you use tabs, commas, or other separator characters, Word will begin your table by creating columns. Choose paragraph marks as your separator character if you want the new table to contain only one column.

WORD

FIGURE   4.9
Example of nested tables

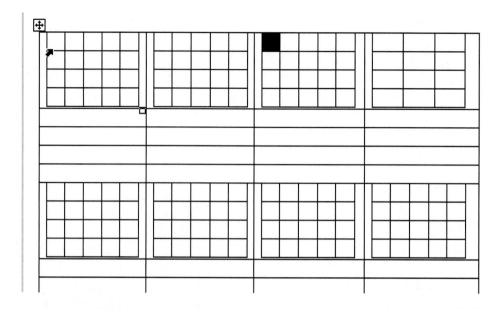

---

task reference   **Converting Text into a Table**

- Select the text you want to convert

- On the **Table** menu, point to **Convert**, and then click **Text to Table**

- Under **Separate text at**, click the option for the separator character you want (see Figure 4.10)

- Select any other options you want

- Click **OK**

FIGURE   4.10

Convert Text to Table
dialog box

Convert Text to Table   ✕

Table size

  Number of columns: 5 ▲▼

  Number of rows: 1 ▲▼

AutoFit behavior

  ● Fixed column width: Auto ▲▼

  ○ AutoFit to contents

  ○ AutoFit to window

Table style: (none)   AutoFormat...

Separate text at

  ○ Paragraphs   ● Commas

  ○ Tabs   ○ Other: -

          OK   Cancel

How Much Do I Need?

Fruit or Vegetable	Volume	Weight	Will Make–
Beans	1 bushel	33 pounds	30-45 pints frozen
Carrots	1 bushel	50 pounds	32-40 pints frozen
Corn, in husks	1 bushel	35 pounds	14-17 pints frozen
Peas, in shell	1 bushel	30 pounds	12-15 pints frozen
Tomatoes	1 bushel	50-60 pounds	20 quarts canned whole
Tomatoes	1 bushel	50-60 pounds	12-14 quarts juice
Cucumbers (4-inch)	-----	6 pounds	4 quarts canned

FIGURE 4.11
Taylor's list of vegetables and how much they will produce

Taylor created a document listing the amount of vegetables required when attempting to can or freeze vegetables (Figure 4.11). Taylor wants to place this information in a table.

Converting a list to a table:

1. Open the data file named **wd04Vegetable.doc**

2. Save the file as **Vegetable1.doc**

3. Select all the text except the title

tip: *Be sure to click the Show/Hide button so you can see the ¶ marks*

4. Click **Table**, point to **Convert**, and click **Text to Table**

5. In the Convert Text to Table dialog box, select **4** for the Number of Columns

6. Click the **AutoFormat** button and select **Table Columns 3** in the Table Styles window

7. Click **OK**

8. Choose **Tabs** under **Separate text at** on the Convert Text to Table dialog box

9. Click **OK**, and click anywhere to deselect the table

10. Compare your table to Figure 4.12

11. Save your document

Table to Text

Often someone will provide information to you in a table and you will determine that the information is more useful to you in a text format. For example, suppose you need to use the information in the cells of a table in different paragraphs of a document. Word allows you to convert from table format to text format. When you convert a table to text, Word substitutes row endings with paragraph marks and column boundaries with tabs, commas, or other marks you choose. Choose paragraph marks as your separator characters if you want the text in each cell to be its own paragraph.

WORD

F I G U R E   4.12
Taylor's list converted to a
table in the Columns 3
format

How Much Do I Need?

Fruit or Vegetable	Volume	Weight	Will Make--
Beans	1 bushel	33 pounds	30-45 pints frozen
Carrots	1 bushel	50 pounds	32-40 pints frozen
Corn, in husks	1 bushel	35 pounds	14-17 pints frozen
Peas, in shell	1 bushel	30 pounds	12-15 pints frozen
Tomatoes	1 bushel	50-60 pounds	20 quarts canned whole
Tomatoes	1 bushel	50-60 pounds	12-14 quarts juice
Cucumbers (4-inch)	----	6 pounds	4 quarts canned

---

task reference　　　　　　　Converting a Table to Text

- Select the rows or table that you want to convert to paragraphs

- On the **Table** menu, point to **Convert**, and then click **Table to Text**

- Under **Separate text with**, click the option for the separator character (comma, tab, space, paragraph, or other) you want to use in place of the column boundaries

- Paragraph marks separate rows

Taylor created a table about some of the common legumes found in the average garden. She now wants to use the information in paragraph form for her newsletter, so she must convert the table to text (shown in Figure 4.13).

Converting a table to text:

1. Open the data file named **wd04Legumes.doc**

2. Save the file as **Legumes1.doc**

3. Click in the table

4. Click **Table**, point to **Convert**, and click **Table to Text**

5. In the Convert Table to Text dialog box, select **Paragraph marks** for Separate text with

6. Click **OK**, and click anywhere to deselect the text

7. Compare your results to Figure 4.14

8. Save your document

help yourself _Click the Ask a Question combo box, type_ **Table**_, and press_ **Enter**. _Click the hyperlink_ **About tables** _to display information about parts of a table and different ways you can work with a table. Click the Help screen_ **Close** _button when you are finished_

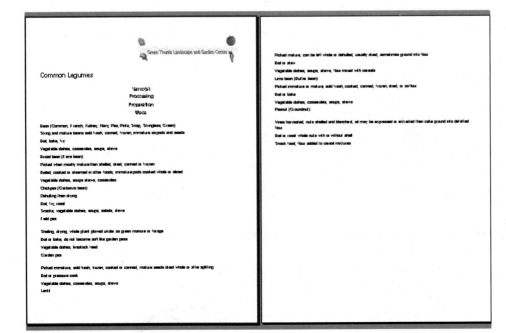

F I G U R E 4.13

Taylor's table about legumes that will be converted to text

F I G U R E 4.14

Table converted to text

WORD

To	Do this
Select a cell	Click the left edge of the cell.
Select a row	Click to the left of the row.
Select a column	Click the column's top gridline or border.
Select multiple cells, rows, or columns	Drag across the cell, row, or column; or select a single cell, row, or column, and then hold down Shift while you click another cell, row, or column.
Select text in the next cell	Press Tab
Select text in the previous cell	Press Shift+Tab
Select the entire table	Click the table, and then press Alt+5 on the numeric keypad. NumLock must be off.

Besides clicking and dragging to select items in a table, Word provides other methods for selecting specific cells, rows, columns, or the entire table. These are shown in Figure 4.15.

S E S S I O N   4 . 1

making *the grade*

1. Identify two ways to insert a table.

2. When entering data into a table the _____ key moves the mouse pointer from column to column.

3. To insert a row using the menu bar, first click _____, then click Insert.

4. _____ characters are characters such as paragraph marks, tabs, or commas you choose to indicate where you want text to separate when you convert a table to text.

5. _____ represents the spacing between the boundary or the cell and the text inside the cell.

SESSION 4.2 ADVANCED TABLE FEATURES

Formatting a Table

You can enhance your table by adding borders and filling cells with colors, patterns, or shading. You can quickly give your table a polished design by using the AutoFormat command. For the beginner, using the AutoFormat command provides some guidelines you can use when you start designing your own table.

anotherword   . . . on Table Formatting

When you create a table, be sure to use a format that is simple and easy to read. With so many great table formatting features available in Word it is easy to create a table that has too many formatting features. Too much formatting will take away from the information

Applying a Table AutoFormat

By default, tables have a black ½-pt, single-line, solid-line border that will be printed. If you remove this border, you will still see the gridlines that form the cell boundaries. Gridlines are not printed. AutoFormat can change the types of borders, gridlines, and even the colors used in a table.

---

task reference   Applying a Table AutoFormat

- Click the table

- On the **Table** menu, click **Table AutoFormat**

- In the **Formats** box, click the format you want (see Figure 4.16)

After looking at some of the options on AutoFormat, Taylor decides to try a different format for her table.

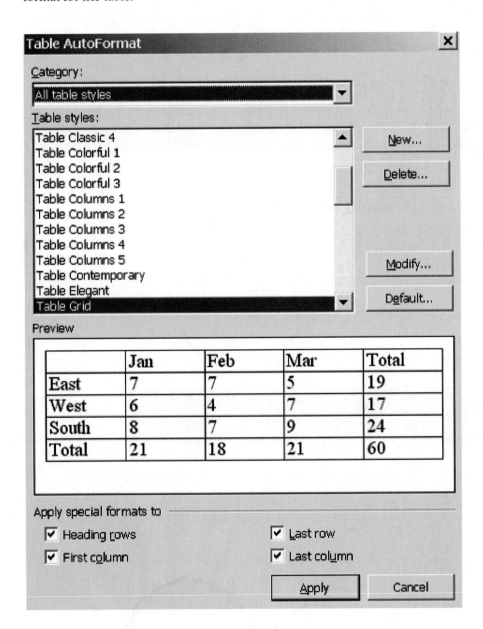

FIGURE 4.16

The AutoFormat options available

Taylor's planting guide
with new format applied

When Do I Plant?

Plant	Planted As	Planting Time
Beans	Seeds	Jun
Beets	Seeds	May-Jun
Broccoli	Plants	Apr-Jun
Cabbage	Plants	May-Jun
Carrots	Seeds	May-Jun
Cauliflower	Plants	May-Jun
Celery	Plants	Jun-Jul
Corn	Seeds	Jun
Cucumbers	Seeds	Jun
Eggplant	Plants	May-Jun
Lettuce	Seeds	Mar-Aug
Melons	Seeds	May-Jun
Peas	Seeds	Feb-May
Peppers	Plants	May
Potatoes	Sets	May
Pumpkins	Seeds	Jun
Radishes	Seeds	Apr-Jun
Spinach	Seeds	Apr-May
Tomatoes	Plants	May-Jun
Turnips	Seeds	Apr-May

Applying a Table AutoFormat to Taylor's table:

1. Ensure your file named **Plantguide1.doc** is opened

2. Click somewhere in the table

3. On the menu bar click **Table**, and then click **Table AutoFormat**

4. In the Table Styles list box, click **Table List 7** format

5. Click **Apply**

6. Compare your table to Figure 4.17

7. Save your document

tip: *If you don't like the format you choose, use the Undo typing button or apply another format with AutoFormat*

Positioning and Resizing a Table

The table move handle can be used to move a table to another place on a page. Dragging the table resize handle will change the size of a table.

---

task reference　　　　　　　　　　　　　　　**Moving a Table**

- Be certain that you are in the **Print Layout view**

- Rest the pointer on the table until the table move handle appears on the upper-left corner of the table

- Rest the pointer on the table move handle until a four-headed arrow appears (Figure 4.18)

- Click and drag the table to the new location

F I G U R E　4.18

Moving a table with the table move handle

table move handle

drag from here

four-headed arrow

to here

task reference
Resizing a Table, Columns, or Rows

- Rest the pointer on the table until the table resize handle appears on the lower-right corner of the table

- Rest the pointer on the table resize handle until a double-headed arrow appears

- Click and drag the table boundary until the table is the size you want (Figure 4.19)

or

- To resize a column, rest the pointer on the column boundary you want to move until it becomes a double-headed arrow and then drag the boundary until the column is the width you want (Figure 4.19)

or

- To resize a row, rest the pointer on the row boundary you want to move until it becomes a double-headed arrow and then click and drag the boundary (Figure 4.19)

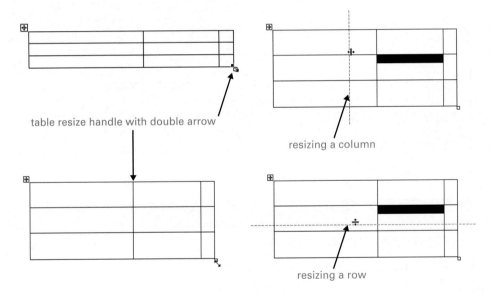

table resize handle with double arrow

resizing a column

resizing a row

FIGURE 4.19
Use of the table resize, column resize, and row resize

Merging and Splitting Cells

Merging cells takes two or more cells and merges them into one cell. Merging cells is a useful feature when you are creating table headings and you want the title of the table to expand across the entire table. *Splitting cells* takes one cell and splits it into two or more cells. Splitting cells is useful when you have one cell that contains too much information and it would be easier for your reader to understand if the cell was split into several cells. Taylor decides to add a title to her table to make it look more professional.

WORD

F I G U R E   4.20

Changing table column
and row size using the
Table menu

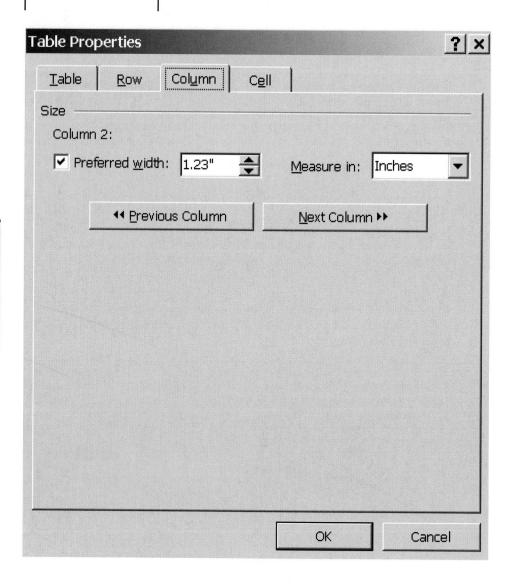

anotherway
. . . on Changing Column and Row Measurements

You can use the Table menu and Table Properties command box to change column and row heights. To change a column width to a specific measurement, click a cell in the column. Then on the Table menu, click Table Properties. After you click the Column tab, you can choose the options you want (see Figure 4.20)

---

task reference   **Merging and Splitting Cells**

- Select the cells you want to merge
- From the **Table** menu, click **Merge Cells**

or

- From the **Table** menu, click **Split Cells**

Merging cells to add a title:

1. Ensure your **Plantguide1.doc** is opened
2. Delete **When Do I Plant?** from the top of the document
3. Select the first row, right-click, and select **Insert rows**
4. Select the first row

5. Click on the **Table** menu, and select **Merge Cells**

6. Type **PLANTING GUIDE** in all caps in the first cell

7. Compare your document with Figure 4.21

8. Save your document

FIGURE 4.21

Taylor's planting guide with title cell merged

PLANTING GUIDE		
Plant	**Planted As**	**Planting Time**
Beans	Seeds	Jun
Beets	Seeds	May-Jun
Broccoli	Plants	Apr-Jun
Cabbage	Plants	May-Jun
Carrots	Seeds	May-Jun
Cauliflower	Plants	May-Jun
Celery	Plants	Jun-Jul
Corn	Seeds	Jun
Cucumbers	Seeds	Jun
Eggplant	Plants	May-Jun
Lettuce	Seeds	Mar-Aug
Melons	Seeds	May-Jun
Peas	Seeds	Feb-May
Peppers	Plants	May
Potatoes	Sets	May
Pumpkins	Seeds	Jun
Radishes	Seeds	Apr-Jun
Spinach	Seeds	Apr-May
Tomatoes	Plants	May-Jun
Turnips	Seeds	Apr-May

help yourself *Click the Ask a Question combo box, type* **Merge cells**, *and press* **Enter**. *Click the hyperlink* **Merge cells into one cell in a table** *to display information about how you can change the orientation of text in a merged cell. Click the Help screen* **Close** *button when you are finished*

Repeating the Header Row

The heading of a table is the first row of the table which typically describes the contents of each column. If your table is larger than one page, the header will not be displayed on the table in the following pages. If you want the heading to be displayed on every page where the table is located, click on the Table menu and the Heading Rows Repeat item. This is a useful feature since your reader won't have to flip back to the first page of the table to understand what is located in each of the columns. Taylor decides to have the headings on her table repeat so that as the list grows to multiple pages, the heading rows will be included on each page. This will save her customers from having to flip back to the first page to find out what title is on each row.

---

task reference　　　　　　　**Heading Rows Repeated**

- Select the rows you want to repeat on each page of the table
- Click on the **Table** menu
- Select **Heading Rows Repeat**

Repeating a row header:

1. Ensure your **Plantguide1.doc** is opened
2. Select the first two rows in the table
3. Click on the **Table** menu, and select **Heading Rows Repeat**
4. Place the cursor on the top of the page before the table and press **Enter** several times until the table is forced onto the next page
5. The heading rows will now repeat on the new page
6. Compare your document with Figure 4.22

F I G U R E 4.22

Taylor's planting guide with heading rows repeating

PLANTING GUIDE		
Plant	Planted As	Planting Time
Beets	Seeds	May-Jun
Broccoli	Plants	Apr-Jun
Cabbage	Plants	May-Jun
Carrots	Seeds	May-Jun
Cauliflower	Plants	May-Jun
Celery	Plants	Jun-Jul
Corn	Seeds	Jun
Cucumbers	Seeds	Jun
Eggplant	Plants	May-Jun
Lettuce	Seeds	Mar-Aug

PLANTING GUIDE		
Plant	Planted As	Planting Time
Melons	Seeds	May-Jun
Peas	Seeds	Feb-May
Peppers	Plants	May
Potatoes	Sets	May
Pumpkins	Seeds	Jun
Radishes	Seeds	Apr-Jun
Spinach	Seeds	Apr-May
Tomatoes	Plants	May-Jun
Turnips	Seeds	Apr-May

7. Remove the blank lines you inserted so there are only two blank lines above the table
8. Save your document

Adding Borders and Shading

You can add borders and shading to your tables. This is similar to adding borders and shading to text, which you learned in Chapter 3. Taylor decides to add some borders and shading to her table to help improve the document's appearance.

---

task reference	Adding Borders and Shading to a Table

- Select the cell or cells where you want to apply a border or shading
- On the **Format** menu, click **Borders and Shading**
- Select the **Borders** tab and apply the desired border

or

- Select the **Shading** tab and apply the desired shading

Applying a border and shading:

1. Ensure your **Plantguide1.doc** is opened
2. Click on the **Table** menu, and choose **Select**, **Table**. Select the entire table
3. Click **Format**, and select **Borders and Shading**
4. Click on the **Borders** tab
5. Select **All**, Color **Automatic**, Style **Single Line**, Width **3 pt**, and click **OK**
6. Compare your document to Figure 4.23
7. Save your document

FIGURE 4.23

Taylor's planting guide with a border applied

Plant	Planted As	Planting Time
Beans	Seeds	Jun
Beets	Seeds	May-Jun
Broccoli	Plants	Apr-Jun
Cabbage	Plants	May-Jun
Carrots	Seeds	May-Jun
Cauliflower	Plants	May-Jun
Celery	Plants	Jun-Jul
Corn	Seeds	Jun
Cucumbers	Seeds	Jun
Eggplant	Plants	May-Jun
Lettuce	Seeds	Mar-Aug
Melons	Seeds	May-Jun
Peas	Seeds	Feb-May
Peppers	Plants	May
Potatoes	Sets	May

Using Sort and Formulas in Tables

You can perform a simple sort of the information in your table by clicking on the column and then clicking the Sort item from the Table menu. You can also apply a mathematical formula to a Word table by selecting Formula from the Table menu. This feature is similar to using a formula in Microsoft Excel.

making the grade

1. _____ cells takes two or more cells and changes them into one cell.

2. _____ cells takes one cell and turns it into two or more cells.

3. Gridlines are not _____.

4. The table _____ handle can be used to change the position of a table to another place on a page.

5. Header rows can be _____ across pages.

SESSION 4.3 USING GRAPHICS

Two basic types of graphics can be used to enhance your Microsoft Word documents: drawing objects and pictures. ***Drawing objects*** include AutoShapes, curves, lines, and WordArt that are part of a Word document. Use the Drawing toolbar to change and enhance these objects with colors, patterns, borders, and other effects. ***Pictures*** are graphics that were created from another file using different software. They include bitmaps, scanned pictures, scanned photographs, and clip art.

You can insert many popular graphics file formats into your document either directly or with the use of separate graphic filters. ***Graphic filters*** allow images with different formats to be imported into a Word document. Using a graphic filter you can import images such as Enhanced Metafiles (.emf), Joint Photographic Experts Group (.jpg), Portable Network Graphics (.png), Windows Bitmap (.bmp), Graphics Interchange Format (.gif), and Windows Metafiles (.wmf). You will need a separate graphic filter installed to insert all other graphics file formats shown in Figure 4.24. If you didn't install the graphic filter when you installed Word on your computer, you can always run the setup program again and add the graphic filter.

help yourself *Click the Ask a Question combo box, type Image formats, and press **Enter**. Click the hyperlink **Graphic File Types Word Can Use** to display information about graphic file types Word can use and file types that require filters. Click the Help screen **Close** button when you are finished*

Inserting an Image

Microsoft Word comes with AutoShapes that you can use in your documents. ***AutoShapes*** are a group of ready-made shapes that include such basic shapes as rectangles and circles, plus a variety of lines and connectors, block arrows, flowchart symbols, stars and banners, and callouts. You can resize, rotate, flip, and color the AutoShapes. The AutoShapes are accessed from the menu on the Drawing toolbar (Figure 4.25) and you find the specific shapes in the flyout menus (see Figure 4.26).

The ***drawing canvas*** is an area upon which you can draw multiple shapes; shapes contained within the drawing canvas can be moved and resized as a unit. The drawing canvas can be used to help arrange and resize the objects in your drawing. The ***Drawing toolbar*** contains the buttons for Draw, Rotate, AutoShapes, Line, Arrow, Rectangle, Oval, Text Box, Insert WordArt, Insert Clip Art, Fill Color, Line Color, Font Color, Line Style, Dash Style, Arrow Style, Shadow, and 3-D.

Type of File	Extension
Computer Graphics Metafile	.cgm
CorelDRAW	.cdr
Encapsulated PostScript	.eps
Enhanced Metafile	.emf
FlashPix graphics filter	.fpx
Graphics Interchange Format	.gif
Hanako graphics filter	.jsh, .jah, & .jbh
JPEG File Interchange Format	.jpg
Kodak Photo CD	.pcd
Macintosh PICT	.pct
PC Paintbrush	.pcx
Portable Network Graphics	.png
Tagged Image File Format	.tif
Windows Bitmap	.bmp
Windows Metafile	.wmf
WordPerfect Graphics	.wpg

FIGURE 4.24
Graphics file formats

FIGURE 4.25
Drawing toolbar

FIGURE 4.26
Examples of AutoShapes

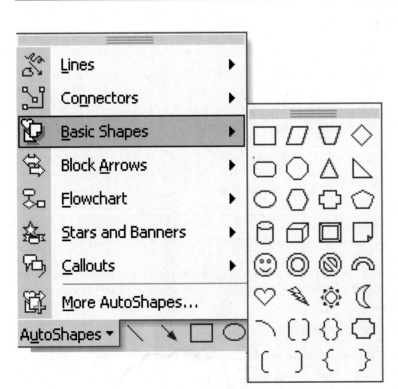

WORD

task reference   Inserting an AutoShape

- On the Drawing toolbar, click **AutoShapes**, point to a category, and then click the shape you want

- To insert a shape with a predefined size, click the document

- To insert a different size, click and drag the shape to the size you want

- To maintain the shape's width-to-height ratio, hold down **Shift** while you drag the shape

- To add color, change borders, rotate, add shadow, or 3-D effects, select the object, and then use the buttons on the Drawing toolbar

Adding star AutoShape to Taylor's planting guide:

1. Ensure your **Plantguide1.doc** is opened

tip: *Before inserting the star, click* **Tools**, **Options**, **General** *tab and clear the check box.* **Automatically create drawing canvas when inserting Autoshapes**

2. On the Drawing toolbar click **AutoShapes**, and point to **Stars and Banners**

tip: *If the Drawing toolbar is not available, click* **View**, **Toolbars**, **Drawing**

3. Select the 32-point star (see Figure 4.27)

FIGURE 4.27

Selecting the 32-point star AutoShape

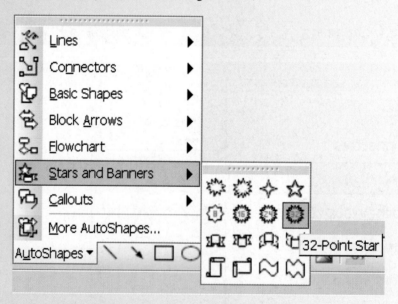

4. Click in the upper left of the document and hold down on left mouse button and drag until the star is about one inch in diameter and release the mouse button

5. Click the star (See Figure 4.28)

6. On the Drawing toolbar, **click** the **Fill Color list box arrow** and select a yellow color

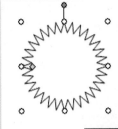

PLANTING GUIDE		
Plant	Planted As	Planting Time
Beans	Seeds	Jun
Beets	Seeds	May-Jun
Broccoli	Plants	Apr-Jun
Cabbage	Plants	May-Jun

7. Compare your work to Figure 4.29

PLANTING GUIDE		
Plant	Planted As	Planting Time
Beans	Seeds	Jun
Beets	Seeds	May-Jun
Broccoli	Plants	Apr-Jun
Cabbage	Plants	May-Jun
Carrots	Seeds	May-Jun

8. Save your document

You can also insert a picture or a scanned photo that you import from other programs and locations. When you select a picture, the Picture toolbar (Figure 4.30) appears with tools that you can use to crop the picture, add a border, or adjust brightness and contrast. To see the Picture toolbar, click View, Toolbars, and Picture. This toolbar can be docked if it is in your way.

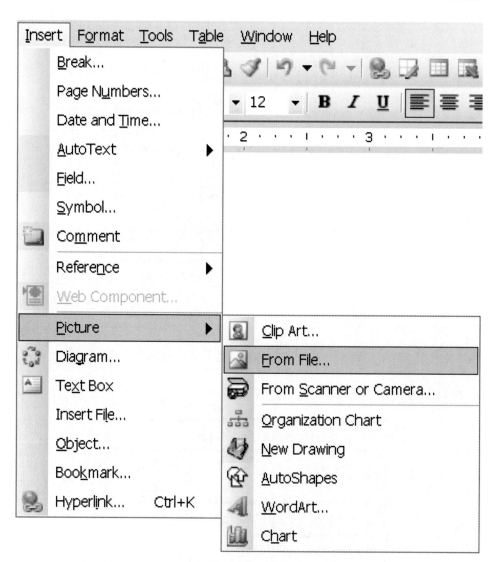

task *reference*   **Inserting a Picture**

- Click where you want to insert the picture

- On the **Insert** menu, point to **Picture**, and then click **From File** (see Figure 4.31)

- Locate the picture you want to insert

- Double-click the picture you want to insert

Sizing an Image

When you select a graphic object, sizing handles appear around your object (see Figure 4.32). *Sizing handles* are square handles that appear at each corner and along the sides of the rectangle that surround a selected drawing object. You can resize an object by

FIGURE 4.32

Sizing handles along the edge of the selection rectangle

FIGURE 4.33

Maintain the proportions of a drawing object while resizing it

To resize a selected object	Hold down
Proportionally from a corner	Shift and drag a corner sizing handle
Vertically, horizontally, or diagonally from the center outward	Ctrl and drag a sizing handle
Proportionally from the center outward	Ctrl+Shift and drag a corner sizing handle
While temporarily overriding the settings for the grid	Alt and drag a sizing handle

dragging its sizing handles, or you can resize it more precisely by specifying a percentage for the object's height and width (see Another Way below). If the object is a picture, photo, bitmap, or clip art, you can crop it and restore it later to its original image. The table in Figure 4.33 describes how to size a graphic and maintain its proportions.

Taylor created a logo for her business, and she wants to insert this image on her planting guide table.

task **reference**   Sizing an Image

- Select the drawing object or image you want to resize
- Drag a sizing handle until the object is the shape and size you want
- Refer to Figure 4.33 to maintain the proportions during resizing

anotherway

. . . to Resize an Image

To resize an object by a specific percentage, click on the Format menu. Then choose the command for the type of object you selected; for example, click AutoShape or Picture, and then click the Size tab. Under Scale, enter the percentages you want in the Height and Width boxes. To maintain the ratio between the object's height and width whenever you resize the object, select the Lock aspect ratio check box on the Size tab. You can also reach the Format option by right-clicking the object

Inserting and sizing an image on a document:

1. Ensure your **Plantguide1.doc** is opened
2. Click somewhere in the top of the document
3. Click **Insert**, point to **Picture**, and click **From File**
4. Locate the file named **wd04Greenthlogo.bmp**
5. Click on the filename and click **Insert**
6. Select the entire table
7. Click on **Center** button on the Standard toolbar
8. Compare your work to Figure 4.34
9. Save your document

Moving an Image

Once an image is inserted in a document you can drag or copy it to another location.

FIGURE 4.34

Taylor's planting guide
with the logo

PLANTING GUIDE		
Plant	**Planted As**	**Planting Time**
Beans	Seeds	Jun
Beets	Seeds	May-Jun
Broccoli	Plants	Apr-Jun
Cabbage	Plants	May-Jun
Carrots	Seeds	May-Jun
Cauliflower	Plants	May-Jun
Celery	Plants	Jun-Jul

***task* reference** Moving or Copying an Image a Short Distance

- Use drag-and-drop editing
- Select the item you want to move or copy
- To move the item, drag the selection to the location you want

or

- To copy the item, hold down **Ctrl** as you drag the selection

---

You can also move or copy items by holding down the right mouse button and dragging the selection. When you release the mouse button, a shortcut menu shows the available options for moving and copying.

Wrapping Text around an Image

How text flows around an image is referred to as ***wrapping***. Word offers several choices for wrapping text around an image. You can try several different text-wrapping options until you get the results that look the best.

***task* reference** Wrapping Text around a Picture or Drawing Object

- Select the picture or drawing object
- On the **Format** menu, click the command for the type of object you selected
- Click **Layout** tab
- Choose the **Wrapping style** you want to apply (see Figure 4.35)

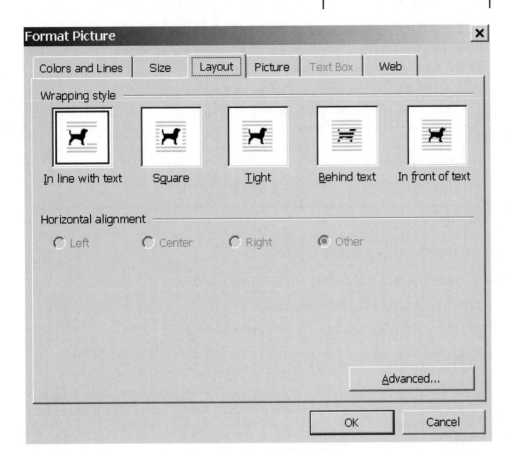

For more wrapping styles and options for the direction of text flow and its distance
from text, you can go to Advanced on the Layout tab and select the Text Wrapping tab.

Creating a Text Box

A *text box* is a movable, resizable container for text or graphics (see Figure 4.36). You
can use text boxes to position several blocks of text on a page or change text orientation. You can add callouts, labels, and other text to your graphics by using text boxes.
After you have inserted a text box, you can use the options on the Drawing toolbar to
enhance it as you would for any other drawing object.

**This is a text box as the
text is being added.**

task reference   Creating a Text Box

- On the Drawing toolbar, click the **Text Box** ▣ button
- To insert a text box with a predefined size, click the document
- To insert a text box with a different size, drag its sizing handles until the text box is the size you want
- To maintain the text box's width-to-height ratio, hold down **Shift** while you drag the sizing handles
- Position the text box by dragging it to the location you want

Adding a text box:

1. Open the data file named **wd04Gardenplan.doc**

2. Save the file as **Gardenplan1.doc**

3. On the **Drawing toolbar**, click the **Text Box** button

4. Click the document near the end of the fourth bullet under **Some Planning Tips**

5. In Times New Roman 10-point font, type this text into the box: **A complete commercial fertilizer with a ratio of 1-1-1 is suitable for the vegetable garden.**

6. Drag the Text Box sizing handles until the text box is large enough to just accommodate the text you typed

tip: *To maintain the text box's width-to-height ratio, hold down **Shift** while you drag the sizing handles. Hold down the Alt key as well to bypass the grid, adjusting the size more precisely*

7. Click **Format** on the menu bar

8. Click **Text Box** on the **Layout** tab

9. Select **Tight** for the Wrapping style on the Format Text Box dialog box

10. Select **Other** for the Horizontal alignment on the Format Text Box dialog box and click **OK**

11. Position the text box by dragging it to the location you want (see Figure 4.37 for location)

12. Save your document

FIGURE 4.37

Location of text box in Taylor's garden planning document

Some Planning Tips

❖ Put perennial vegetables like asparagus and rhubarb along with small fruits on one side of the garden where they will not interfere with garden preparation.

❖ Group the crops according to the time they mature to facilitate succession plantings, rotation, or planting of green manure crops after harvest of the early crop.

❖ Vine crops such as melons, squash, and cucumbers can be planted on one side so they can spread into the fencerow.

❖ To insure good pollination of sweet corn, plant several short parallel rows in blocks rather than one long single row.

❖ Do not crowd the plants; allow ample room for each vegetable to develop properly.

❖ Do not plant too much of crops such as chard, leaf lettuce, and parsley.

❖ Do not plant vegetables that are disliked by the family.

> A complete commercial fertilizer with a ratio of 1-1-1 or 1-2-2 (N-P-K) is suitable for the vegetable garden.

Soil Needs Nutrients, Too

In addition to organic matter and proper acidity, the soil should contain plenty of readily available nutrients. These are best supplied by liberal applications of manure and super phosphate or commercial fertilizers. This can be applied at the rate of three pounds per one hundred square feet at the time the garden is prepared in the spring.

You can use the options on the Drawing toolbar to enhance a text box, for example, to change the fill color. *Fill* is the color, pattern, or image inside a drawing object. You can also format the text box from the menu bar by using the Format button. For Taylor's Garden Plan she decides to use a green fill color inside the text box and then to change the color of the typing to white.

---

task reference   Selecting a Fill Color

- Select the drawing object you want to change
- On the **Drawing toolbar**, click the **arrow** next to **Fill Color** 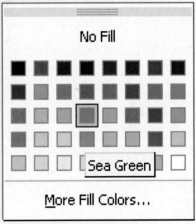 button
- Click the **color** you want
- If you don't see the color you want, click **More Fill Colors**
- Click a color on the Standard tab, or click the **Custom** tab to mix your own color
- Click **OK**

Adding a fill color to text box:

1. Ensure that you have **Gardenplan1.doc** opened
2. Select all of the text in the text box
3. On the Drawing toolbar, click the **arrow** next to **Fill Color** button
4. Click the **Sea Green** color (see Figure 4.38)
5. Click the **Font Color** button
6. Select **White**, and click anywhere outside the text box to deselect it
7. Compare your work to Figure 4.39
8. Save your document

FIGURE 4.38

Selecting the Sea Green fill color

No Fill

Sea Green

More Fill Colors...

FIGURE 4.39

Text box with Sea Green fill and white text

Some Planning Tips
- ❖ Put perennial vegetables like asparagus and rhubarb along with small fruits on one side of the garden where they will not interfere with garden preparation.
- ❖ Group the crops according to the time they mature to facilitate succession plantings, rotation, or planting of green manure crops after harvest of the early crop.
- ❖ Vine crops such as melons, squash, and cucumbers can be planted on one side so they can spread into the fencerow.
- ❖ To insure good pollination of sweet corn, plant several short parallel rows in blocks rather than one long single row.
- ❖ Do not crowd the plants; allow ample room for each vegetable to develop properly.
- ❖ Do not plant too much of crops such as chard, leaf lettuce, and parsley.
- ❖ Do not plant vegetables that are disliked by the family.

A complete commercial fertilizer with a ratio of 1-1-1 or 1-2-2 (N-P-K) is suitable for the vegetable garden.

Soil Needs Nutrients, Too
In addition to organic matter and proper acidity, the soil should contain plenty of readily available nutrients. These are best supplied by liberal applications of manure and super phosphate or commercial fertilizers. This can be applied at the rate of three pounds per one hundred square feet at the time the garden is prepared in the spring.

F I G U R E   4.40

Shadow options

task reference   Adding a Shadow to a Text Box

- Select the text box or drawing object you want to add a shadow to
- On the Drawing toolbar, click **Shadow** button
- Click the shadow option you want (see Figure 4.40)

Adding a shadow to text box:

1. Ensure your file **GardenPlan1.doc** is opened
2. Click to select the text box
3. On the **Drawing toolbar**, click **Shadow** ▪ button
4. Click the **Shadow Style 6**
5. Compare your work to Figure 4.41

F I G U R E   4.41

Text box with shadow

> A complete commercial fertilizer with a ratio of 1-1-1 or 1-2-2 (N-P-K) is suitable for the vegetable garden.

6. Save your document

tip: *To change the color or offset of a shadow, click Shadow button, click Shadow Settings, and then click the options you want on the Shadow Settings toolbar*

Using WordArt

You can insert decorative text by inserting WordArt on the Drawing toolbar. *WordArt* is a feature of Word that allows you to create special effects on text by inserting a Microsoft Office drawing object. You can create shadowed, skewed, rotated, and stretched text as well as text that has been fitted to predefined shapes. Because a special text effect is a drawing object, you can also use other buttons on the Drawing toolbar to change the effect, for example, to fill a text effect with a picture. The WordArt button is located on the Drawing toolbar (see Figure 4.42).

FIGURE   4.42
WordArt Gallery

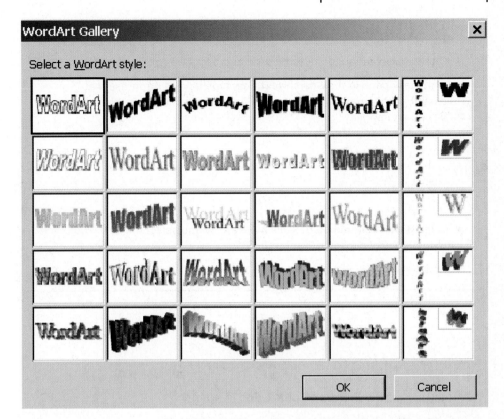

WordArt Gallery

Select a WordArt style:

OK   Cancel

---

task reference   Inserting WordArt

- On the **Drawing toolbar**, click **Insert WordArt**
- Click the type of **WordArt drawing object** you want, and then click **OK**
- In the **Edit WordArt Text** dialog box, type the text you want to format; select any other options you want
- Click **OK**
- WordArt toolbar appears when you click the WordArt special text
- To add or change effects to the text, use the buttons on the WordArt and Drawing toolbars

---

anotherword   . . . on Changing Text in WordArt

Even after you create WordArt, you can modify it. Using the WordArt toolbar you can rotate, change letter height, and create vertical text. By using the Drawing toolbar you can also add shadows and 3-D effects to WordArt, as well as change its color

---

Using Clip Art

Clip art is a stored image that you can insert into a Word document. Word comes with many different types of clips that you can use to enhance your documents. Inserting a clip art image is an easy way to make your document look professional.

WORD

Clip art selection

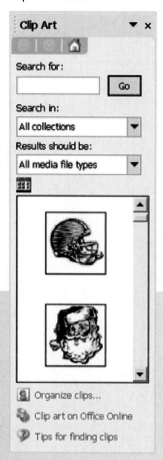

task reference   Inserting a Clip Art

- On the **Insert** menu, point to **Picture**, and click **Clip Art**
- In the task pane in the **Search text** box, type a word or phrase that describes the image you want or leave the Search text box blank to display all clip art images

or

- In the **Search in** box, click the arrow and select the collections you want to search

or

- In the **Results should be** box, click the arrow and select the check box next to the types of clips you want to find
- Click **Search** (see Figure 4.43)

Adding clip art to a new document:

1. Ensure your file **PlantingGuide1.doc** is opened
2. Insert a few blank lines after the bottom of the table
3. Click the **Insert** menu, point to **Picture**, and click **Clip Art**
4. In the task pane in the Search text box, type **Vegetable** and click **Search**
5. Click on one of the images to paste it into your document
6. Click on the **Modify** button
7. In the task pane in the Search text box, type **Gardener** and click **Search**
8. Click on one of the images to paste it into your document
9. Click on the **Modify** button
10. Clear the Search text box so it is blank and click **Search**; all clip art images are displayed
11. Click on one of the images to paste it into your document
12. Save your document

Inserting Symbols

The *Insert Symbol command* allows you to enter symbols into your documents. Symbols can include such things as special, foreign language, and measurement characters.

---

task reference   Inserting Symbols

- Click the **Insert** menu, select **Symbol**, and click on the **Symbol** tab
- Select the font
- Double-click on the symbol you want to insert into your document (see Figure 4.44)

or

- Select the **Special Characters** tab
- Double-click on the special character you want to insert into your document (see Figure 4.45)

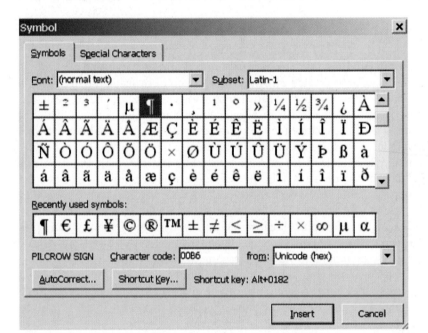

F I G U R E   4.44

Symbol tab

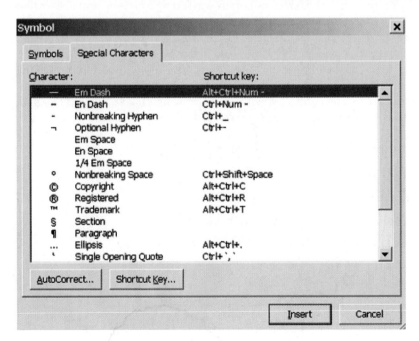

F I G U R E   4.45

Special Character tab

making the grade

1. To maintain an image's width-to-height ratio, hold down the _____ while dragging to resize.

2. _____ objects include AutoShapes, curves, lines, and WordArt.

3. _____ are graphics that are created from another file using different software.

4. Sizing _____ are square handles that appear at each corner and along the sides of the rectangle that surrounds a selected drawing object.

5. How text flows around an image is referred to as _____.

SESSION 4.4 SUMMARY

Word makes creating and modifying tables an easy task. Tables with varying numbers of columns and rows can be created using the Table menu or by using the Insert Table button on the Standard toolbar. Tables can also be drawn and text can be converted to a table and vice versa. Once a table is in place, columns and rows can be added and deleted and their size can be changed to match the contents of each cell. Moreover, using the resize handle in the lower right corner can change the size of the entire table.

AutoFormat creates tables with attractive formats, and the Table menu allows changes in the table properties such as borders, shading, row size, column size, and the placement of text. A handle just outside the top left corner of a table can be grabbed to move the table to a new position in the document.

Two main categories of graphics are inserted into Word—drawing objects and pictures. Once drawing objects or pictures are inserted, they can be sized, moved, or copied. They can also be modified with the Drawing toolbar and the Picture toolbar.

From the Format menu you control how text wraps around an image. Resizing handles enlarge or reduce images; using the Format menu, images can be resized to an exact percentage. By dragging or copying a drawing object or picture it can be moved to another location.

Text boxes are movable, resizable containers for text or graphics, and are treated like other drawing objects. They can be moved, resized, filled with color, or they can have their line color and text color changed. In addition, shadows and 3-D effects can be added to text boxes.

WordArt is text created with special effects by inserting a Microsoft Office drawing object. The WordArt Galley provides 30 types of art formats that can be applied to text. In addition WordArt can be combined with other drawing objects, colored, rotated, sized, and the font can be changed. WordArt is treated like other images.

MICROSOFT OFFICE SPECIALIST OBJECTIVES SUMMARY

- Insert and modify tables—MOS WW03S-2-1
- Insert, position, and size graphics—MOS WW03S-1-4
- Sort content in lists and tables—MOS WW03E-2-1
- Perform calculations in tables—MOS WW03E-2-2
- Modify table formats—MOS WW03E-2-3
- Format, position, and resize graphics using advanced layout features—MOS WW03E-1-3

making the grade *answers*

SESSION 4.1

1. Click Table Insert button on Standard toolbar or click Table, Insert on menu

2. Tab

3. Table

4. Separator

5. Cell padding

SESSION 4.2

1. Merging

2. Splitting

3. Printed

4. Move

5. Repeated

SESSION 4.3

1. Shift

2. Drawing

3. Pictures

4. Handles

5. Wrapping

task reference *summary*

Task	Page #	Preferred Method
Inserting an empty table	WD 4.5	• Click where you want to create a table • Click **Insert Table** button on the Standard toolbar • Drag to select the number of columns and rows you want • Release the mouse button to insert the blank table
Adding columns or rows to a table	WD 4.5	• Click the position in the table where you want to add columns or rows • Select the number of columns or rows to insert • On the **Table** menu, click **Insert** • Click **Columns to the Right** or **Columns to the Left** or • On the **Table** menu, click **Insert** • Click **Rows Above** or **Rows Below**
Deleting columns or rows in a table	WD 4.6	• Click the position in the table where you want to delete columns or rows • Click **Table**, **Delete** • Choose Columns or rows
Converting text into a table	WD 4.8	• Select the text you want to convert • On the **Table** menu, point to **Convert**, and then click **Text to Table** • Under **Separate text at**, click the option for the separator character you want • Select any other options you want • Click **OK**
Converting a table to text	WD 4.10	• Select the rows or table that you want to convert to paragraphs • On the **Table** menu, point to **Convert**, and then click **Table to Text** • Under **Separate text with**, click the option for the separator character (comma, tab, space, paragraph, or other) you want to use in place of the column boundaries • Paragraph marks separate rows
Applying a Table AutoFormat	WD 4.13	• Click the table • On the **Table** menu, click **Table AutoFormat** • In the **Formats** box, click the format you want

task reference *summary*

Task	Page #	Preferred Method
Moving a table	WD 4.14	• Be certain that you are in the **Print Layout view** • Rest the pointer on the table until the table move handle appears on the upper-left corner of the table • Rest the pointer on the table move handle until a four-headed arrow appears • Drag the table to the new location
Resizing a table, columns, or rows	WD 4.15	• Rest the pointer on the table until the table resize handle appears on the lower-right corner of the table • Rest the pointer on the table resize handle until a double-headed arrow appears • Drag the table boundary until the table is the size you want or • To resize a column, rest the pointer on the column boundary you want to move until it becomes a double-headed arrow and then drag the boundary until the column is the width you want or • To resize a row, rest the pointer on the row boundary you want to move until it becomes a double-headed arrow and then drag the boundary
Merging and splitting cells	WD 4.16	• Select the cells you want to merge • From the **Table** menu click **Merge Cells** or • From the **Table** menu click the **Split Cells**
Heading rows repeated	WD 4.18	• Select the rows you want to repeat on each page of the table • Click on the **Table** menu • Select **Heading Rows Repeat**
Adding borders and shading to a table	WD 4.19	• Select the cell or cells where you want to apply a border or shading • Click **Borders and Shading** on the **Format** menu • Select the **Borders** tab and apply the desired border or • Select the **Shading** tab and apply the desired shading
Inserting an AutoShape	WD 4.22	• On the Drawing toolbar, click **AutoShapes**, point to a category, and then click the shape you want • To insert a shape with a predefined size, click the document • To insert a different size, drag the shape to the size you want • To maintain the shape's width-to-height ratio, hold down **Shift** while you drag the shape • To add color, change borders, rotate, add shadow, or 3-D effects, select the object, and then use the buttons on the Drawing toolbar
Inserting a picture	WD 4.24	• Click where you want to insert the picture • On the **Insert** menu, point to **Picture**, and then click **From File** • Locate the picture you want to insert • Double-click the picture you want to insert
Sizing an image	WD 4.25	• Select the drawing object or image you want to resize • Drag a sizing handle until the object is the shape and size you want
Moving or copying an image a short distance	WD 4.26	• Use drag-and-drop editing • Select the item you want to move or copy • To move the item, drag the selection to the location you want or • To copy the item, hold down **Ctrl** as you drag the selection

task reference *summary*

Task	Page #	Preferred Method
Wrapping text around a picture or drawing object	WD 4.26	• Select the picture or drawing object • On the **Format** menu, click the command for the type of object you selected • Click **Layout** tab • Choose the **Wrapping style** you want to apply
Creating a text box	WD 4.28	• On the Drawing toolbar, click **Text Box** button • To insert a text box with a predefined size, click the document • To insert a text box with a different size, drag its sizing handles until the text box is the size you want • To maintain the text box's width-to-height ratio, hold down **Shift** while you drag the sizing handles • Position the text box by dragging it to the location you want
Selecting a fill color	WD 4.29	• Select the drawing object you want to change • On the **Drawing toolbar**, click the **arrow** next to **Fill Color** button • Click the **color** you want • If you don't see the color you want, click **More Fill Colors** • Click a color on the Standard tab, or click the **Custom** tab to mix your own color • Click **OK**
Adding a shadow to a text box	WD 4.30	• Select the text box or drawing object you want to add a shadow to • On the Drawing toolbar, click **Shadow** button • Click the shadow option you want
Inserting WordArt	WD 4.31	• On the **Drawing toolbar**, click **Insert WordArt** • Click the type of **WordArt drawing object** you want, and then click **OK** • In the **Edit WordArt Text** dialog box, type the text you want to format; select any other options you want • Click **OK** • WordArt toolbar appears when you click the WordArt special text • To add or change effects to the text, use the buttons on the WordArt and Drawing toolbars
Inserting a clip art	WD 4.32	• On the **Insert** menu, point to **Picture**, and click **Clip Art** • In the task pane in the **Search text** box, type a word or phrase that describes the image you want or • In the **Search in** box, click the arrow and select the collections you want to search or • In the **Results should be** box, click the arrow and select the check box next to the types of clips you want to find • Click **Search**
Inserting symbols	WD 4.33	• Click the **Insert** menu, and select **Symbol** • Select the font • Double-click on the symbol or • Select the Special Characters tab • Double-click on the special character you want to insert

TRUE/FALSE

1. A border represents the inside rows in a table.

2. A cell is the area at the intersection of a row and a column.

3. Clip art is a stored image that you can insert into a Word document.

4. Fill is the color, pattern, or image you can insert outside of a drawing.

5. Gridlines merge rows and columns in a table.

FILL-IN

1. The _____ represents the outside edges of a table.

2. _____ cells takes two or more cells and merges them into one cell.

3. A text _____ is a movable, resizable container for text or graphics.

4. _____ is text created with special effects by inserting a Microsoft Office drawing object.

5. An _____ mark is used to indicate the end of a row or a cell and is viewable only when the Show/Hide button is clicked.

6. A _____ is graphics created from another file using different software.

MULTIPLE CHOICE

1. Which of the following is a part of AutoShapes?
   a. Rectangles
   b. Circles
   c. Block arrows
   d. All of the above

2. Which of the following is contained on the Drawing toolbar?
   a. Rectangle
   b. Oval
   c. Dash style
   d. All of the above

3. Which of the following is not a separator character?
   a. Space
   b. Paragraph mark
   c. Tab
   d. Comma

4. What takes one cell and splits it into two or more cells?
   a. Merging cells
   b. End marks
   c. Splitting cells
   d. Cell padding

5. What is an area upon which you can draw multiple shapes?
   a. Drawing toolbar
   b. Drawing object
   c. Drawing canvas
   d. None of the above

6. What is used to drag a table to another location by holding down the left mouse button?
   a. Nested table
   b. Table move handle
   c. Table resize handle
   d. None of the above

REVIEW QUESTIONS

1. Identify two ways to insert a table.

2. Name two ways to move from cell to cell in a table.

3. What happens when you press Tab in the last cell on the right of a table?

4. What happens when you press Enter with the mouse pointer on the outside right edge of the last cell in a table?

5. What is a text box and how do you add one to a document?

CREATE THE QUESTION

For each of the following answers, create an appropriate, short question.

ANSWER	QUESTION
1. Text box	_____
2. AutoShape	_____
3. Fill Color button	_____
4. WordArt	_____
5. Wrapping	_____
6. Separator character	_____
7. Cell	_____

FACT OR FICTION

1. Separator characters are characters such as paragraph marks, tabs, or commas that you choose to indicate where you want text to separate when you convert a table to text, or where you want new rows or columns to begin when you convert text to a table.

2. The Drawing toolbar contains buttons for Draw, AutoShapes, Line, Arrow, Rectangle, Oval, Text Box, Insert WordArt, Insert Clip Art, Fill Color, Line Color, Font Color, Line Style, Dash Style, Arrow Style, Shadow, and 3-D.

3. The drawing canvas is an area upon which you can draw multiple shapes, and shapes contained within the drawing canvas cannot be moved or resized as a unit.

4. AutoShapes are a group of ready-made shapes that include such basic shapes as rectangles and circles, plus a variety of lines and connectors, block arrows, flowchart symbols, stars and banners, and callouts.

5. The sizing handle is a square handle that appears at each corner and along the sides of the rectangle that surrounds a selected drawing object; drag a sizing handle to resize an object.

1. Completing the Planting Guide

Taylor is excited about her new professional looking documents. The only part that she still wants to add is her company address, phone number, fax, and e-mail address. This will allow her customers to contact her directly if they have any questions.

Help Taylor complete her Planting Guide and Planning a Garden handouts by adding the above mentioned information in a text box that looks similar to a business card.

1. Open the file named **Plantguide1.doc**

2. Save the file as Plantguide2.doc

3. Click **Text Box** button on the Drawing toolbar

4. Insert a text box about halfway down on the right side of the table

5. In the text box type the following:

    **1200 West 300 North
    Ames, MI 99999
    Ph: 207-555-6796
    Fax: 207-555-6543
    greenthmb@melon.com**

6. Select the text in the box and convert it to Arial Black, 9-point font

7. Fill the text box with light yellow

8. Add Shadow Style 1 to the text box

9. Compare your work to Figure 4.46

10. Save your document

11. Copy the text box you just created

12. Save your document

F I G U R E 4.46

Taylor's planting guide with contact information in a text box

2. Creating a Weekly Schedule

Using a weekly schedule to track your tasks and activities is a great way to stay focused and ensure you don't miss anything. Using Word, create a generic weekly schedule that you can print and fill out each week. Once you have completed the schedule, try to add some clip art images and different borders and shading to enhance your schedule. See Figure 4.47 for an example schedule.

1. Create a new document and save it as **Schedule1.doc**

2. In the **Table** menu, click **Insert**, and click **Table**

3. In the Table dialog box type in **8** columns and **15** rows, click **OK**

4. Select the first row

5. Select the **Table** menu and click **Merge Cells**

6. Click on the first row and type **<YourName>'s Weekly Schedule**

7. Click on the **Align Center** button on the Formatting toolbar

8. Type **Monday** in row 2 column 2, **Tuesday** in row 2 column 3, **Wednesday** in row 2 column 4, **Thursday** in row 2 column 5, **Friday** in row 2 column 6, **Saturday** in row 2 column 7, and **Sunday** in row 2 column 8

9. Select the first two rows

10. Select the **Format** menu, click **Borders and Shading**, and select the **Shading** tab

11. Select any color to shade the first two columns and click **OK**

12. Type **Morning** in row 3 column 1, **Afternoon** in row 7 column 1, **Evening** in row 11 column 1, and **Notes** in row 15 column 1

13. Select the last row

14. Select the **Table** menu and click **Merge Cells**

15. Select the **Table** menu, click on **Table Properties**, and click on the **Row** tab

16. Specify the row height to be **1** inch

17. Click **OK**

18. Save your document

FIGURE 4.47

Generic schedule

challenge!

1. Creating an Animal Care Checklist

Veterinarian Dr. Janus Rockett runs a small-animal clinic in Vermont. The clinic hires many veterinary technicians who help take care of the animals, attend pet appointments, and administer shots. A critical part of a technician's daily duties is to care for all the sick animals that are being housed at the clinic. To ensure that the care is consistent no matter which technician is on duty, Janus wants to create a series of daily checklists that the technicians will fill out. Janus would like a checklist for each different type of animal that is housed at the clinic. Figure 4.48 shows an example of the checklist Janus created for chinchillas.

You have recently been hired by Janus as the senior veterinary technician. Your first task is to begin creating the checklists for all the other animals. Create the following checklist for the daily care of hamsters and dogs. Follow the same format as displayed in Figure 4.48 and save your file as **Checklist1.doc**.

HAMSTERS

- Clean cage twice per week
- Room thermostat set to maintain temperature of 68 degrees F
- Clean food dishes and water bottles
- Wash hands between handling hamsters
- Check the function of room ventilation
- Feed fresh fruits and vegetables in small amounts

DOGS

- Clean kennel daily
- Clean food and water dishes
- Feed each day at 4:00 p.m.
- Exercise 1 hour in the morning and 1 hour in the evening
- Take dog to training during morning
- Take dog to group kennel during afternoon

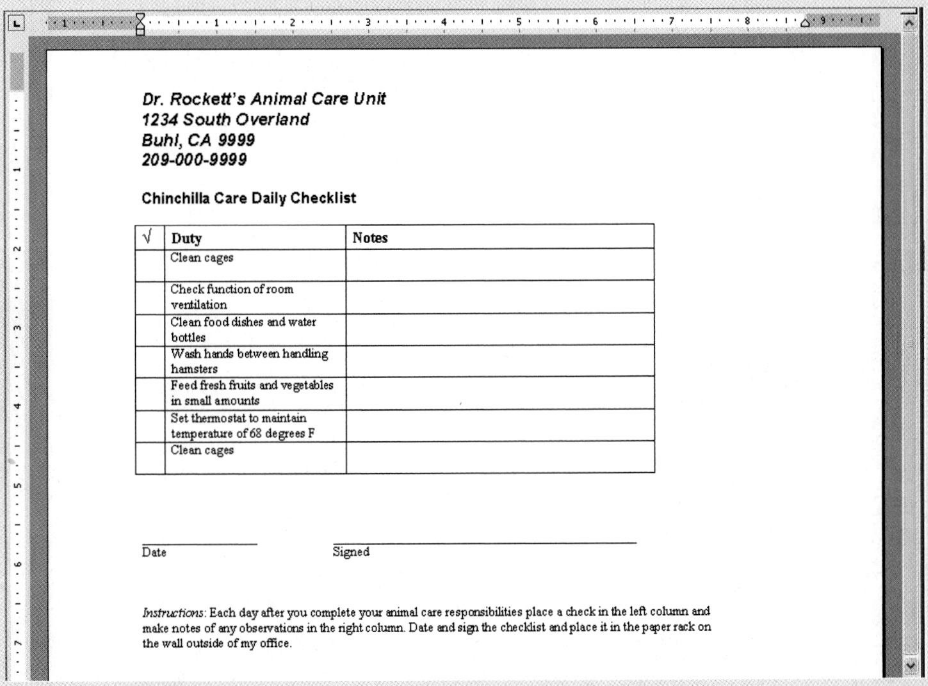

Dr. Rockett's Animal Care Unit
1234 South Overland
Buhl, CA 9999
209-000-9999

Chinchilla Care Daily Checklist

√	Duty	Notes
	Clean cages	
	Check function of room ventilation	
	Clean food dishes and water bottles	
	Wash hands between handling hamsters	
	Feed fresh fruits and vegetables in small amounts	
	Set thermostat to maintain temperature of 68 degrees F	
	Clean cages	

Date ______ Signed ______

Instructions: Each day after you complete your animal care responsibilities place a check in the left column and make notes of any observations in the right column. Date and sign the checklist and place it in the paper rack on the wall outside of my office.

FIGURE 4.48
Completed checklist for chinchillas

2. Calculating the cost of owning a horse

You are the resident horse expert at Mount Timp Stables & Training. You have worked at the stables for the last five years and one of your activities is to help people understand the real cost of buying a horse before they make a horse purchase. You decide to put together a document discussing all of the important information each customer should be aware of before purchasing a horse. The document has experienced tremendous success, and it is now going to be used throughout the community and by the local 4-H clubs. You decide to "dress it up" with a new design for the table and a logo for the stables.

Retrieve the file named **wd04Horsecost.doc** and save it as **Horsecost1.doc**. Using AutoFormat, convert the table to the Contemporary format. Insert the logo from your data files named **wd04mounttlogo.bmp** at the top of the table and resize it to fit across the top of the table. Compare your final document to Figure 4.49.

FIGURE 4.49

Final cost of owning a horse table with Contemporary format and logo

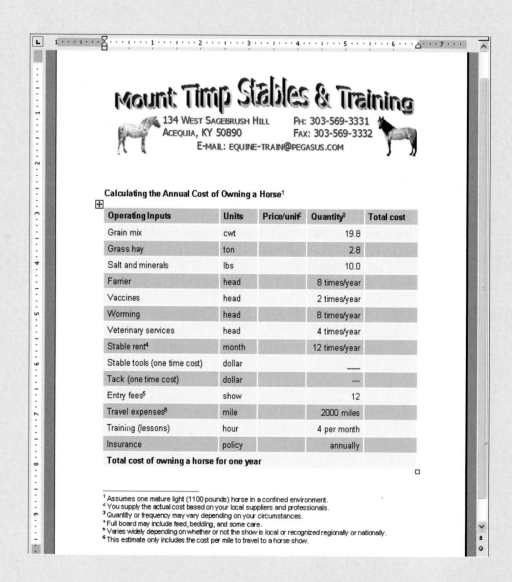

Operating Inputs	Units	Price/unit[2]	Quantity[3]	Total cost
Grain mix	cwt		19.8	
Grass hay	ton		2.8	
Salt and minerals	lbs		10.0	
Farrier	head		8 times/year	
Vaccines	head		2 times/year	
Worming	head		8 times/year	
Veterinary services	head		4 times/year	
Stable rent[4]	month		12 times/year	
Stable tools (one time cost)	dollar		—	
Tack (one time cost)	dollar		---	
Entry fees[5]	show		12	
Travel expenses[6]	mile		2000 miles	
Training (lessons)	hour		4 per month	
Insurance	policy		annually	

Calculating the Annual Cost of Owning a Horse[1]

Total cost of owning a horse for one year

[1] Assumes one mature light (1100 pounds) horse in a confined environment.
[2] You supply the actual cost based on your local suppliers and professionals.
[3] Quantity or frequency may vary depending on your circumstances.
[4] Full board may include feed, bedding, and some care.
[5] Varies widely depending on whether or not the show is local or recognized regionally or nationally.
[6] This estimate only includes the cost per mile to travel to a horse show.

1. Creating a Price List for Organic Produce Sold Online

Nature's Way, an upscale produce company, is located in New Hampshire and owned by Jenny Welch. Jenny started the company in 1985 in her kitchen. The company now maintains 23 employees and specializes in jams and jellies produced from organically grown fruit. You have just been hired as Jenny's technical assistant. Jenny is very interested in creating a Web site for her business. Jenny wants you to put together a professional looking document that details all of the jam and jelly information that she can put on the Web site. Use the following information to create a price list table:

- Raspberry $3.25
- Currant $4.
- Grape $2.75
- Strawberry $4.25
- Apple $2.75
- Peach $3.50
- Apricot $2.75
- Loganberry $5.

For the table format choose the Web 3 from the AutoFormat list. Add Nature's Way logo to the top of this price list. Resize the logo until it is about 2.5 inches wide. Use Figure 4.50 as a guide. The company logo is named **Naturelogo.bmp**. Save the file as **Pricelist1.doc**.

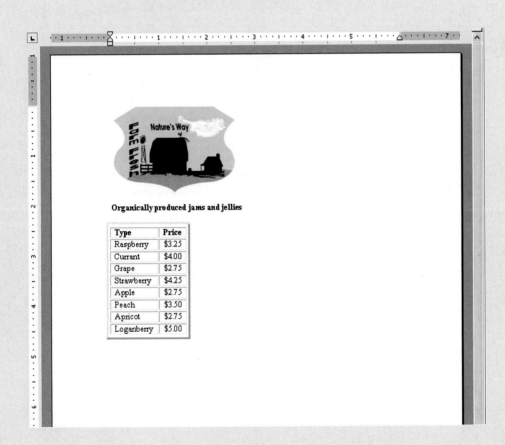

FIGURE   4.50

Price list for Nature's Way

2. Drawing a Table and Adding a Logo

Forest Hills Community College is excited to begin offering online classes. Originally, the college decided to publish a one-page description of their online courses in the local newspapers in order to attract students. Now the college has decided to publish the one-page description in professional business magazines. The one-page description needs to be enhanced since it will be printed in color. The document should have a logo added and a table around the text.

Retrieve the data file named **wd04Classesfinal.doc** and save it as **Classesfinal1.doc**. Add the Forest Hills logo so that it stretches across the top **wd04Forestlogo.bmp**. Draw tables around the text in each column using the Table to Text feature in Word. Format the borders and the gridlines of the tables. Use shading to enhance the color of the text in the title and the background in the courses. Figure 4.51 is one example of how the final Forest Hills online class list might look.

FIGURE 4.51

Forest Hills online classes with logo and table drawn around each set of classes

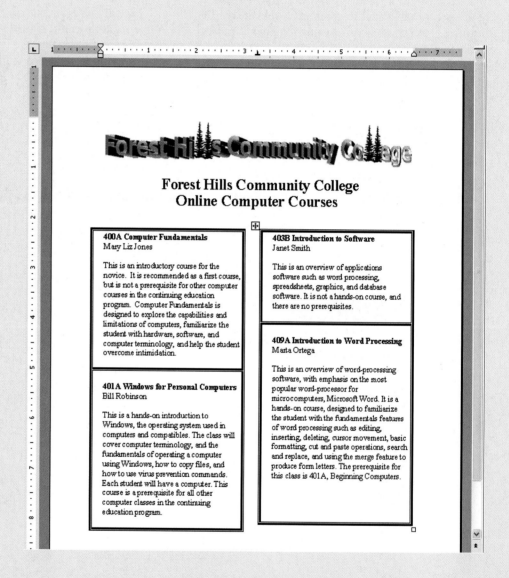

on the web

1. Using Tables to Create an Invoice

Annette Pool recently started a business creating Web page designs. Her business is called Shoshone Web Design. Her first customer, Maxine Hess, was extremely pleased with her work. After finishing her first job Annette realized that she didn't have an official company invoice that she could send to Maxine. An invoice must be used in order to receive payment for her services. Annette decides to hire you to create her invoice. Figure 4.52 displays the sample invoice that Annette wants you to create using Word.

Using tabs, alignment, and tables develop the invoice for Annette that matches the one displayed in Figure 4.52. Annette wants you to use the Arial font since it is her favorite. Be sure to change the font size and font appearance to match the figure. Save your file as **Invoice1.doc**. Once you have completed the invoice, Annette would like you to produce the final invoice for Maxine Hess. Use the information provided below to complete the final invoice. Save the file as **Invoice2.doc**.

- Maxine Hess
- Environ-Safe Garbage Collection
- Building 34 Westside Industrial Park
- Ashton, TX 66666
- Invoice # 2455
- Today's date
- Description: Development of company logo for trucks and collection containers
- Amount and Total: $1,200.00

FIGURE 4.52

Finished invoice for Shoshone Web Design

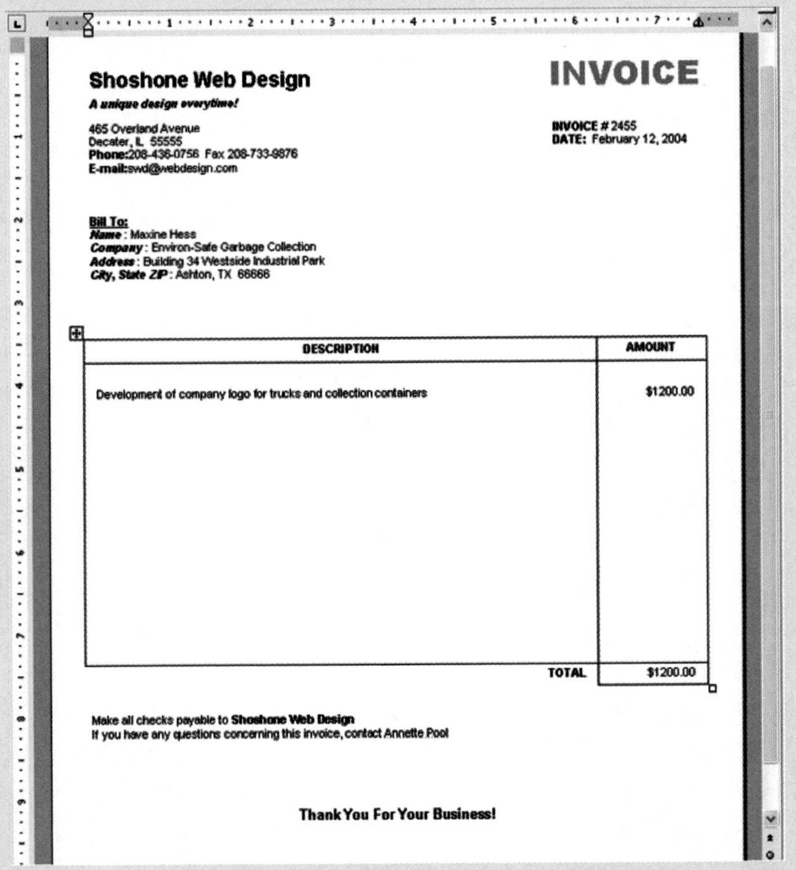
Shoshone Web Design

A unique design everytime!

465 Overland Avenue
Decater, IL 55555
Phone:208-436-0756 Fax 208-733-9876
E-mail:swd@webdesign.com

INVOICE

INVOICE # 2455
DATE: February 12, 2004

Bill To:
Name : Maxine Hess
Company : Environ-Safe Garbage Collection
Address : Building 34 Westside Industrial Park
City, State ZIP : Ashton, TX 66666

DESCRIPTION	AMOUNT
Development of company logo for trucks and collection containers	$1200.00
TOTAL	$1200.00

Make all checks payable to **Shoshone Web Design**
If you have any questions concerning this invoice, contact Annette Pool

Thank You For Your Business!

2. Adding Clip Art to a Flyer

You have created a flyer to advertise features of an Internet service provider called AccessHostPro. You have decided to add some clip art from the Clip Art Gallery that comes with Word. Retrieve the document **wd04Accesshost.doc** and save it as **Access1.doc**. From the Clip Art Gallery insert the lightbulb found in the Business category. Size this clip art to fit in the upper-left corner and then copy it and place it in the other three corners of the flyer. Save your document.

around the world

1. Learning the English and Metric Systems

The metric system, used in almost every country in the world, was devised by French scientists in the late 18th century to replace the difficult collection of units then in use. The goal of this effort was to produce a system that was easy to use and to use the decimal system rather than fractions.

You are preparing to take a group of high school seniors for a summer abroad. You are going to visit England, France, Spain, and Germany. The United States still uses the English system for measurements, and you are worried that your students might have a difficult time understanding the metric system. The countries you will be visiting all use the metric system, so you want to give students a quick overview of the metric system that they can use during their visit. Ideally, a student should be able to figure out how far is 16 kilometers and how much is 10 kilograms.

Using the Table function create a table that looks like Figure 4.53 and contains the same information. Save your work as **Metric1.doc**.

2. Finalizing an International Newsletter

Environment 4-Sure.com specializes in international environmental issues. Open the document **wd04Enviro.doc** and save it as **Enviro1.doc**. Use WordArt to create a new masthead out of the title of the newsletter. Then place the logo (Enviro2_logo.bmp) in the empty space at the bottom of the center column on the first page and at the bottom of the third column on the second page. Save your work.

FIGURE 4.53

Metric system overview and conversion table

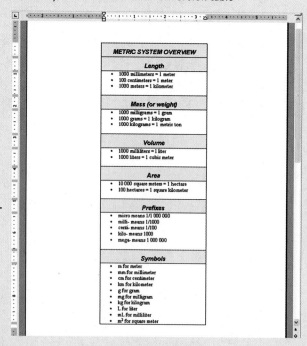

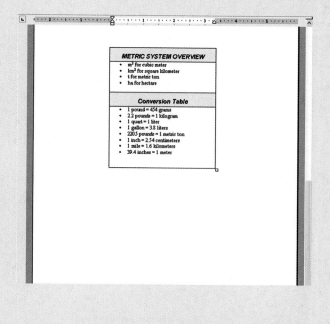

Creating a Schedule for Career Days

The Kasota School District provides high school juniors and seniors with a list of colleges, universities, and employers that will be at the upcoming Career Day. Tom Gould, senior student counselor, plans to put this information into a document containing a table. For each college, university, or employer the table will include the name of the organization, a contact person, and a classroom number for the Career Day. The Kasota School District logo also needs to be added to the document. The following is a list of information that will be in Tom's table:

Figure 4.54 displays Tom's finished product. The table title is Tahoma 16-point bold type, and the text of the table is Times New Roman 12-point font with bold and italic applied to some of the column headings. Using the Table AutoFormat under the Table button on the menu bar generated the table format. Table format in Figure 4.54 is List 1. The logo for the Kasota School District is supplied in your data files with the filename of **KUSDlogo.bmp**. Save your work as **Careerdays1.doc**.

Organization	Contact	Classroom
Colleges and Universities		
South-central Community College	Merlin Stock	B-16
Saint Joan University	Terry Spackman	B-108
Mid-city Community College	Teresa Solomon	C-23
El Camino University	Heidi Troy	
Businesses		
Triple T Concrete and Construction	Todd Morrison	Auditorium
State Department of Agriculture	Cindi Hernandez	A-24
AgriTech Corporation	Alan Harris	A-21
Jones, Talbot, & Tarter Contractors	Liane Tarter	Band room
IMCO Manufacturing	Jason Jones	B-01
Ortega Pre-School & Day Care	Marta Ortega	C-22
Motion Motors Repair	Jerry Olmstead	B-46
Phaze Enviro Action	Ralph Nader	Science lab
The Computer School	Rick Parker	A-34
Sheila's Landscape and Nursery	Sheila Herrera	B-05
Town Square Florist	Justin Metts	B-06

F I G U R E   4.54

Table of participants for Kasota High School Career Fair

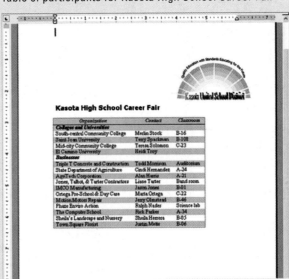

analysis

1. Clip Art

Use the Help feature in Word to learn how to save clip art from the Web. Using the Internet, locate a Web site that allows free downloading of clip art and download several new art images to your computer. Discuss the pros and cons of using Web-accessible clip art.

2. Calendar

Discuss what elements of Word are available to help you make a calendar.

reference 1

Word *File Finder*

Location in Chapter	Data File to Use
CHAPTER 1	
Session 1.1	
Starting Word	
Obtaining help from the Office Assistant	
Session 1.2	
Opening an existing document	wd01Mission.doc
Session 1.3	
Previewing a document	wd01Mission.doc
Saving a document	wd01Mission.doc
Closing a document	wd01Mission.doc
Exiting Word	
Hands-On Projects	
Practice Exercise 1	
Practice Exercise 2	wd01Memo.doc
Challenge Exercise 1	
Challenge Exercise 2	
E-Business Exercise 1	wd01Internet.doc
E-Business Exercise 2	wd01ISP.doc
On the Web Exercise 1	
On the Web Exercise 2	
Around the World Exercise 1	wd01Vacation.doc
Around the World Exercise 2	
Running Project	
CHAPTER 2	
Session 2.1	
Cutting and pasting text	wd02MagicSlopes.doc
Using Find and Replace	wd02MagicSlopes.doc
Practicing Undo and Redo	wd02MagicSlopes.doc

REFERENCE

Location in Chapter	Data File to Use
Checking spelling in a document	wd02MagicSlopes.doc
Session 2.2	
Changing font and font size	wd02MagicSlopes.doc
Underlining selected text	wd02MagicSlopes.doc
Bolding selected text	wd02MagicSlopes.doc
Applying italics	wd02MagicSlopes.doc
Highlighting text	wd02MagicSlopes.doc
Changing case	wd02MagicSlopes.doc
Session 2.3	
Setting the left margin	wd02MagicSlopes.doc
Setting the bottom margin using **Page Setup**	wd02MagicSlopes.doc
Double spacing lines	wd02MagicSlopes.doc
Centering text	wd02MagicSlopes.doc
Indenting practice	wd02MagicSlopes.doc
Setting tabs in a document	wd02MagicSlopes.doc
Show or hide formatting marks	wd02MagicSlopes.doc
Hands-On Projects	
Practice Exercise 1	
Practice Exercise 2	wd02Memo.doc
Challenge Exercise 1	wd02Recommendation.doc
Challenge Exercise 2	wd02Resume.doc
E-Business Exercise 1	wd02CoverLetter.doc
E-Business Exercise 2	wd02Agenda.doc
On the Web Exercise 1	
On the Web Exercise 2	wd02Mission.doc
Around the World Exercise 1	
Around the World Exercise 2	
Running Project	wd02LessonPlan.doc
CHAPTER 3	
Session 3.1	
Automatically hyphenating text	wd03Videos.doc
Inserting the date automatically	wd03Videos.doc

Location in Chapter	Data File to Use
Adding numbers	wd03Videos.doc
Creating a border	wd03Videos.doc
Creating a shaded area	wd03Videos.doc
Session 3.2	
Learning to apply a default style	wd03Videos.doc
Learning to use Style Gallery	wd03Videos.doc
Creating a template for Videos1.doc	wd03Videos.doc
Session 3.3	
Inserting page numbers on the bottom center of a page	wd03Videos.doc
Inserting page breaks	wd03Videos.doc
Adding a footer	wd03Videos.doc
Inserting a table of contents	wd03Videos.doc
Marking words for the index	wd03Videos.doc
Building an index	wd03Videos.doc
Hands-On Projects	
Practice Exercise 1	
Practice Exercise 2	
Challenge Exercise 1	wd03Evaluation.doc
Challenge Exercise 2	wd03Lecture.doc
E-Business Exercise 1	wd03Glossary.doc
E-Business Exercise 2	wd03Whitepaper.doc
On the Web Exercise 1	
On the Web Exercise 2	
Around the World Exercise 1	
Around the World Exercise 2	
Running Project	wd03Syllabus.doc
CHAPTER 4	
Session 4.1	
Creating a table and entering text into a table	wd04GardenPlan.doc
Converting a list to a table	wd04Vegetable.doc
Converting a table to text	wd04Legumes.doc

Location in Chapter	Data File to Use
Session 4.2	
Applying a table AutoFormat to Taylor's table	wd04GardenPlan.doc
Merging cells to add a title	wd04GardenPlan.doc
Repeating a row header	wd04GardenPlan.doc
Applying a border and shading	wd04GardenPlan.doc
Session 4.2	
Adding Star AutoShape to Taylor's planting guide	wd04GardenPlan.doc
Inserting and sizing an image on a document	wd04GardenPlan.doc
Adding a text box	wd04GardenPlan.doc
Adding a fill color to text box	wd04GardenPlan.doc
Adding a shadow to text box	wd04GardenPlan.doc
Adding a clip art to a new document	wd04GardenPlan.doc
Hands-On Projects	
Practice Exercise 1	
Practice Exercise 2	
Challenge Exercise 1	wd04Horsecost.doc
Challenge Exercise 2	
E-Business Exercise 1	wd04Classesfinal.doc
E-Business Exercise 2	
On the Web Exercise 1	wd04Accesshost.doc
On the Web Exercise 2	
Around the World Exercise 1	
Around the World Exercise 2	wd04Enviro.doc
Running Project	

reference 2

Microsoft Office Specialist Objective	Task	Session Location	End-of-Chapter Location
CHAPTER 1	**Working with a Document**		
WW03S-5-4	Save documents in appropriate formats for different uses	1.3	1.24
WW03S-5-5	Print documents, envelopes, and labels	1.3	1.24
WW03S-5-6	Preview documents and Web pages	1.3	1.24
WW03S-1-1	Insert and edit text, symbols, and special characters	1.2	1.24
WW03S-5-3	Organize documents using file folders	1.2	1.24
WW03S-5-7	Change and organize document views and windows	1.2	1.24
CHAPTER 2	**Editing and Formatting Documents**		
WW03S-1-1	Insert and edit text, symbols, and special characters	2.1	2.33
WW03S-1-2	Insert frequently used and predefined text	2.1	2.33
WW03S-1-3	Navigate to specific content	2.1	2.33
WW03S-1-6	Locate, select, and insert supporting information	2.1	2.33
WW03S-3-1	Format text	2.2	2.33
WW03S-3-2	Format paragraphs	2.3	2.33
WW03S-5-7	Change and organize document views and windows	2.3	2.33
CHAPTER 3	**Advanced Editing and Formatting**		
WW03S-1-2	Insert frequently used and predefined text	3.1	3.35
WW03S-2-2	Create bulleted lists, numbered lists, and outlines	3.1	3.35
WW03S-3-5	Modify document layout and page setup	3.1	3.35
WW03S-3-1	Format text	3.2	3.35
WW03S-5-1	Create new documents using templates	3.2	3.35

Microsoft Office Specialist Objective	Task	Session Location	End-of-Chapter Location
WW03S-3-4	Insert and modify content in headers and footers	3.3	3.35
WW03S-3-5	Modify document layout and page setup	3.3	3.35
WW03E-1-1	Create custom styles for text, tables, and lists	3.2	3.35
WW03E-3-2	Create and modify document background	3.2	3.35
WW03E-1-2	Control pagination	3.3	3.35
CHAPTER 4	**Using Graphics and Tables**		
WW03S-2-1	Insert and modify tables	4.1	4.34
WW03S-1-4	Insert, position, and size graphics	4.3	4.34
WW03E-2-1	Sort content in lists and tables	4.2	4.34
WW03E-2-2	Perform calculations in tables	4.2	4.34
WW03E-2-3	Modify table formats	4.2	4.34
WW03E-1-3	Format, position, and resize graphics using advanced layout features	4.3	4.34

reference 3

Word *Task Reference Summary*

Task	Page #	Preferred Method
Opening a Word document	WD 1.11	• Click on the **File** menu, click **Open**, click on the document's name, click the **Open** button located on the Open dialog box, or double-click on the document's name
Deleting text	WD 1.17	• Select the text you would like to delete, press the **Delete** key on your keyboard, or insert the cursor behind the text you want to delete, press the **Backspace** key on your keyboard
Printing the active Word document	WD 1.19	• Click **Print** on the Standard toolbar, or click **Print** on the File menu, make any needed changes in the Print dialog box, click the **OK** button in the Print dialog box (see Figure 1.20)
Saving a new unnamed Word document	WD 1.20	• Click the **Save As** item in the File menu, change the folder if you want to save the document in a different location than the default folder, type the document's name in the File name box, click **Save**
Saving an active Word document	WD 1.20	• Click the **Save** item in the File menu
Closing a document	WD 1.22	• Click **Close** on the File menu, click **Yes** to save changes
Exiting Word	WD 1.22	• Click **Exit** on the File menu, or click the **Close** button at the top right of the screen
Cutting, copying, and moving text	WD 2.5	• Select the item you want to move or copy; to move the item, click **Cut** on the Standard toolbar, click where you want the item to appear, click **Paste** on the Standard toolbar or • To copy the item, click **Copy** on the Standard toolbar, click where you want the item to appear
Finding text	WD 2.6	• On the Edit menu, click **Find** to open the Find and Replace dialog box; in the Find what box, enter the text you want to search for, select any other options that you want, click **Find Next**; to cancel a search in progress, press **Esc**; to close the Find and Replace dialog box, click the **Cancel** button or the **Close** button
Replacing text	WD 2.7	• On the Edit menu, click **Replace**; in the Find what box, enter the text that you want to search for; in the Replace with box, enter the replacement text, select any other options that you want, click Find Next, Replace, or Replace All; to cancel a search in progress, press Esc; to close the Find and Replace dialog box, click the Cancel button or the Close button
Checking spelling	WD 2.9	• Choose the error you want to correct by right-clicking a word with a wavy red underline, click the correct word or spelling from the list or • Click on the **Spelling and Grammar** 🔡 button in the Standard toolbar to check the spelling and grammar in the entire document, choose the correct spelling of the word; or correct the word in the **Spelling and Grammar** dialog box, click **Ignore** to ignore any words that are spelled correctly and just not recognized by Word

Task	*Page #*	*Preferred Method*
Changing the font and size	WD 2.15	• To apply text formatting to a single character, word, or several words, select the text you want to change, click on a font name in the Font box on the Formatting toolbar or • To change the size of text or numbers, select the text you want to change, click a point size in the Font size box on the Formatting toolbar
Adding a basic underline	WD 2.16	• Select the text you want to underline, click the **Underline** button on the Formatting toolbar or • Select the text you want to underline, select **Ctrl+U** on the keyboard
Making text bold	WD 2.17	• Select the text you want to bold, click the **Bold** button on the Formatting toolbar or • Select the text you want to bold, select **Ctrl+B** on the keyboard
Applying italic formatting to text or numbers	WD 2.18	• Select the text you want to italicize, click the **Italic** button on the Formatting toolbar or • Select the text you want to italicize, select **Ctrl+I** on the keyboard
Opening the Format Font window	WD 2.19	• Select the **Format** menu, select **Font**; the Format Font window is displayed; select the Font type, size, or style you want
Highlighting text	WD 2.20	• Click the **Highlight** button on the Formatting toolbar; the mouse pointer will change shape to a highlighter-marking pen; drag the mouse I-beam over the text and the active color is applied; to turn off highlight, click on the **Highlight** button again or • Select the text you want highlighted, click on the **Highlight** button
Changing text color	WD 2.21	• Click the **Font Color** button on the Formatting toolbar, start typing in the new color; to turn off the color, click on the Font Color button and select a different color or Automatic for black or • Select the text you want colored, click on the **Font Color** button
Changing case	WD 2.22	• Select the text requiring the case change, click on the **Format** menu, click **Change Case**, select the type of case change you are making—sentence case, lowercase, uppercase, title case, or toggle case
Changing left and right page margins	WD 2.23	• Switch to Print Layout view button, point to a margin boundary on the horizontal ruler or vertical ruler. When the pointer changes to a double-headed arrow, drag the margin boundary, to specify exact margin measurements, hold down **Alt** as you drag the margin boundary; the ruler displays the measurements of the margins or • On the **File menu** click **Page Setup** and click the **Margins** tab, enter the settings you want, click **Default** to have Word save the new default settings in the template on which the document is based
Adjusting line spacing	WD 2.26	• Select the lines, paragraphs, or pages where you want to set the line spacing, click the **Format** menu, click **Paragraph**, click the **Indents and Spacing** tab; under Spacing select the options you want in the **Line spacing** box

Task	Page #	Preferred Method
Aligning text left, right, centered, and justified	WD 2.27	• Select the text you want to align left, click the **Align Left** button on the Formatting toolbar or use **Ctrl+L** from the keyboard or • Select the text you want to align right, click the **Align Right** button on the Formatting toolbar or use **Ctrl+R** from the keyboard or • Select the text you want to center, click the **Center** button on the Formatting toolbar or use **Ctrl+E** from the keyboard or • Select the text you want to justify, click the **Justify** button on the Formatting toolbar or use **Ctrl+J** from the keyboard
Changing the indent	WD 2.28	• Select the paragraph where you want to create a first line indent; if you don't see the horizontal ruler, click **Ruler** on the **View** menu; on the horizontal ruler drag the First Line Indent marker to the position where you want the text to start or • Select the paragraph where you want to increase or decrease the left indent of an entire paragraph; on the Formatting toolbar click the **Increase Indent** button or **Decrease Indent** button or • Select the paragraph where you want to create a hanging indent; on the horizontal ruler drag the **Hanging Indent** marker to the position where you want the text to start or • Select the paragraph you want to out-dent or extend into the left margin; if you don't see the horizontal ruler click **Ruler** on the **View** menu; on the horizontal ruler drag the **Left Indent** marker to the position where you want the paragraph to start
Setting tabs	WD 2.30	• Select the paragraph(s) that will receive a new tab setting, select **Tabs** from the **Format** menu, select the type of tab you want, click **OK** **Using Tabs** • To use a tab, place the insertion point where you want text to align with the tab and press the Tab key on your keyboard **Moving Tabs** • Click the tab you want to move and drag the tab to the new location and release the mouse button **Deleting Tabs** • Click the tab you want to delete on the gray bar under the horizontal ruler and drag the tab into the document area of the screen and release the mouse button
Hyphenating text with three different methods	WD 3.5	• On the **Tools** menu, point to **Language**, and then click **Hyphenation** • Select the **Automatically hyphenate document** check box • In the **Hyphenation zone box**, enter the amount of space to leave between the end of the last word in a line and the right margin • To reduce the number of hyphens, make the hyphenation zone wider • To reduce the raggedness of the right margin, make the hyphenation zone narrower • In the **Limit consecutive hyphens to** box, enter the number of consecutive lines that can be hyphenated or • On the **Tools** menu, point to **Language**, and then click **Hyphenation** • Click **Manual** • If Word identifies a word or phrase to hyphenate, do one of the following: • To insert an **optional hyphen** in the location Word proposes, click **Yes**

REFERENCE

Task	Page #	Preferred Method
		• To insert an optional hyphen in another part of the word, use the arrow keys or mouse to move the insertion point to that location, and then click **Yes** or • Click where you want to insert the optional hyphen • Press **Ctrl+- (hyphen)**
Inserting the date and time	WD 3.7	• Insert the cursor where you want the date and time to be located • Click on the **Insert** menu and choose **Date and Time** • Click on the date and time format you require • Check **Update Automatically** if you require the date and time to be updated every time the document is opened • Click **OK**
Adding bullets or numbers	WD 3.7	• **Select** the items you want to add bullets or numbers • On the Formatting toolbar, do one of the following: • To add bullets, click **Bullets** button or • To add numbering, click **Numbering** button
Creating a border	WD 3.9	• Select the paragraph where you want the border • Click on the **Format** menu and choose **Borders and Shading** • Select the **Borders** tab and set the border style, color, and width • Click **OK**
Printing multiple pages on a document	WD 3.10	• On the **File** menu, click **Print** • Under Zoom, click **2, 4, 6, 8, or 16** pages in the Pages per sheet box • Click **OK**
Changing page orientation	WD 3.12	• On the **File** menu, click **Page Setup**, and then click the **Paper Size** tab • Under **Orientation**, click **Portrait** or **Landscape** • Click **OK**
Applying a style with the Formatting toolbar	WD 3.14	• Position the insertion point anywhere in the paragraph or select any amount of text in the paragraph • On the Formatting toolbar, from the **Style** pull-down listing, select the paragraph or character style you want to apply or • From the Format menu, select **Styles and Formatting** or • Click on the **Styles and Formatting** button on the Formatting toolbar and • Select the style(s) you want to apply • If the style you want is not listed in the Style task pane, select another category of styles from the Show pull-down listing at the bottom of the task pane
Reapplying original formatting to a style	WD 3.15	• Select the section of document you want to revert to the default style • On the Formatting toolbar, from the Style pull-down listing, select the original style—the style you wish to reapply or • Select Clear Formatting to restore the formatting to the normal style for your document
Using Word's predefined styles	WD 3.15	• Click **Styles and Formatting** from the Format menu • Highlight the paragraph you want to add the style to • Click on the style
Previewing styles	WD 3.16	• On the Format menu, click **Theme** • Click **Style Gallery** • In the Template box, select the template that contains styles you want to use • To preview how your document will look with the different styles, click **Document** under Preview

Task	Page #	Preferred Method
		• To see a sample document with styles from the selected template, click **Example** • To see a list of the styles used in the selected template, click **Style samples**
Creating a paragraph style by example	WD 3.17	• Place your cursor within the newly formatted example paragraph • On the Formatting toolbar, in the Style text box, click the name of the existing style (often Normal) • Type a new name for the style you want to create • To create the style, press **Enter**
Creating a paragraph style using the task pane	WD 3.19	• From the Formatting toolbar, click on **Styles and Formatting** button and the task pane appears • To create a new style, click **New Style** • The New Style dialog box appears • In the Name text box, type a name for the new style • In the Style type pull-down list, to create a character style select **Character**; to create a paragraph style select **Paragraph** • From the Style based on pull-down list, select an existing style to base the new style on • Click **Format** to show a pull-down listing • Select the attribute you want to change and the Font dialog or Paragraph dialog box appears • Fill out the corresponding dialog box • Click **OK** • To do more formatting or to create additional styles, repeat the steps • To apply your new style to the selected text, in the task pane, click on the formatting you wish to apply • Close the **task pane**
Deleting styles from a document or template	WD 3.20	• If the Styles and Formatting task pane is not open, click **Styles and Formatting** on the Formatting toolbar • In the Styles and Formatting task pane, right-click the style you want to delete, and then click **Delete** • Close the **task pane**
Selecting a template	WD 3.21	• Click **New** on the File menu • Click on **General Templates** on the task pane • Select a template
Creating templates two ways	WD 3.21	• To base a template on an existing document • On the File menu, click **Open** • Open the document you want or • To base a new template on an existing template • On the File menu, click **New** • In the New Document task pane under New from template, click **General Templates** • Click a template similar to the one you want to create • Click **Template** under Create New, and then click **OK** Or for a document • On the File menu, click **Save As** • In the Save as type box, click **Document Template** • Click **Save**
Inserting page numbers	WD 3.23	• On the **Insert** menu, click **Page Numbers** • In the **Position box**, specify whether to print page numbers in the header at the top of the page or in the footer at the bottom of the page • **Select** any other options you want, for example, to show or hide the page number on the first page or other format options • Click **OK**

Task	Page #	Preferred Method
Inserting page breaks	WD 3.24	• Click where you want to insert a page break • On the **Insert** menu, click **Break** • Under Section break types, click **Page Break** • Click **OK**
Keeping lines together	WD 3.25	• Select the paragraphs that contain lines you want to keep together • On the **Format** menu, click **Paragraph** • Click the **Line and Page Breaks** tab • Select the **Keep lines together** check box • Click **OK** or • Select **Keep with next** (depending on whether you are dealing with lines or paragraphs or both) • Click **OK**
Inserting section break	WD 3.26	• Click where you want to insert a section break • On the **Insert** menu, click **Break** • Under Section break types, **click** the option that describes where you want the new section to begin • Click **OK**
Adding a header	WD 3.28	• On the **View** menu, click **Header and Footer** • To create a header, enter text or graphics in the header area • Or click a button on the Header and Footer toolbar (see Figure 3.26) • When you finish, click **Close**
Adding a footer	WD 3.29	• On the **View** menu, click **Header and Footer** • Click Header and Footer button to switch between the header and the footer • To create a footer, enter text or graphics or page options in the footer area • When you finish, click **Close**
Inserting a footnote or an endnote	WD 3.30	• In Print Layout view, click where you want to insert the footnote or endnote reference mark • On the **Insert** menu, click **Reference**, click **Footnote** • Select **Footnote** or **Endnote** • Under Numbering, **click** the option you want • Click **Insert** (Word inserts the note number and places the insertion point next to the note number.) • Type the note text • Scroll to your place in the document and click to continue typing
Creating a table of contents	WD 3.31	• Be certain that your document contains built-in heading styles (Heading 1 through Heading 9) to the headings you want to include in your table of contents • Click where you want to insert the table of contents • On the Insert menu, click **Reference, Index and Tables**, and then click the **Table of Contents** tab on the Index and Tables dialog box • Click a design in the Formats box or • To specify a custom table of contents layout, choose the options you want • Select any other table of contents options you want • Click **OK**
Marking an index entry	WD 3.32	• Select the text you want to mark as an index entry • Click **Insert, Reference, Index and Tables, Index** tab • Click **Mark Entry** button in dialog box • Selected text appears in the Main Entry field • Edit the entry if necessary (for example, changing capitalization) • Click **Mark**

Task	Page #	Preferred Method
		• Mark Index Entry dialog box remains open • Click **Close** • The Mark Index Entry dialog box closes • Click the **Show/Hide** button to hide nonprinting characters
Building an index	WD 3.33	• Mark all of the index entries in your document • Insert the cursor where you want to place the index • On the Insert menu, click **Reference**, **Index and Tables**, and then click the **Index** tab • To use one of the available designs, click a design in the Formats box or • To design a custom index layout, choose the options you want • Select any other index options that you want • Click **OK**
Updating an index or table of contents	WD 3.34	• Click to the left of the index or table of contents • Press F9
Inserting an empty table	WD 4.5	• Click where you want to create a table • Click **Insert Table** [icon] button on the Standard toolbar • Drag to select the number of columns and rows you want • Release the mouse button to insert the blank table
Adding columns or rows to a table	WD 4.5	• Click the position in the table where you want to add columns or rows • Select the number of columns or rows to insert • On the **Table** menu, click **Insert** • Click **Columns to the Right** or **Columns to the Left** or • On the **Table** menu, click **Insert** • Click **Rows Above** or **Rows Below**
Deleting columns or rows in a table	WD 4.6	• Click the position in the table where you want to delete columns or rows • Click **Table**, **Delete** • Choose Columns or rows
Converting text into a table	WD 4.8	• Select the text you want to convert • On the **Table** menu, point to **Convert**, and then click **Text to Table** • Under **Separate text at**, click the option for the separator character you want • Select any other options you want • Click **OK**
Converting a table to text	WD 4.10	• Select the rows or table that you want to convert to paragraphs • On the **Table** menu, point to **Convert**, and then click **Table to Text** • Under **Separate text with**, click the option for the separator character (comma, tab, space, paragraph, or other) you want to use in place of the column boundaries • Paragraph marks separate rows
Applying a Table AutoFormat	WD 4.13	• Click the table • On the **Table** menu, click **Table AutoFormat** • In the **Formats** box, click the format you want
Moving a table	WD 4.14	• Be certain that you are in the **Print Layout view** • Rest the pointer on the table until the table move handle appears on the upper-left corner of the table • Rest the pointer on the table move handle until a four-headed arrow appears • Drag the table to the new location

Task	Page #	Preferred Method
Resizing a table, columns, or rows	WD 4.15	• Rest the pointer on the table until the table resize handle appears on the lower-right corner of the table • Rest the pointer on the table resize handle until a double-headed arrow appears • Drag the table boundary until the table is the size you want or • To resize a column, rest the pointer on the column boundary you want to move until it becomes a double-headed arrow and then drag the boundary until the column is the width you want or • To resize a row, rest the pointer on the row boundary you want to move until it becomes a double-headed arrow and then drag the boundary
Merging and splitting cells	WD 4.16	• Select the cells you want to merge • From the **Table** menu click **Merge Cells** or • From the **Table** menu click **Split Cells**
Heading rows repeated	WD 4.18	• Select the rows you want to repeat on each page of the table • Click on the **Table** menu • Select **Heading Rows Repeat**
Adding borders and shading to a table	WD 4.19	• Select the cell or cells where you want to apply a border or shading • Click **Borders and Shading** on the **Format** menu • Select the **Borders** tab and apply the desired border or • Select the **Shading** tab and apply the desired shading
Inserting an AutoShape	WD 4.22	• On the Drawing toolbar, click **AutoShapes**, point to a category, and then click the shape you want • To insert a shape with a predefined size, click the document • To insert a different size, drag the shape to the size you want • To maintain the shape's width-to-height ratio, hold down **Shift** while you drag the shape • To add color, change borders, rotate, add shadow, or 3-D effects, select the object, and then use the buttons on the Drawing toolbar
Inserting a picture	WD 4.24	• Click where you want to insert the picture • On the **Insert** menu, point to **Picture**, and then click **From File** • Locate the picture you want to insert • Double-click the picture you want to insert
Sizing an image	WD 4.25	• Select the drawing object or image you want to resize • Drag a sizing handle until the object is the shape and size you want
Moving or copying an image a short distance	WD 4.26	• Use drag-and-drop editing • Select the item you want to move or copy • To move the item, drag the selection to the location you want or • To copy the item, hold down **Ctrl** as you drag the selection
Wrapping text around a picture or drawing object	WD 4.26	• Select the picture or drawing object • On the **Format** menu, click the command for the type of object you selected • Click **Layout** tab • Choose the **Wrapping style** you want to apply
Creating a text box	WD 4.28	• On the Drawing toolbar, click **Text Box** button • To insert a text box with a predefined size, click the document • To insert a text box with a different size, drag its sizing handles until the text box is the size you want

Task	Page #	Preferred Method
		• To maintain the text box's width-to-height ratio, hold down **Shift** while you drag the sizing handles • Position the text box by dragging it to the location you want
Selecting a fill color	WD 4.29	• Select the drawing object you want to change • On the **Drawing toolbar**, click the **arrow** next to **Fill Color** button • Click the **color** you want • If you don't see the color you want, click **More Fill Colors** • Click a color on the Standard tab, or click the **Custom** tab to mix your own color • Click **OK**
Adding a shadow to a text box	WD 4.30	• Select the text box or drawing object you want to add a shadow to • On the Drawing toolbar, click **Shadow** button • Click the shadow option you want
Inserting WordArt	WD 4.31	• On the **Drawing toolbar**, click **Insert WordArt** • Click the type of **WordArt drawing object** you want, and then click **OK** • In the **Edit WordArt Text** dialog box, type the text you want to format; select any other options you want • Click **OK** • WordArt toolbar appears when you click the WordArt special text • To add or change effects to the text, use the buttons on the WordArt and Drawing toolbars
Inserting a clip art	WD 4.32	• On the **Insert** menu, point to **Picture**, and click **Clip Art** • In the task pane in the **Search text** box, type a word or phrase that describes the image you want or • In the **Search in** box, click the arrow and select the collections you want to search or • In the **Results should be** box, click the arrow and select the check box next to the types of clips you want to find • Click **Search**
Inserting symbols	WD 4.33	• Click the **Insert** menu, and select **Symbol** • Select the font • Double-click on the symbol or • Select the Special Characters tab • Double-click on the special character you want to insert

glossary

1.5 lines: Line spacing that is one-and-one-half times that of single line spacing.

At least line spacing: Minimum line spacing that Word can adjust to accommodate larger font sizes or graphics.

At line spacing: Amount of line spacing selected by the user.

AutoCorrect: A feature to automatically detect and correct typos, misspelled words, grammatical errors, and incorrect capitalization.

AutoShapes: A group of ready-made shapes that include such basic shapes as rectangles and circles, plus a variety of lines and connectors, block arrows, flowchart symbols, stars and banners, and callouts.

AutoText: Allows you to insert text or graphics into documents quickly and with a minimum of keystrokes.

Backspace: Moves cursor to left one space at a time deleting characters with each space backwards.

Borders: Outside edges of a table.

Case: Refers to whether the text is in uppercase (all capital letters) or lower case (all small letters).

Cell padding: Spacing between the boundary or the cell and the text inside the cell.

Cells: Area at the intersection of a row and column.

Character style: Include any of the options available from the Font dialog box, such as bold, italic, and small caps.

Click and Type: A feature that allows quick insertion of text, graphics, tables, or other items in a blank area of a document; automatically applies the formatting necessary to position the item where the user double-clicked.

Clip art: A stored image that you can insert into a Word document.

Continuous section break: Inserts a section break and starts the new section on the same page.

Delete key: Moves the cursor to the right while deleting a single character one space at a time.

Document properties: Details about a file that help identify it—for example, a descriptive title, the author name, the subject, and keywords that identify topics or other important information in the file.

Document window: Where text, tables, charts, and graphics will be displayed as they are entered.

Double line spacing: Twice that of single line spacing.

Drag: To hold down on the left mouse button and move the mouse pointer across text or to move toolbars and scroll bars.

Drawing canvas: An area upon which you can draw multiple shapes; shapes contained within the drawing canvas can be moved and resized as a unit. The drawing canvas helps arrange and resize the objects in your drawing.

Drawing objects: AutoShapes, curves, lines, and WordArt that are part of a Word document.

Drawing toolbar: Toolbar containing the buttons for Draw, Rotate, AutoShapes, Line, Arrow, Rectangle, Oval, Text Box, Insert WordArt, Insert Clip Art, Fill Color, Line Color, Font Color, Line Style, Dash Style, Arrow Style, Shadow, and 3-D.

End marks: Used to indicate the end of a row or a cell (_); viewed when the Show/Hide button (¶) is clicked.

Endnotes: References or explanations that typically appear at the end of a document.

Even-page section break: Inserts a section break and starts the new section on the same page.

Exactly line spacing: Spacing that Word does not adjust.

Fill: Color, pattern or image inside a drawing object.

Find: Allows you to find a particular word or phrase in a document.

First line indent: Often used to indicate the first line of a new paragraph.

Font: Overall design for a set of characters.

Footers: Displayed and printed in the margin at the bottom of a page.

Footnotes: References or explanations at the end of a page in a document.

Format Painter: Speedy way to copy text, titles, and paragraph formats that contain specific fonts and appearances from one place in a document to another.

Formatting: Organizing the appearance of text on the page.

Formatting toolbar: Normally appears below the Standard toolbar and contains buttons that change the appearance of a text in a document, for example, bold, italicize, underline, justify, number, or bullet text.

Graphic filters: Allow images with different formats imported into Word.

Gridlines: Lines separating rows and columns in a table.

Gutter margin: A margin setting that adds extra space to the side or top margin of a document you plan to bind.

Gutter space: Space between columns.

Hanging indent: First line or phrase against the left margin with remaining text indented a set amount from the left margin.

Hard page break: Inserted manually at a specific point.

Headers: Displayed and printed in the margin at the top of a page.

Highlighted: Marked text with colored background and often white lettering.

Highlighting: A transparent colored bar over selected text.

Horizontal ruler: A bar marked off in units of measure (such as inches) that is displayed across the top of the document window.

Icons: Small symbols representing the command.

EOB 1.1

Index: A list of key word locations placed at the end of a long document.

Insert Symbol command: Allows you to enter symbols into your documents.

Insertion point: Indicates the position where you will be entering text.

Landscape: Orientation of text and graphics on the width of a page.

Line spacing: Determines the amount of vertical space between lines of text.

Margin: Blank space around the edges of the page.

Menu bar: Contains File, Edit, View, Insert, Format, Tools, Table, Window, and Help as pull-down menu options.

Merging cells: Takes two or more cells and merges them into one cell.

Mirror margin: Margins of the left page are a mirror image of those of the right page. That is, the inside margins are the same width, and the outside margins are the same width.

Mouse pointer: Indicates the current position of the mouse.

Multiple line spacing: Increased or decreased by a percentage specified by the user.

Negative indent: Text extends beyond the horizontal margin set for the rest of the text.

Nested table: Table inside of the cell of another table.

Next-page section break: Inserts a section break and starts the new section on the next page.

Nonbreaking hyphen: Prevents a hyphenated word from breaking if it falls at the end of a line.

Nonbreaking space: Prevents a line break between two words.

Nonprinting character: Characters like spaces, tabs, and paragraphs.

Odd-page section break: Inserts a section break and starts the new section on the next odd-numbered page.

Office Assistant: Provides a wide variety of help and tips on Word features and functions.

Optional hyphen: Used to control where a word or phrase breaks if it falls at the end of a line, for example, to specify that the word "nonprinting" break as "non-printing" rather than "nonprint-ing."

Orientation: Flow of text or graphics across the width or length of a page.

Orphans: First line of a paragraph printed by itself at the bottom of a page.

Overtype mode: To replace existing characters as you type; displayed as OVR in the status bar.

Paragraph style: Include character and paragraph formatting, tab settings, paragraph positioning, borders, and shading.

Pictures: Graphics created from another file.

Points: Units of measurement for type.

Portrait: Orientation of text and graphics on the length of a page.

Print dialog: Provides printing options applied to document and printer.

Print Preview: Displays text and graphics as they will appear when printed on paper.

Redo: Perform an editing change again.

Redo: Reverses the action of the Undo command. To redo more than one action at a time, click the arrow next to the Redo button, and then click the actions you want to redo.

Replace: Allows you to replace any particular word or phrase in a document with a new word or phrase.

Scaled: Text and graphics enlarged or reduced to fit the size of a printed page.

Scroll bar: Shaded bars along the right side and bottom of a document window that allow scrolling to another part of the document by dragging the box or clicking the arrows in the scroll bar.

Scrolling: Moving left and right and up and down through the document.

Section break: Stores the formatting elements, such as the margins, page orientation, headers and footers, and sequence of page numbers for a specific area of a document.

Select: Specifying text or some option.

Separator character: Characters such as paragraph marks (¶), tabs (_), or commas you choose to indicate where you want text to separate when you convert a table to text, or where you want new rows or columns to begin when you convert text to a table.

Shortcut menu: A menu that shows a list of commands relevant to a particular item; evoked with right click of mouse button.

Single line spacing: Accommodates the largest font in that line, plus a small amount of extra space.

Sizing handles: Square handle that appears at each corner and along the sides of the rectangle that surrounds a selected drawing object; drag a sizing handle to resize an object.

Smart Tags: Buttons shared across Microsoft Office that appear automatically to correct or help the user with an action.

Soft page break: Inserted automatically at a point determined by Word.

Splitting cells: Takes one cell and splits it into two or more cells.

Standard toolbar: Appears below the menu bar, contains buttons that execute popular menu bar commands such as Open, Save, Print, Cut, and Insert Table.

Status bar: Bar at the bottom of the document window that displays information about a command or toolbar button, an operation in progress, or the location of the insertion point.

Style: A set of formatting characteristics identified by name that you can apply to text in your document to quickly change its appearance.

Style Gallery: Allows copying of the style formatting from the new template into the active document, only replacing the style definitions.

Tab stops: Insert a space for formatting text, as in indenting a line or block of text.

Table move handle: Used to drag table to another location by holding down the right mouse button.

Table resize handle: Used to enlarge or reduce a table by clicking and holding down the right mouse button.

Task pane: A dockable dialog window that provides a convenient way to use a command, gather information, and modify a document.

Template: A collection of styles, keyboard assignments, and toolbar assignments saved to a file.

Text box: Movable, resizable container for text or graphics.

Title bar: This area displays the current document name and the program.

Typeface: Overall design of a font's characters.

Typography: Style and appearance of printed matter or the arrangement of composed type.

Undo: Cancels editing changes.

Undo: Ability to change a mistake in typing, deleting, formatting, and so on.

Widows: Last line of a paragraph printed by itself at the top of a page.

Word wrap: Flow of text between the right and left margins without pressing Enter.

WordArt: Text created with special effects by inserting a Microsoft Office drawing object.

Word-processing software: Helps you create papers, letters, memos, and other basic documents.

Wrapping: How text flows around an image.

index